OVER 175 GREAT IDEAS FOR CLEVER CRAFTERS

"You're so clever!"

Get ready to hear these words of praise all year long, as you breeze through the creative projects in this fun-packed book. Wow your family and friends this *winter* with the simple season's greetings wreath … celebrate *spring* with perky posies to paint or découpage … make *summer* sizzle with microwave tie-dye and other cool stuff for kids … and welcome *fall* with a quick-and-cozy afghan or an awesome beaded lamp. This diverse collection is a sampling of the best projects ever offered by the world's leading publisher of crafts and needlework designs, and even beginners can be confident of success with the clear instructions. So dive in today and get hooked on the soul-pleasing satisfaction of creating something down-right clever!

LEISURE ARTS, INC.
Little Rock, Arkansas

Editorial Staff

Vice President and Editor-in-Chief:
Sandra Graham Case
Executive Director of Publications:
Cheryl Nodine Gunnells
Senior Publications Director: Susan White Sullivan
Director of Designer Relations: Debra Nettles
Licensed Product Coordinator: Lisa Truxton Curton
Editorial Director: Susan Frantz Wiles
Art Operations Director: Jeff Curtis
Director of Public Relations and Retail Marketing:
Stephen Wilson

EDITORIAL
Associate Editors: Steven M. Cooper, Linda L. Garner,
and Kimberly L. Ross

ART
Art Publication Director: Rhonda Hodge Shelby
Art Imaging Director: Mark Hawkins
Art Category Manager: Lora Puls
Freelance Artists: Jessica Puls and Jessica Riddle
Imaging Technicians: Stephanie Johnson and
Mark Potter
Publishing Systems Administrator: Becky Riddle
Publishing Systems Assistants: Clint Hanson,
John Rose, and Chris Wertenberger

Business Staff

Publisher: Rick Barton
Vice President, Finance: Tom Siebenmorgen
Director of Corporate Planning and Development:
Laticia Mull Dittrich
Vice President, Retail Marketing: Bob Humphrey
Vice President, Sales: Ray Shelgosh
Vice President, National Accounts: Pam Stebbins
Director of Sales and Services: Margaret Reinold
Vice President, Operations: Jim Dittrich
Comptroller, Operations: Rob Thieme
Retail Customer Service Manager: Stan Raynor
Print Production Manager: Fred F. Pruss

International Standard Book Number 1-57486-369-X

10 9 8 7 6 5 4 3 2 1

Contents

Contents (continued)

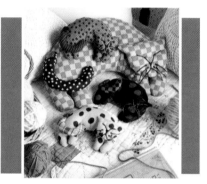

Hummingbird Banquet

It's not often that one is treated to an up-close vision of the dainty hummingbird's mid-air dance. Captured on the throw pillow shown here, our winged ballerina dines on a banquet of nectar from an awaiting blossom. What a delightful treasure for any fan of our feathered friends!

CROSS STITCH

96w x 69h

X	DMC	1/4X	B'ST	ANC.	COLOR
•	blanc	•		2	white
	310	◢	◢	403	black
◉	326	◢		59	dk rose
✖	349	◢		13	vy dk coral
	352	◢		9	coral
V	353			6	lt coral
	434		◢	310	brown
▲	451	◢		233	dk grey
Π	452			232	grey
%	453			231	lt grey
◪	500		◢	683	vy dk blue green
✣	603	◢		62	dk pink
•	605	◢		50	pink
T	676			891	dk yellow
♡	745			300	yellow
∅	815		◢	43	vy dk rose
+	818			23	lt pink
★	946			332	orange
◓	3345	◢		268	dk green
✔	3347	◢		266	green
☆	3348			264	lt green
▪	3777			1015	rust
d	3813			875	lt blue green
◩	3815	◢		877	dk blue green
2	3816			876	blue green

On Facing Page: The design was stitched over 2 fabric threads on a 16" x 14" piece of White Lugana (25 ct). Three strands of floss were used for Cross Stitch and 1 for Backstitch. It was made into a pillow.

For pillow, trim stitched piece 1½" larger than design on all sides. Cut a piece of fabric the same size as stitched piece for backing.

For cording, cut one 2" x 36" bias fabric strip and one 36" length of ¼" dia. purchased cord. Center cord on wrong side of bias strip; matching long edges, fold strip over cord. Using zipper foot, baste along length of strip close to cord; trim seam allowance to ½". Matching raw edges and beginning at bottom edge, pin cording to right side of stitched piece, making a ⅜" clip in seam allowance of cording at each corner. Ends of cording should overlap approximately 2"; pin overlapping end out of the way. Starting 2" from

beginning end of cording and ending 4" from overlapping end, remove 2½" of basting; fold end of fabric back and trim cord so it meets beginning end of cord. Fold end of fabric under ½"; wrap fabric over beginning end of cording. Finish sewing cording to stitched piece.

For ruffle, cut a 6" x 85" fabric strip. Press short ends ½" to wrong side. Matching wrong sides and long edges, press fabric strip in half. Machine baste ½" from raw edges and gather fabric strip to fit stitched piece. Matching raw edges and beginning at bottom edge, pin ruffle to right side of stitched piece, overlapping short ends ¼". Using a ½" seam allowance, sew ruffle to stitched piece. Matching right sides and leaving an opening for turning, use a ½" seam allowance to sew stitched piece and backing fabric together. Trim corners diagonally. Turn pillow right side out, carefully pushing corners outward. Stuff pillow with polyester fiberfill and blind stitch opening closed.

Design by Barbara Baatz.

Marks of Praise

To mark your daily progress in reading The Good Book, turn to these oversized page-keepers. Rich linen sets the tone for their inspiring words and traditional designs.

27w x 112h   30w x 113h   28w x 114h

Sing Unto the Lord

As for me and my house we will serve The Lord

How Great Thou Art

Each design was stitched on a 6" x 11" piece of Zweigart® Summer Khaki Belfast Linen (32 ct). They were stitched over 2 fabric threads. Two strands of floss were used for Cross Stitch and 1 for Backstitch and French Knots. They were made into bookmarks.

For each bookmark, trim stitched piece ³/₄" larger than design on all sides. Cut a piece of Summer Khaki Belfast Linen the same size as stitched piece for backing. Matching right sides and leaving an opening for turning, use a ¹/₂" seam allowance to sew fabric pieces together. Trim seam allowances diagonally at corners. Turn bookmark right side out, carefully pushing corners outward. Blind stitch opening closed; press bookmark flat.

Designs by Diane Williams.

X	DMC	B'ST	ANC.	COLOR
•	ecru	✓	387	ecru
◉	355		1014	terra cotta
◆	420		374	brown
☐	729		890	gold
‰	758		882	peach
◼	869	✓	944	dk brown
◘	895		1044	dk green
◣	918		341	dk copper
Σ	930		1035	dk blue
Π	931		1034	blue

X	DMC	ANC.	COLOR
★	3023	1040	grey
■	3051	681	dk olive green
T	3052	262	olive green
▬	3345	268	green
2	3346	267	lt green
▼	3787	273	dk grey
‖	3828	373	lt brown
●	3371	382	brown black
			French Knot

9

COFFEE ACCLAIM

Stitched in colors as rich as the brew it celebrates, this eye-opening accent is destined to delight coffee lovers. The handsome framed piece features robust sentiments that'll wake up a kitchen or breakfast area!

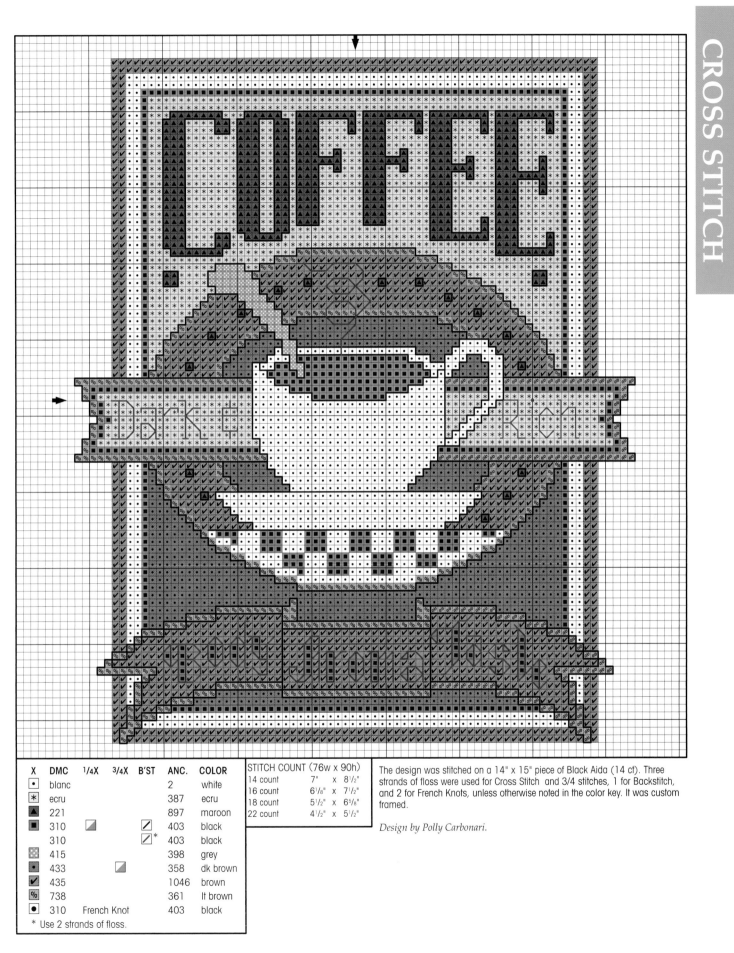

X	DMC	1/4X	3/4X	B'ST	ANC.	COLOR
•	blanc				2	white
*	ecru				387	ecru
▲	221				897	maroon
■	310	◪		◪	403	black
	310			◪*	403	black
▨	415				398	grey
•	433		◪		358	dk brown
✔	435				1046	brown
%	738				361	lt brown
●	310	French Knot			403	black

* Use 2 strands of floss.

STITCH COUNT (76w x 90h)

14 count	7" x 8½"
16 count	6⅛" x 7½"
18 count	5½" x 6⅝"
22 count	4½" x 5½"

The design was stitched on a 14" x 15" piece of Black Aida (14 ct). Three strands of floss were used for Cross Stitch and 3/4 stitches, 1 for Backstitch, and 2 for French Knots, unless otherwise noted in the color key. It was custom framed.

Design by Polly Carbonari.

Garden Birdsong

The garden would be very silent if no birds sang there except for those who sang the best.
—Audubon

This charming little bird, paired with a delightful verse, conveys the artist's immense love of natural themes and gardening.

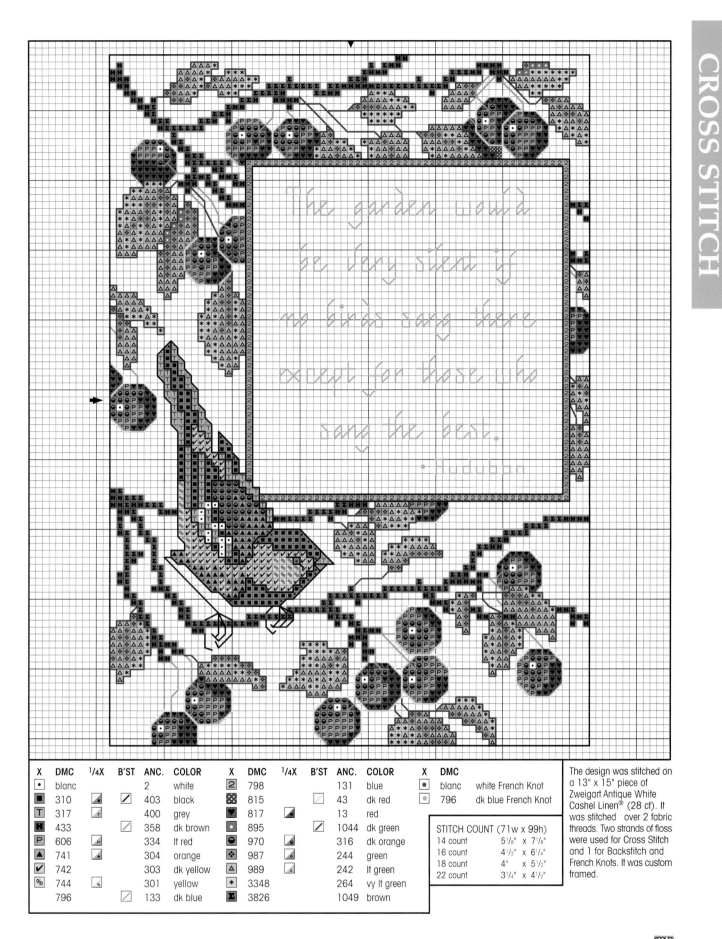

The garden would be very silent if no birds sang there except for those who sang the best. — Audubon

X	DMC	1/4X	B'ST	ANC.	COLOR	X	DMC	1/4X	B'ST	ANC.	COLOR	X	DMC	
•	blanc			2	white	2	798			131	blue	•	blanc	white French Knot
■	310	▨	✓	403	black	▨	815			43	dk red	◉	796	dk blue French Knot
T	317	T		400	grey	♥	817	▨		13	red			
H	433		✓	358	dk brown	◉	895			1044	dk green			
P	606	▨		334	lt red	◉	970	▨		316	dk orange			
▲	741	▲		304	orange	✤	987	▨		244	green			
✔	742	▨		303	dk yellow	△	989	△		242	lt green			
%	744	▨		301	yellow	*	3348			264	vy lt green			
	796	✓		133	dk blue	Σ	3826			1049	brown			

STITCH COUNT (71w x 99h)

14 count	5 1/8" x 7 1/8"
16 count	4 1/2" x 6 1/4"
18 count	4" x 5 1/2"
22 count	3 1/4" x 4 1/2"

The design was stitched on a 13" x 15" piece of Zweigart Antique White Cashel Linen® (28 ct). It was stitched over 2 fabric threads. Two strands of floss were used for Cross Stitch and 1 for Backstitch and French Knots. It was custom framed.

Design by Barbara Baatz

*T*he next time you decide to cook up some fun for your Christmas kitchen, reach for these whimsical towels. Embellished with a trio of designs, the decorative cloths will add a dash of merriment to the hub of the household.

Christmas Towels

X	DMC	1/4X	B'ST	ANC.	COLOR	X	DMC	1/4X	B'ST	ANC.	COLOR	X	DMC	1/4X	B'ST	ANC.	COLOR
•	blanc	•		2	white	n	738	n		361	lt tan	#	3328			1024	salmon
■	310		/	403	black	5	743	s		302	yellow	7	3712			1023	lt salmon
↑	318	↑		399	grey	◉	762	◉		234	lt grey	w	3755	•		140	lt blue
★	322			978	dk blue	Z	776			24	pink		3799		/	236	dk grey
◓	334	◔		977	blue	H	839			360	dk brown	◦	blanc		white French Knot		
✖	347	◪		1025	red	◗	840	◪		379	brown	◉	310		black French Knot		
●	436	◢		1045	dk tan	%	841			378	lt brown	●	938		vy dk brown French Knot		
✦	437	✦		362	tan	X	842	ꙇ		388	vy lt brown						
8	676	8		891	lt gold	T	911	◿		205	green						
C	677			886	vy lt gold	6	913	6		204	lt green						
✔	721			324	orange	✳	938	◿	/	381	vy dk brown						
Σ	729			890	gold	♥	948			1011	flesh						

The designs were stitched on the 11 ct insert of a prefinished towel. Three strands of floss were used for Cross Stitch and 2 for Backstitch and French Knots.

80w x 36h

80w x 35h

75w x 35h

Designs by Deborah Lambein.

Sweetheart Jar Lids

Whether topping off a jar of scrumptious candy or heart-shaped
bath beads, these adorable jar lids make precious Valentine's Day gifts! The heartfelt
keepsakes can be used year-round to hold anything from decorative soaps
in the bathroom to cookies in the kitchen.

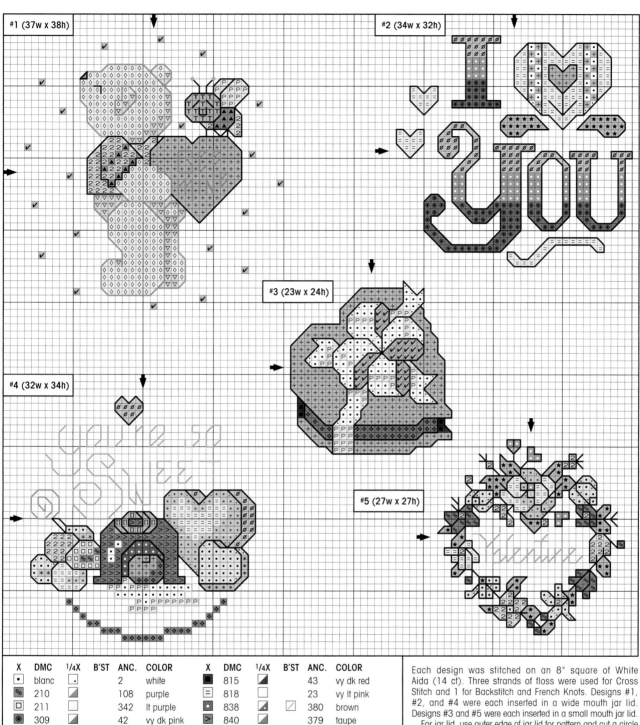

#1 (37w x 38h) **#2 (34w x 32h)** **#3 (23w x 24h)** **#4 (32w x 34h)** **#5 (27w x 27h)**

X	DMC	1/4X	B'ST	ANC.	COLOR	X	DMC	1/4X	B'ST	ANC.	COLOR
•	blanc			2	white	■	815			43	vy dk red
%	210			108	purple	=	818			23	vy lt pink
□	211			342	lt purple	•	838		✓	380	brown
◉	309			42	vy dk pink	>	840			379	taupe
▲	310		✓ *	403	black	Ⅱ	841			378	lt taupe
❖	321		✓ †	9046	dk red	∅	899			52	pink
▣	335		✓ *	38	dk pink	★	913			204	green
✳	352			9	dk peach	◇	945			881	lt peach
•	353			6	peach		975		✓ †	355	rust
▽	402			1047	lt rust		3799		✓	236	grey
+	666			46	red	T	3827				gold
2	744			301	yellow	⊙	3799				grey French Knot
P	775			128	lt blue						
•	776			24	lt pink						
✔	809			130	blue						

* Use 310 for Design #1 and 335 for all other.

† Use 321 for Design for #4 and 975 for all other.

Each design was stitched on an 8" square of White Aida (14 ct). Three strands of floss were used for Cross Stitch and 1 for Backstitch and French Knots. Designs #1, #2, and #4 were each inserted in a wide mouth jar lid. Designs #3 and #5 were each inserted in a small mouth jar lid.

For jar lid, use outer edge of jar lid for pattern and cut a circle from adhesive mounting board. Using opening of jar lid for pattern, cut a circle of batting. Center batting on adhesive board and press in place. Center stitched piece on batting and press edges onto adhesive board; trim edges close to board. Glue board inside jar lid.

Designs by Linda Gillum.

Love Letters

*T*he romantic at heart will cherish our dainty throw pillow with
its message of love stitched on a cheery yellow background. We finished it
with frilly ruffles for a pretty decorative touch.

STITCH COUNT (56w x 64h)

14 count	4" x 5⅝"
16 count	3½" x 4"
18 count	3⅛" x 3⅝"
22 count	2⅝" x 3"

X	DMC	B'ST	ANC.	COLOR
☆	blanc		2	white
	318	╱	399	grey
△	335		38	dk pink
+	776		24	pink
◤	813		161	blue
	912	╱ *	209	green
◯	954		203	lt green

*Use 2 strands of floss.

The design was stitched on a 13" x 14" piece of Yellow Aida (14 ct). Three strands of floss were used for Cross Stitch and 1 for Backstitch, unless otherwise noted in the color key.

For pillow, trim stitched piece 1½" larger than design on all sides. Cut a piece of fabric the same size as stitched piece for backing. For cording, you will need a 28" length of ¼" dia. purchased cording with attached seam allowance. For ruffle, cut one 5" x 56" fabric strip and 56" length of 1"w flat lace.

Note: Use a ½" seam allowance for all seams.

If necessary, trim seam allowance of cording to ½". Matching raw edges and beginning at bottom edge, pin cording to right side of stitched piece, making a ⅜" clip in seam allowance of cording at corners. Ends of cording should overlap approximately 4". Turn overlapped ends of cording toward outside edge of stitched piece; baste cording to stitched piece.

For ruffle, press short ends of fabric strip ½" to wrong side. Matching wrong sides and long edges, press fabric strip in half. Matching raw edges of fabric strip and straight edge of lace, baste layers together close to raw edge. Gather fabric strip and lace to fit stitched piece. Matching raw edges and beginning at bottom edge, pin ruffle to right side of stitched piece, overlapping short ends ¼". Sew ruffle to stitched piece. Matching right sides and leaving an opening for turning, sew stitched piece and backing fabric together. Trim corners diagonally. Turn pillow right side out, carefully pushing corners outward. Stuff pillow with polyester fiberfill and blind stitch opening closed.

A UNION OF HEARTS

Romantic posies and clear-toned bells serve as reminders of a joyful wedding day and the blissful years yet to come. Personalized and custom-framed, this tender piece is sure to capture the hearts of your favorite newlyweds.

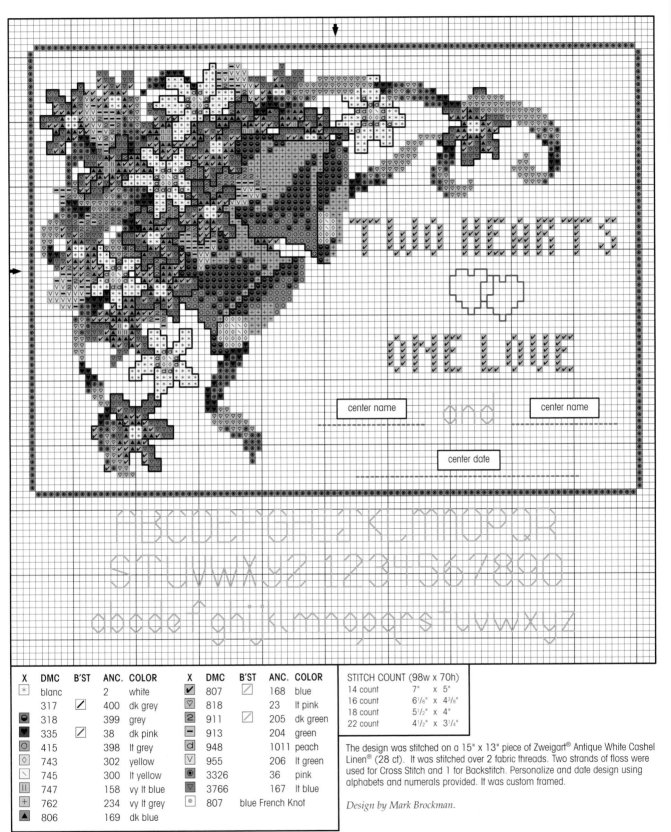

X	DMC	B'ST	ANC.	COLOR	X	DMC	B'ST	ANC.	COLOR
*	blanc		2	white	✔	807	∕	168	blue
	317	∕	400	dk grey	▽	818		23	lt pink
◐	318		399	grey	2	911	∕	205	dk green
▼	335	∕	38	dk pink	–	913		204	green
○	415		398	lt grey	d	948		1011	peach
◇	743		302	yellow	V	955		206	lt green
◣	745		300	lt yellow	◉	3326		36	pink
‖	747		158	vy lt blue	▽	3766		167	lt blue
+	762		234	vy lt grey	◦	807			blue French Knot
▲	806		169	dk blue					

STITCH COUNT (98w x 70h)

14 count	7"	x	5"
16 count	6¹⁄₈"	x	4³⁄₈"
18 count	5¹⁄₂"	x	4"
22 count	4¹⁄₂"	x	3¹⁄₄"

The design was stitched on a 15" x 13" piece of Zweigart® Antique White Cashel Linen® (28 ct). It was stitched over 2 fabric threads. Two strands of floss were used for Cross Stitch and 1 for Backstitch. Personalize and date design using alphabets and numerals provided. It was custom framed.

Design by Mark Brockman.

*M*ark Baby's arrival in the world with this cute photo frame featuring a locket and lots of sweet baby charms. Personalized with the name and birth date, the design provides a perfect spot for a first-day photo of the little bundle of joy.

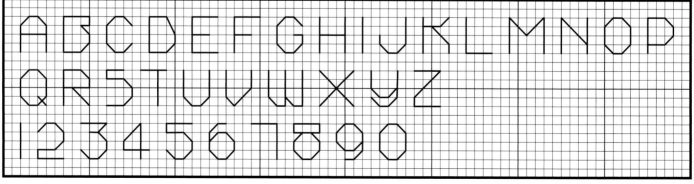

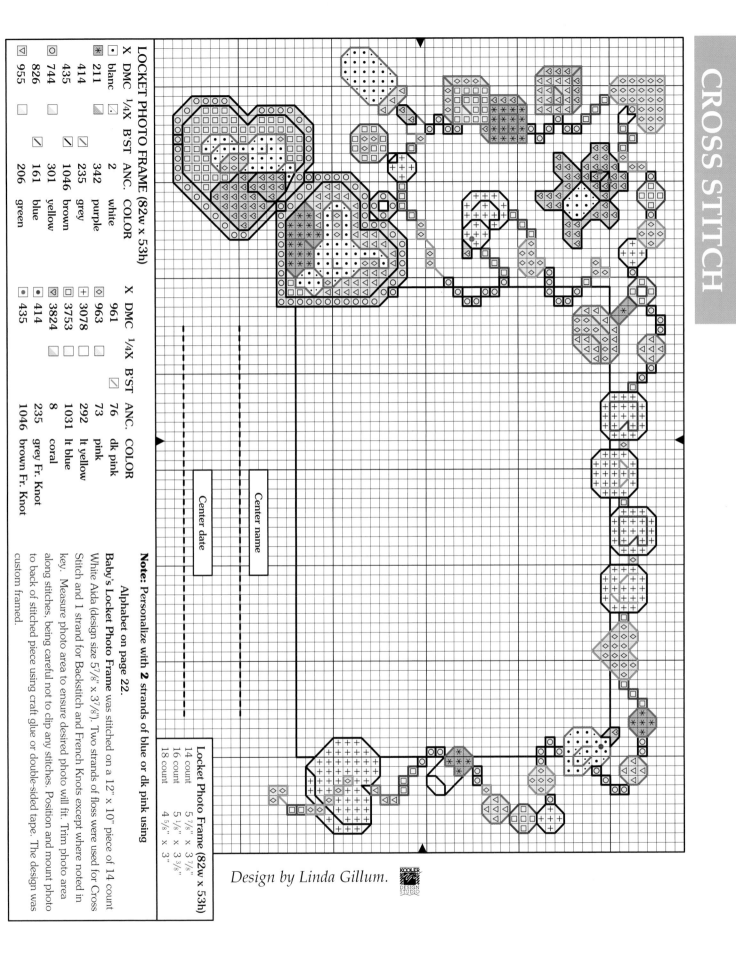

LOCKET PHOTO FRAME (82w x 53h)

X	DMC	1/4X	B'ST	ANC.	COLOR
•	blanc			2	white
✳	211			342	purple
◢	414			235	grey
◹	435			1046	brown
◉	744			301	yellow
◺	826		◹	161	blue
▽	955			206	green

X	DMC	1/4X	B'ST	ANC.	COLOR
◇	961		◹	76	dk pink
◇	963			73	pink
+	3078			292	lt yellow
☐	3753			1031	lt blue
◹	3824			8	coral
◥	414			235	grey Fr. Knot
•	435			1046	brown Fr. Knot

Center name

Center date

Note: Personalize with 2 strands of blue or dk pink using
Alphabet on page 22.

Baby's Locket Photo Frame was stitched on a 12" x 10" piece of 14 count
White Aida (design size 5⅞" x 3⅞"). Two strands of floss were used for Cross
Stitch and 1 strand for Backstitch and French Knots except where noted in
key. Measure photo area to ensure desired photo will fit. Trim photo area
along stitches, being careful not to clip any stitches. Position and mount photo
to back of stitched piece using craft glue or double-sided tape. The design was
custom framed.

Locket Photo Frame (82w x 53h)		
14 count	5⅞" x	3⅞"
16 count	5⅛" x	3⅜"
18 count	4⅝" x	3"

Design by Linda Gillum.

KOOLER DESIGN STUDIO

Friendship Road

Although life's journeys can take us far from those we love, how wonderful it is to be reminded that there is a road by which we can return. This charming portrait of an inviting home and a peaceful phrase offers solace in knowing that close friends are never far away.

X	DMC	1/4X	B'ST	ANC.	COLOR
•	blanc	•		2	white
Π	300	Π		352	brown
◊	301	◊		1049	lt brown
▲	335			38	pink
□	349	◰		13	lt red
♥	498			1005	red
▣	553			98	purple
☆	743			302	yellow
✳	744	⁘		301	lt yellow
♡	827			160	lt blue
✖	895			1044	dk green
★	932	◪		1033	blue
$	987			244	green
▽	3347			266	lt green
T	3348			264	vy lt green
	3799		╱	236	dk grey
⦿	3799		dk grey French Knot		

The design was stitched on an 8" x 10" piece of White Lugana (25 ct). It was stitched over 2 fabric threads. Three strands of floss were used for Cross Stitch and 1 for Backstitch and French Knots. It was custom framed.

Design by Terrece Beesley.

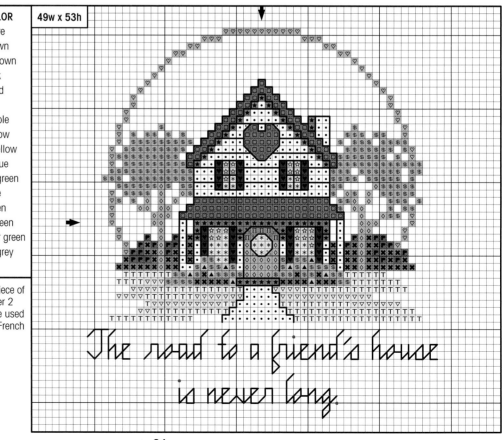

49w x 53h

Redwork Wreath

Good times are best...

When shared with friends

You will need a 20" square of white fabric for redwork, water soluble marking pen, 17$\frac{1}{2}$" dia. grapevine wreath, assorted red and white kitchen utensils, red and white check bow, mat board, craft knife, paper-backed fusible web, and hot glue gun.

1. Center fabric over pattern and trace sunbonnet girls using fabric marking pen. Repositioning fabric to allow a 1" space between top words and design and a 1$\frac{1}{4}$" space between bottom words and design, trace words.

2. Embroider design using one strand of floss for woodgrain areas and two strands of floss for remaining design. Follow manufacturer's instructions to fuse web to wrong side of redwork piece.

3. Use craft knife to cut a piece of mat board to fit back of wreath.

4. Fuse redwork piece to mat board. Trim redwork piece same size as mat board.

5. Glue bow and kitchen utensils to wreath. Glue mat board to back of wreath.

Continued on page 26.

Re-create the charm of turn-of-the-century needlework with this precious Sunbonnet Sue design in redwork. The sweet, shy little girls were popular then as illustrations in children's books and on quilts, embroidered linens, and other items. This design's tender sentiment reminds us to enjoy life's quiet moments with those who are dear.

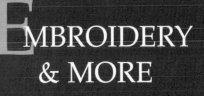

EMBROIDERY & MORE

Good times are best...

When shared with friends

Embroidering Design
The majority of the design is worked in Stem Stitch. We recommend working all Stem Stitch first, then French Knots.

Refer to Embroidery Stitches, page 29, and use number of floss strands stated in project instructions.
Note: You may wish to set the floss

color before stitching by soaking floss in a mixture of 1 tablespoon vinegar and 8 ounces of water. Allow floss to air dry.

26

Crazy Quilt Pillow

Delicate embroidery stitches and lace make this crazy quilt pillow a work of art. We substituted buttons and bows for stitchery in some of the sections and made a simple beaded fringe for the edges. To create your own precious pillow, start with scraps of six different fabrics in your favorite color scheme.

Design by Patricia Eaton.

EMBROIDERY & MORE

INSTRUCTIONS

1. Trace heavy lines of block pattern, page 28, onto paper. Turn paper over and re-trace lines to reverse pattern (reversed side of paper will face up when you are ready to sew).

2. Using 6 different scraps of purple cottons, label fabrics A-F to match sections on block pattern. Use the non-reversed paper pattern as a guide to roughly cut out one fabric piece for each area of the pattern. Pieces should be at least $^1/_2$" larger on all sides than the corresponding section on the block.

3. With non-reversed side of paper pattern facing up, center fabric piece A on section A with right side of fabric facing out. Holding fabric and pattern in front of a light source, make sure that fabric extends beyond all section A seamlines; pin in place.

4. Place fabric piece B on top of A, with right sides together. Use your light source to check that when you sew A and B pieces together along the line separating those sections, that fabric piece B will completely cover section B on the pattern when it is opened up. Once adjusted, place paper pattern, with fabric side down, under your

sewing machine needle. Using a short straight stitch, sew directly on top of line separating sections A and B. Turn paper over and trim fabric seam allowance to $^1/_4$". Open fabric piece B and press; pin in place.

5. Repeat Step 4 to add remaining fabric pieces to paper pattern.

6. Using a medium stitch length, stay-stitch along outer lines of block. Trim excess fabric $^1/_2$" from edges to complete block. Tear away paper pattern.

7. Referring to photo, embroider block for pillow front. No seam-covering stitches were used. Lace trims were stitched along two seams, and buttons and a bow were stitched to unembroidered areas.

8. For pillow back, cut a square of fabric same size as pillow front. With right sides facing, sew pillow front and back together, leaving an opening for turning. Turn pillow

right side out; press. Stuff with fiberfill and sew opening closed.

9. To add beaded fringe, thread beading needle with an 18" length of nylon thread. Take several small stitches at one corner of pillow to secure thread. Thread 7 purple, 3 pink, and 1 purple seed bead onto thread. Referring to Beaded Fringe Diagram, skip last bead on thread, then thread needle back through pink beads. Thread 7 more purple beads onto thread. Take a small stitch in seamline of pillow about $^3/_8$" from first stitch. Continue to repeat sequence around entire edge of pillow.

Beaded Fringe Diagram

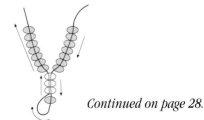

Continued on page 28.

Transferring the Design to the Block

Pat's Pointer: *Transferring the design to your fabric doesn't have to be a big deal. Transfer as few lines to the fabric as possible, just so you know where to place the major components of the design.*

Method 1: For light-colored fabrics, use a light source, such as a light table or a window, to simply trace the design onto the fabric using a pencil.

Method 2: For dark-colored fabrics or fabrics that you don't want to risk leaving permanent marks on, trace design onto a piece of heat-sensitive brush-off fabric stabilizer or water-soluble fabric stabilizer (available at fabric stores) using a permanent fine-point pen. Baste the stabilizer onto the right side of the block. Embroider design, stitching through stabilizer. When stitching is complete, remove basting threads and stabilizer.

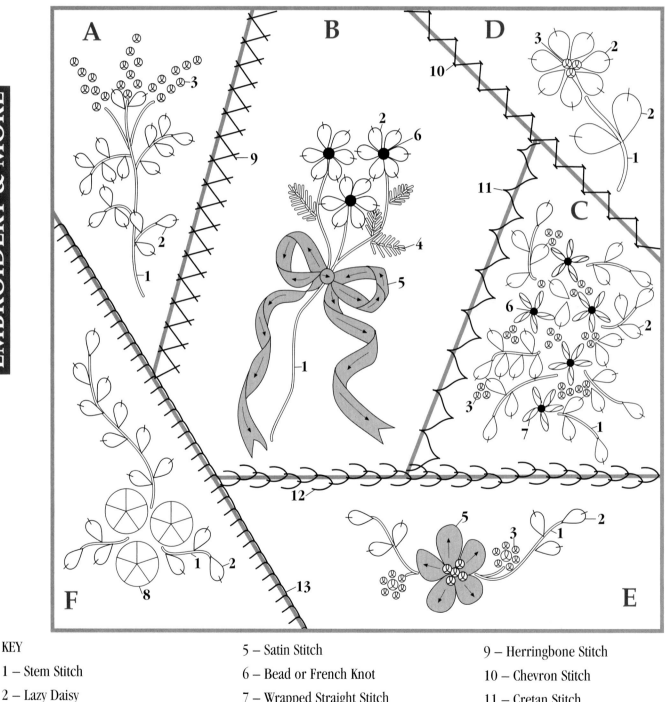

EMBROIDERY & MORE

KEY

1 – Stem Stitch

2 – Lazy Daisy

3 – French Knot or Bead

4 – Fishbone Stitch

5 – Satin Stitch

6 – Bead or French Knot

7 – Wrapped Straight Stitch

8 – Woven Rose

9 – Herringbone Stitch

10 – Chevron Stitch

11 – Cretan Stitch

12 – Feather Stitch

13 – Blanket Stitch

The Embroidery Stitches

Blanket Stitch – Use 2 or 3 strands of floss

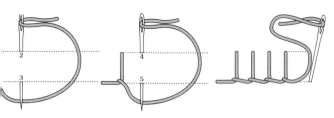

Chevron Stitch – Use 3 strands of floss

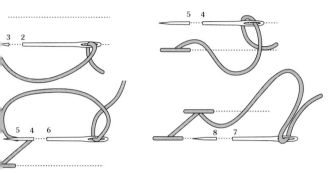

Cretan Stitch – Use 3 strands of floss

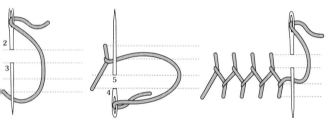

Feather Stitch – Use 2 or 3 strands of floss

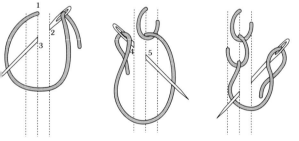

Fishbone Stitch – Use 2 or 3 strands of floss

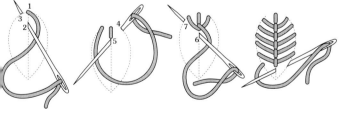

French Knot – Use 3 to 12 strands of floss

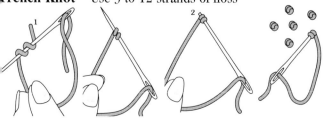

Herringbone Stitch – Use 2 or 3 strands of floss

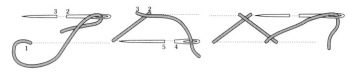

Lazy Daisy – Use 2 to 6 strands of floss

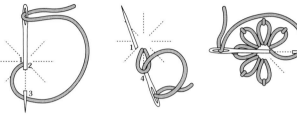

Satin Stitch – Use 2 or 3 strands of floss

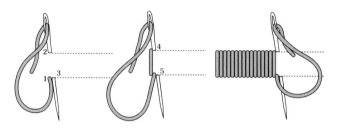

Stem Stitch – Use 2 or 3 strands of floss

Woven Rose – Use 2 strands of floss for spokes, and 6 strands of floss for weaving

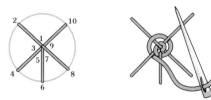

Wrapped Straight Stitch – Use 3 to 6 strands of floss

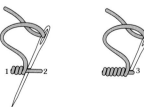

For more embroidery stitches, see page 201.

"Beary" Good

Our tiny bear is big on sharing his opinion! Whether used as a gift tag for our yummy Espresso Brownies or even to post a little one's good grades, this cute cub and his brightly beaded banner tell one and all that life is "beary good!"

ESPRESSO BROWNIES

1   teaspoon instant espresso powder
2   tablespoons warm water
1   package (10$^1/_4$ ounces) brownie mix
1   egg
3   tablespoons vegetable oil
$^1/_2$ teaspoon ground cinnamon

Preheat oven to 350 degrees. In a medium bowl, combine espresso powder and warm water. Add remaining ingredients; stir until well blended. Spread batter into a greased 8-inch square baking pan. Bake 18 to 22 minutes. Cool in pan on a wire rack. Cut into 1$^1/_2$ x 2-inch bars.

Yield: about 1 dozen brownies

Design by Monica Brady.

The design was stitched on a 4" x 5" piece of Crafter's Pride Black Vinyl-Weave™ (14 ct). Three strands of floss were used for Cross Stitch and 1 for Backstitch, unless otherwise noted in the color key. Beads were attached using 1 strand of DMC 310 floss. See Attaching Beads, below. It was made into a gift ornament. To finish gift ornament, trim Vinyl-Weave one square from edge of design. **Attaching Beads:** Refer to chart for bead placement and sew bead in place using a fine needle that will pass through bead. Bring needle up at 1 and then down at 2. Secure floss on back or move to next bead as shown.

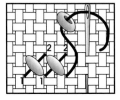

DMC	B'ST	ANC.	COLOR
310		403	black
310		403	black
321		9046	red
434		310	dk tan
436		1045	tan
437		362	lt tan
743		302	yellow
783		307	gold
Mill Hill Bead - 00020			

Use 3 strands of floss.

STITCH COUNT (31w x 42h)
14 count	2$^1/_4$" x	3"
16 count	2" x	2$^5/_8$"
18 count	1$^3/_4$" x	2$^3/_8$"
22 count	1$^1/_2$" x	2"

Hardanger Coaster

*W*ith their simple stitching and cutwork, these coasters emulate a
timeless technique known as Hardanger embroidery. The name comes from the
Hardanger Fjord region of Norway, where the ancient technique was commonly
stitched in the white-on-white style we know today. Like cross stitch, Hardanger
embroidery involves a few basic stitches worked on evenweave fabric, often using
perle cotton thread. Over the years, a particular 22 count fabric became
so closely associated with the technique that it, too, took on the
traditional name. We used Hardanger fabric for our lovely coasters,
but Lugana and various types of linen will also work.

HARDANGER COASTER
Chart and all figures on page 33.

For each coaster, you will need an 8" square of White Hardanger (22 ct) fabric, #5 DMC blanc perle cotton, #8 DMC blanc perle cotton, and small sharp scissors.

1. Referring to Stitch Diagrams and using #5 perle cotton, work Kloster Blocks indicated on chart.
2. After all Kloster Blocks have been completed, refer to chart and locate the red lines that indicate threads to be cut. Begin with the three squares in each corner which are surrounded on all four sides by Kloster Blocks. Run scissors blade under four fabric threads indicated (Fig. 1) and cut. All threads are cut and removed from these areas. Continue cutting as indicated on the chart. Carefully remove the remaining cut threads with tweezers, leaving groups of four horizontal and vertical threads. These threads will be worked with Needlewoven Bars and Dove's Eye Stitch.
3. Referring to Stitch Diagrams and using #8 perle cotton, work Needlewoven Bars and Dove's Eye Stitch as indicated on chart.
4. Referring to Stitch Diagrams and using #5 perle cotton, work Buttonhole Stitch as indicated in chart.
5. Cut excess fabric from around the outside edge of design, being careful not to cut Buttonhole Stitches.
6. Wash and press coaster.

EMBROIDERY & MORE

STITCH DIAGRAMS

Kloster Block
The **Kloster Block** is a group of 5 Satin Stitches worked over 4 fabric threads. Come up with needle at the bottom of all blocks (odd numbers in Fig. 2) and go down with needle at the top of all blocks (even numbers in Fig. 2). When turning a corner clockwise, thread is carried behind the last stitch in a block. The bottom of this last stitch serves as a pivot point and shares a fabric hole with the bottom of the first stitch in the next block (#19 & #21). When turning a corner counter-clockwise, thread is carried behind the first stitch in the next block. The top of the last stitch in a block serves as a pivot point and shares a fabric hole with the top of the first stitch in the next block (#30 & #32).

Needlewoven Bars and Dove's Eye Stitch
After fabric threads have been cut and removed, there will be groups of four fabric threads that criss-cross the cut area. For **Needlewoven Bars**, these 4 fabric threads are woven together to form a bar. Holding thread behind the 4 fabric threads, follow Fig. 3 to begin weaving over the first two fabric threads and under the second two. Using tight tension, continue weaving in a figure eight motion, over two and under two (Fig. 4), until bar is full. Finish bar with thread toward next bar to be woven; begin next bar by going over two fabric threads and under two fabric threads (Fig. 5).

The **Dove's Eye Stitch** is worked at the same time as the Needlewoven Bars in the design. Needleweave three bars around where the Dove's Eye Stitch is to be placed and one-half of the fourth bar. Go down with the needle in the middle of Bar 3 (Fig. 6). Bring needle over the thread going from Bar 4 to Bar 3 and go down in Bar 2. Bring needle over the thread going from Bar 3 to Bar 2 and go down in Bar 1. Bring needle over the thread going from Bar 2 to Bar 1. Then bring needle under the thread from Bar 4 to Bar 3 and go down in the middle of Bar 4 (Fig. 7). Finish needleweaving Bar 4. When the Dove's Eye Stitch is worked next to another Dove's Eye Stitch, begin needleweaving in the first unwoven bar, treating the existing woven bars as part of the Dove's Eye.

Pointers:
• When working Hardanger, use a Tapestry needle. The blunt point helps prevent splitting the fabric threads. Use a size #22 needle when working with #5 perle cotton and a size #24 needle when working with #8 and #12 perle cotton.
• The use of an embroidery hoop is optional. Experiment working with and without a hoop to decide which is more comfortable for you. However, do not use a hoop while cutting fabric threads. If a hoop is used while stitching, position fabric loosely, so the fabric threads are not stretched; if the fabric is stretched while working, the Satin Stitches will buckle when released from the hoop.

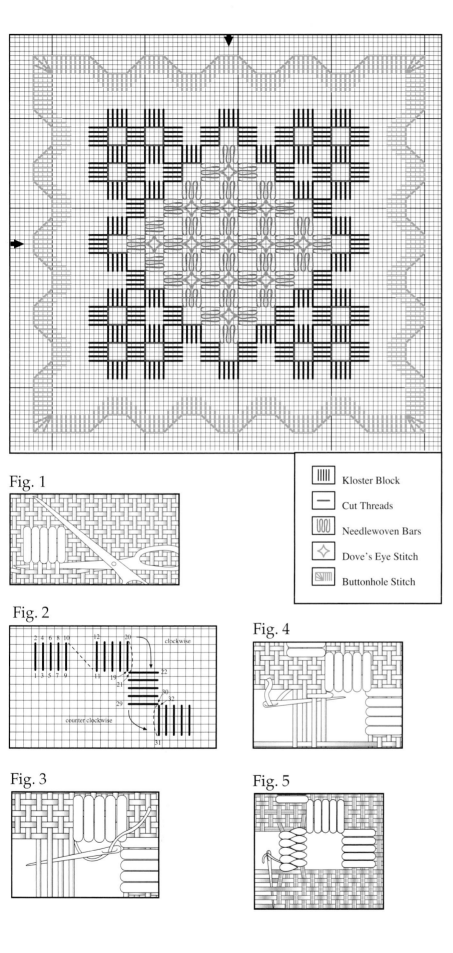

Fig. 1

Buttonhole Stitch

Bring needle up from wrong side at 1. Go down at 2 and come up at 3, keeping floss below point of needle (Fig. a). Referring to chart for placement, continue in this manner around the design (Fig. b).

Fig. a

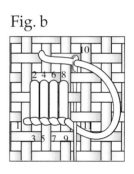

Fig. b

	‖‖‖	Kloster Block
	—	Cut Threads
	ⓊⓊⓊ	Needlewoven Bars
	◇	Dove's Eye Stitch
	▨	Buttonhole Stitch

Fig. 2

clockwise

counter clockwise

Fig. 4

Fig. 3

Fig. 5

Fig. 6

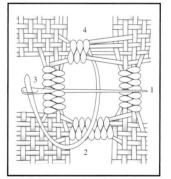

Fig. 7

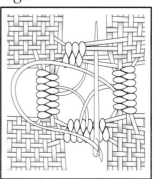

Safari Cats Tissue Topper

If you love a touch of the exotic, here's the accent for you! Our tissue box cover captures the allure of wild jungle cats for any room in your home.

LASTIC CANVAS

34

Side (32 x 38 threads) (stitch 2)

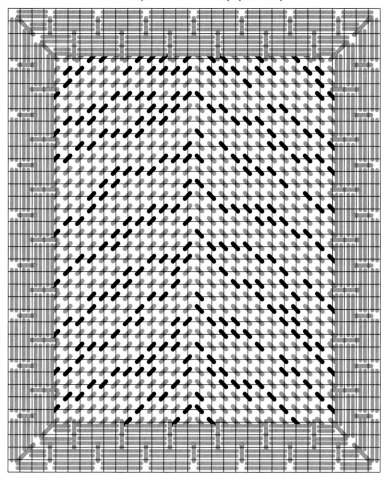

Insert

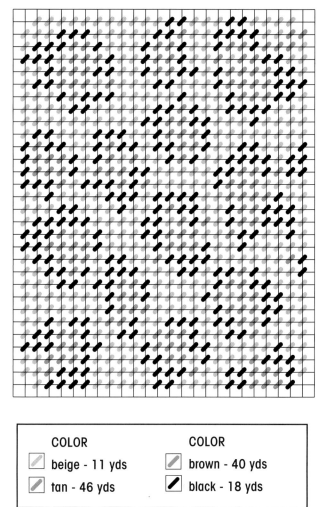

COLOR	COLOR
beige - 11 yds	brown - 40 yds
tan - 46 yds	black - 18 yds

Top (32 x 32 threads)

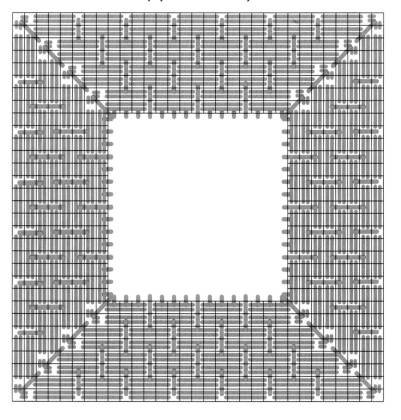

(Please read General Instructions, page 201, before beginning project.)

Skill Level: Beginner
Size: $4^3/_4$"w x $5^3/_4$"h x $4^3/_4$"d
(Fits a $4^1/_4$"w x $5^1/_4$"h x $4^1/_4$"d boutique tissue box.)
Supplies: Worsted weight yarn (refer to color key), two $10^1/_2$" x $13^1/_2$" sheets of 7 mesh plastic canvas, and #16 tapestry needle.
Stitches Used: Backstitch, Gobelin Stitch, Overcast Stitch, and Tent Stitch.
Instructions: Follow charts to cut and stitch Top and two Side pieces. For remaining two Sides, cut two pieces of canvas 32 x 38 threads each. Follow Side chart to stitch bamboo border, leaving area inside border unworked. Follow Insert chart to stitch area inside bamboo border. Using brown overcast stitches, join Sides along long edges; join Top to Sides. Using brown overcast stitches, cover unworked edges.

Design by Conn Baker Gibney.

Jaunty St. Nick

All decked out in North Pole plaid, our bearded St. Nick makes an impressive centerpiece. This jaunty standing figure will be admired by all.

(Please read General Instructions, page 201, before beginning project.)

Skill Level: Beginner

Size: 9"w x 13$^1/_2$"h x 2$^1/_4$"d

Supplies: Worsted weight yarn and metallic gold yarn (refer to color key), two 10$^1/_2$" x 13$^1/_2$" sheets of 7 mesh plastic canvas, #16 tapestry needle, white mini curl doll hair, polyester fiberfill, and craft glue.

Stitches Used: Backstitch, Cross Stitch, French Knot, Gobelin Stitch, Mosaic Stitch, Overcast Stitch, and Tent Stitch.

Instructions: Follow chart to cut and stitch Santa Front; use red tent stitches to cover Santa Back. For Bottom, cut two pieces of canvas 16 x 16 threads each; Bottom pieces are not worked. Referring to photo for yarn colors, join Front to Back along unworked edges, leaving blue shaded area unworked. Lightly stuff Santa with fiberfill. Stack Bottom pieces and join Bottom to Front and Back along blue shaded area. For beard, cut doll hair into short lengths; glue to Santa.

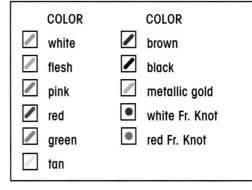

COLOR		COLOR	
▨	white	▧	brown
▨	flesh	▨	black
▨	pink	▨	metallic gold
▨	red	⊙	white Fr. Knot
▨	green	⊙	red Fr. Knot
▨	tan		

Design by Joan Green.

Santa Front/Back
(61 x 91 threads) (cut 2, stitch 1)

Tic-Tac-Toad

You're in for a "toad-ally" good time with our amphibious friend! A new spin on an old-fashioned favorite, the whimsical board is accompanied by game pieces that can be strung on a ribbon for safekeeping. Kids will love this "ribbiting" game for trips and rainy days. It'll also make a great one-of-a-kind gift!

(Please read General Instructions, page 201, before beginning project.)

Skill Level: Beginner
Size: 10¼"w x 7¼"h
Supplies: Worsted Weight Yarn or Needloft® Plastic Canvas Yarn (refer to color key), two 10½" x 13½" sheets of 7 mesh plastic canvas, #16 tapestry needle, and 1 yd of ¼"w red grosgrain ribbon
Stitches Used: Overcast Stitch and Tent Stitch

Instructions: Follow charts to cut and stitch Tic-Tac-Toad pieces. (Note: Back is not worked.) Using green overcast stitches, join Front to Back. Using black overcast stitches, cover unworked edges of remaining pieces. Thread ribbon through center of "X" and "O" pieces. Refer to photo for placement and tie ribbon ends into a bow around Toad.

Design by Michele Wilcox.

NL	COLOR	
✎	00	black - 20 yds
✎	25	lt green - 22 yds
✎	27	green - 30 yds
✎	41	white - 1 yd

"X" (10 x 10 threads)
(stitch 5)

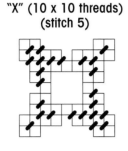

"O" (10 x 10 threads)
(stitch 5)

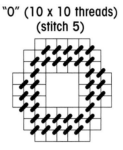

Toad Front/Back (68 x 49 threads) (cut 2, stitch 1)

PLASTIC CANVAS

HAPPY HOLD-UPS

Inspired by the carefree joys of summertime, our cheery magnets will brighten your day — any time of the year!

(Please read General Instructions, page 201, before beginning project.)

Skill Level: Beginner

Approx. Size: 2³/₄"w x 2³/₄"h each

Supplies: Worsted weight yarn or Needloft® Plastic Canvas Yarn (refer to color key and photo), DMC Embroidery Floss (refer to color key and photo), one 10¹/₂" x 13¹/₂" sheet of 7 mesh plastic canvas, #16 tapestry needle, magnetic strip, and clear-drying craft glue.

Stitches Used: Backstitch, Cross Stitch, French Knot, Fringe Stitch, Gobelin Stitch, Mosaic Stitch, Overcast Stitch, Scotch Stitch, and Tent Stitch.

Instructions: Follow chart to cut and stitch desired magnet. Referring to photo for yarn color used, cover unworked edges. Glue magnetic strip to wrong side of magnet.

For Balloon string, cut a 5" length of red yarn. Referring to photo, thread yarn length through Balloon at ★. Secure end of yarn length on wrong side of Balloon.

For Kite tail, cut a 5" length of orange yarn. Referring to photo, secure one end of yarn length on wrong side of Kite. Cut a 4" length each of blue, green, and red yarn. Tie each yarn length into a knot around Kite tail; trim ends.

Designs by Ann Townsend.

Kite (18 x 24 threads)

Butterfly (18 x 15 threads)

YARN (NL)
- red (01)
- gold (11)
- brown (13)
- green (28)
- dk blue (32)
- blue (35)
- white (41)
- orange (52)
- pink (55)
- yellow (57)
- yellow Fr. Knot (57)
- brown Fringe (13)

FLOSS (DMC)
- *black (310)

*Use 6 strands of floss.

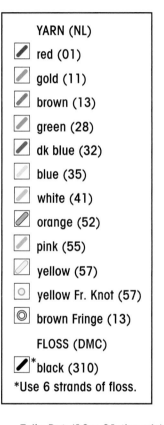

Flower (18 x 18 threads)

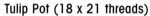

Balloon (16 x 19 threads)

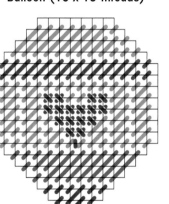

Tulip Pot (18 x 21 threads)

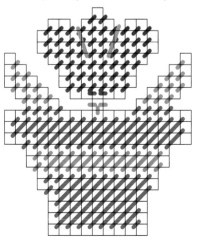

Sun (22 x 14 threads)

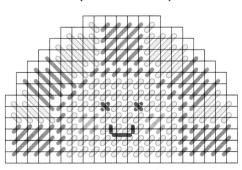

Apple Basket (16 x 16 threads)

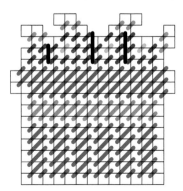

Rabbit Haven

A closer look at our buoyant spring blooms reveals a sweet surprise. Nestled amongst tulips, daffodils, daisies, and brown-eyed Susans, a watchful bunny sits still for a picture-perfect portrait.

PLASTIC CANVAS

(Please read General Instructions, page 201, before beginning project.)

Skill Level: Beginner
Size: 8 1/2"w x 10 1/2"h

Supplies: Worsted weight yarn or Needloft® Plastic Canvas Yarn and embroidery floss (refer to color key), one 10 1/2" x 13 1/2" sheet of 7 mesh plastic canvas, and #16 tapestry needle.

Stitches Used: Backstitch, Gobelin Stitch, and Tent Stitch.
Instructions: Follow chart to cut and stitch Floral Bunny. It was custom framed.

Design by Kathy Wirth and Dianne Davis.

Floral Bunny (57 x 71 threads)

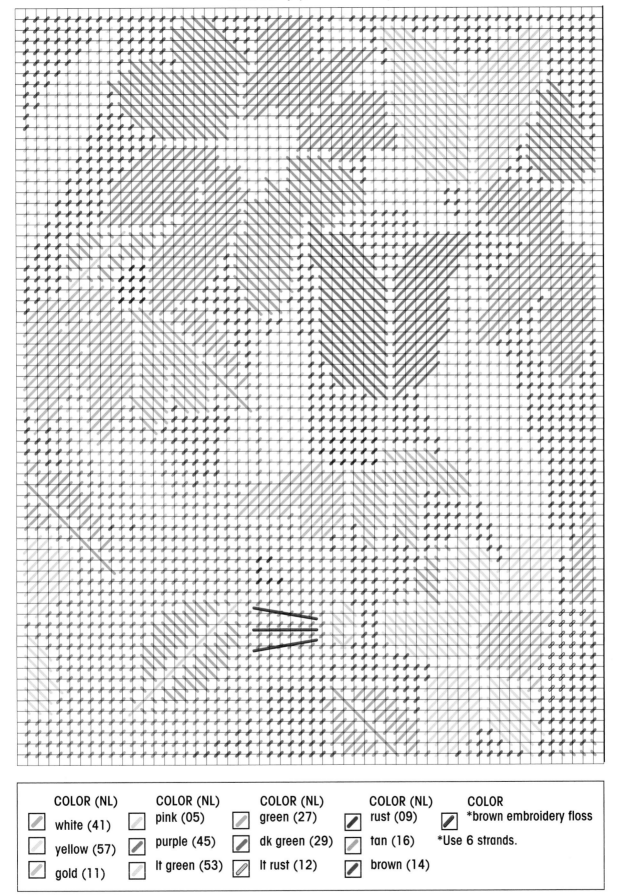

	COLOR (NL)		COLOR (NL)		COLOR (NL)		COLOR (NL)		COLOR
	white (41)		pink (05)		green (27)		rust (09)		*brown embroidery floss
	yellow (57)		purple (45)		dk green (29)		tan (16)		*Use 6 strands.
	gold (11)		lt green (53)		lt rust (12)		brown (14)		

Home "Tweet" Home Coasters

Invite the cheeriness of spring into your home with this quaint little birdhouse! It's home "tweet" home to a matching set of coasters. Simply lift the roof to find the tabletop protectors cleverly nested inside.

(Please read General Instructions, page 201, before beginning project.)

Skill Level: Beginner

Coaster Size: 4 1/2"w x 4 1/2"h each

Holder Size: 5 1/2"w x 5"h x 2 1/2"d

Supplies: Worsted weight yarn (refer to color key), three 10 1/2" x 13 1/2" sheets of 7 mesh plastic canvas, and #16 tapestry needle.

Stitches Used: Backstitch, French Knot, Gobelin Stitch, Lazy Daisy Stitch, Overcast Stitch, and Tent Stitch.

Instructions: Follow charts to cut and stitch coaster set pieces. For Bottom, cut a piece of canvas 16 x 10 threads; Bottom is not worked. Using white yarn, join Perch Side to unworked edges of Perch Top and Bottom. Matching ✖'s and using white yarn, tack Perch Top and Bottom to Front. Using lt blue yarn, join Bottom to Sides along short unworked edges. Using lt blue yarn, join Front and Back to Sides and Bottom. Using lt pink yarn, join Roof pieces along short unworked edges. Referring to photo and using white yarn, join Eaves pieces to Roof pieces along unworked edges. Using blue yarn, tack Wings to Bird; tack Bird to Front. Referring to photo and using matching color yarn, tack Leaves and Flowers to Front.

Design by Virginia Lamp and Michael Lamp.

Wing (8 x 6 threads)

Wing (8 x 6 threads)

Bird (13 x 13 threads)

COLOR	
	white - 29 yds
	yellow - 3 yds
	lt pink - 12 yds
	pink - 5 yds
	purple - 3 yds
	lt blue - 37 yds
	blue - 4 yds
	dk blue - 12 yds
	green - 3 yds
○	*yellow Fr. Knot
●	*black Fr. Knot - 1 yd
	pink Lazy Daisy
	purple Lazy Daisy
	green Lazy Daisy

*Use 2 plies of yarn.

Leaf (4 x 5 threads)
(stitch 4)

Coaster (30 x 30 threads) (stitch 6)

Purple Flower
(6 x 6 threads)

Pink Flower
(6 x 6 threads)

45

Roof (12 x 25 threads)
(stitch 2)

Eaves (25 x 25 threads) (stitch 2)

Perch Top/Bottom
(10 x 5 threads)
(stitch 2)

Perch Side
(15 x 3 threads)

Front/Back (32 x 33 threads) (stitch 2)

Side (10 x 20 threads)
(stitch 2)

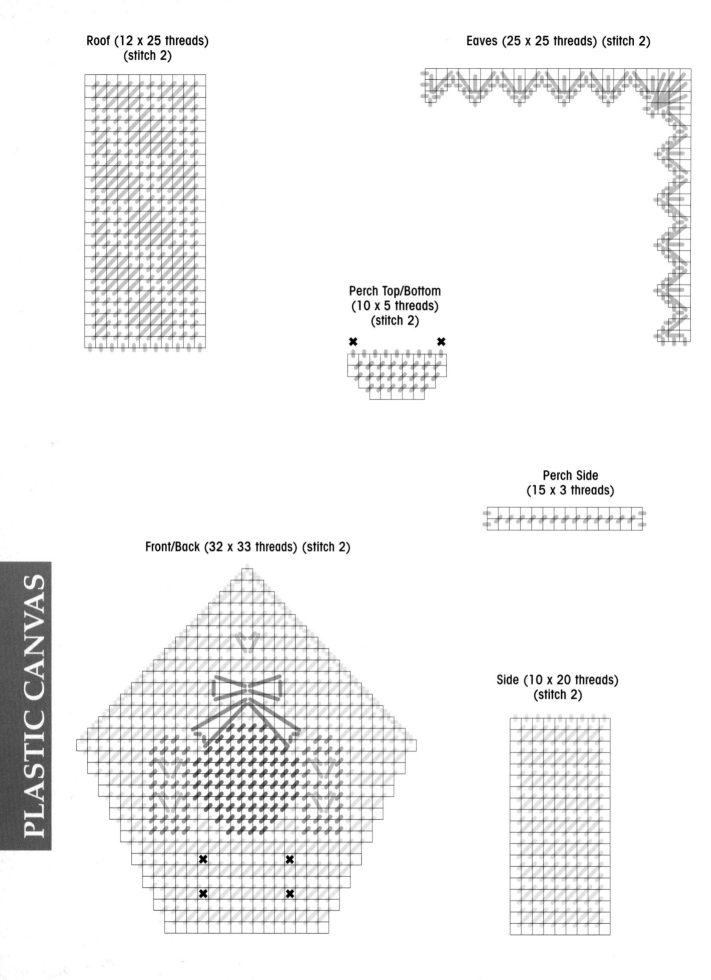

PLASTIC CANVAS

46

Captivating Cables Tee

Cables give this sweater its captivating appeal. Crocheted in cotton thread for cool comfort, the pullover can be made in three sizes.

CROCHE

CAPTIVATING CABLES TEE

Shown on page 47
(Before beginning, see General Instructions, page 202.)

Finished Chest Measurements:
Small - 36", **Medium** - 42",
Large - 48"

Size Note: Instructions are written for size Small with sizes Medium and Large in braces { }. Instructions will be easier to read if you circle all the numbers pertaining to your size. If only one number is given, it applies to all sizes. If a zero is given, it means to do nothing.

MATERIALS

South Maid Cotton Thread (size 10)
[400 yards per ball]:
Natural - 4{5-6} balls
Steel crochet hook, size 5 (1.90 mm) **or** size needed for gauge
Tapestry needle

GAUGE: 16 dc and 8 rows = 2"

BACK

BODY

♡ Ch 146{170-194}.

♡ **Row 1:** Dc in fourth ch from hook **(3 skipped chs count as first dc, now and throughout)** and in each ch across: 144{168-192} dc.

♡ **Row 2** (Right side)**:** Ch 3 **(counts as first dc, now and throughout)**, turn; dc in next dc and in each dc across.

Note: Mark last row as **right** side.

♡ **Rows 3 thru 48{54-60}:** Ch 3, turn; dc in next dc and in each dc across; do **not** finish off.

SLEEVES

To add on dc, YO, insert hook into base of last dc made *(Fig. 1)*, YO and pull up a loop, YO and draw through one loop on hook, (YO and draw through 2 loops on hook) twice **(one dc added)**. Repeat as many times as instructed.

Fig. 1

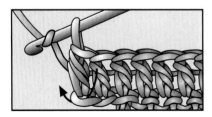

♡ **Row 1:** Ch 26{26-28}, turn; dc in fourth ch from hook and in each ch and each dc across, add on 24{24-26} dc: 192{216-244} dc.

♡ **Rows 2 thru 37{39-42}:** Ch 3, turn; dc in next dc and in each dc across.

♡ Finish off.

FRONT

BODY

♡ Ch 146{170-194}.

♡ **Row 1** (Wrong side)**:** Dc in fourth ch from hook and in each ch across: 144{168-192} dc.

Note: Mark **back** of any dc on last row as **right** side.

To work Front Post treble crochet (abbreviated FPtr), YO twice, insert hook from **front** to **back** around post of st indicated, YO and pull up a loop, (YO and draw through 2 loops on hook) 3 times. Skip st behind FPtr.

♡ **Row 2:** Ch 3, turn; dc in next 40{48-56} dc, work FPtr around each of next 2 sts, dc in next 2 dc, work FPtr around each of next 2 sts, ★ dc in next 8{10-12} dc, work FPtr around each of next 2 sts, dc in next 2 dc, work FPtr around each of next 2 sts; repeat from ★ 3 times **more**, dc in next dc and in each dc across.

To work Back Post treble crochet (abbreviated BPtr), YO twice, insert hook from **back** to **front** around post of st indicated, YO and pull up a loop, (YO and draw through 2 loops on hook) 3 times. Skip st in front of BPtr.

♡ **Row 3:** Ch 3, turn; dc in next 40{48-56} dc, work BPtr around each of next 2 FPtr, dc in next 2 dc, work BPtr around each of next 2 FPtr, ★ dc in next 8{10-12} dc, work BPtr around each of next 2 FPtr, dc in next 2 dc, work BPtr around each of next 2 FPtr; repeat from ★ 3 times **more**, dc in next dc and in each dc across.

♡ **Rows 4 and 5:** Repeat Rows 2 and 3.

To work Front Post double treble crochet (abbreviated FPdtr), YO 3 times, insert hook from **front** to **back** around post of BPtr indicated, YO and pull up a loop, (YO and draw through 2 loops on hook) 4 times. Skip st behind FPdtr.

To work Twist (uses next 6 sts), skip next 4 sts, work FPdtr around each of next 2 BPtr, working **behind** last 2 FPdtr made, dc in next 2 skipped dc, working in **front** of last 2 FPdtr made, work FPdtr around first skipped BPtr and next skipped BPtr.

♡ **Row 6:** Ch 3, turn; dc in next 40{48-56} dc, work Twist, [dc in next 8{10-12} dc, work Twist] 4 times, dc in next dc and in each dc across.

♡ **Row 7:** Ch 3, turn; dc in next 40{48-56} dc, work BPtr around each of next 2 FPtr, dc in next 2 dc, work BPtr around each of next 2 FPtr, ★ dc in next 8{10-12} dc, work BPtr around each of next 2 FPtr, dc in next 2 dc, work BPtr around each of next 2 FPtr; repeat from ★ 3 times **more**, dc in next dc and in each dc across.

♡ **Rows 8 thru 48{54-60}:** Repeat Rows 2-7, 6{7-8} times; then repeat Rows 2-6 once **more**; do **not** finish off.

SLEEVES

♡ **Row 1:** Ch 26{26-28}, turn; dc in fourth ch from hook and in each ch across, dc in next 41{49-57} dc, work BPtr around each of next 2 FPtr, dc in next 2 dc, work BPtr around each of next 2 FPtr, ★ dc in next 8{10-12} dc, work BPtr around each of next 2 FPtr, dc in next 2 dc, work BPtr around each of next 2 FPtr; repeat from ★ 3 times **more**, dc in last 41{49-57} dc, add on 24{24-26} dc: 192{216-244} sts.

♡ **Row 2:** Ch 3, turn; dc in next dc and in each dc across to next BPtr, work FPtr around each of next 2 BPtr, dc in next 2 dc, work FPtr around each of next 2 BPtr, ★ dc in next 8{10-12} dc, work FPtr around each of next 2 BPtr, dc in next 2 dc, work FPtr around each of next 2 BPtr; repeat from ★ 3 times **more**, dc in next dc and in each dc across.

♡ **Row 3:** Ch 3, turn; dc in next dc and in each dc across to next FPtr, work BPtr around each of next 2 FPtr, dc in next 2 dc, work BPtr around each of next 2 FPtr, ★ dc in next 8{10-12} dc, work BPtr around each of next 2 FPtr, dc in next 2 dc, work BPtr around each of next FPtr; repeat from ★ 3 times **more**, dc in next dc and in each dc across.

♡ **Rows 4 and 5:** Repeat Rows 2 and 3.

♡ **Row 6:** Ch 3, turn; dc in next dc and in each dc across to next BPtr, [work Twist, dc in next 8{10-12} dc] twice, skip next 4 sts, work FPdtr around each of next 2 BPtr, working **behind** last 2 FPdtr made, dc in first skipped dc, dc in sp **before** next skipped dc and in skipped dc, working in **front** of last 2 FPdtr made, work FPdtr around first skipped BPtr and next skipped BPtr, [dc in next 8{10-12} dc, work Twist] twice, dc in next dc and in each dc across: 193 {217-245} sts.

To work Front Post double crochet (abbreviated FPdc), YO, insert hook from **front** to **back** around post of st indicated, YO and pull up a loop, (YO and draw through 2 loops on hook) twice. Skip st behind FPdc.

To work Back Post double crochet (abbreviated BPdc), YO, insert hook from **back** to **front** around post of st indicated, YO and pull up a loop, (YO and draw through 2 loops on hook) twice. Skip st in front of BPdc.

♡ **Row 7:** Ch 3, turn; work BPdc around next st, (work FPdc around next st, work BPdc around next st) across to last dc, dc in last dc.

♡ **Row 8:** Ch 3, turn; work FPdc around next BPdc, (work BPdc around next FPdc, work FPdc around next BPdc) across to last dc, dc in last dc.

♡ **Rows 9-13:** Repeat Rows 7 and 8 twice; then repeat Row 7 once **more**; do **not** finish off.

LEFT NECK SHAPING

To work neck decrease (uses next 2 sts), YO, insert hook from **front** to **back** around post of next BPdc, † YO and pull up a loop, YO and draw through 2 loops on hook †, YO and insert hook from **back** to **front** around post of next FPdc, repeat from † to † once, YO and draw through all 3 loops on hook.

♡ **Row 1:** Ch 3, turn; dc in next 86{98-112} sts, (work FPdc around next BPdc, work BPdc around next FPdc) 4 times, work neck decrease, leave remaining 96{108-122} sts unworked: 96{108-122} sts.

♡ **Row 2:** Ch 2, turn; work FPdc around next BPdc, (work BPdc around next FPdc, work FPdc around next st) 4 times, dc in next dc and in each dc across: 95{107-121} sts.

♡ **Row 3:** Ch 3, turn; dc in next dc and in each dc across to last 10 sts, (work FPdc around next st, work BPdc around next FPdc) 4 times, work neck decrease: 94{106-120} sts.

♡ **Rows 4 thru 24{26-29}:** Repeat Rows 2 and 3, 10{11-13} times; then repeat Row 2, 1{1-0} time(s) **more**: 73{83-94} sts.

♡ Finish off leaving a long end for sewing.

RIGHT NECK SHAPING

♡ **Row 1:** With **right** side facing, join thread with slip st from **back** to **front** around post of same st as last leg of neck decrease at end of Row 1 of Left Neck Shaping, ch 2; work FPdc around next BPdc, (work BPdc around next FPdc, work FPdc around next BPdc) 4 times, dc in next FPdc and in each st across: 96{108-122} sts.

♡ **Row 2:** Ch 3, turn; dc in next dc and in each dc across to last 10 sts, (work FPdc around next st, work BPdc around next FPdc) 4 times, work neck decrease: 95{107-121} sts.

♡ **Row 3:** Ch 2, turn; work FPdc around next BPdc, (work BPdc around next FPdc, work FPdc around next st) 4 times, dc in next dc and in each dc across: 94{106-120} sts.

♡ **Rows 4 thru 24{26-29}:** Repeat Rows 2 and 3, 10{11-13} times; then repeat Row 2, 1{1-0} time(s) **more**: 73{83-94} sts.

♡ Finish off leaving a long end for sewing.

FINISHING

♡ On each side of Tee, match stitches and whipstitch shoulder and top of Sleeve seam.

♡ Sew each underarm and side in one continuous seam.

NECK EDGING

♡ With **right** side facing, join thread with sc in right shoulder seam; sc in each dc across Back, sc in next seam; working in end of rows across Left Neck Shaping, [sc, (ch 2, sc) twice] in each row across to last row, 3 sc in last row, sc in next st (same st as last leg of neck decrease); working in end of rows across Right Neck Shaping, 3 sc in first row, [sc, (ch 2, sc) twice] in each row across; join with slip st to first sc, finish off.

SLEEVE EDGING

To work treble crochet (abbreviated tr), YO twice, insert hook in sp indicated, YO and pull up a loop, (YO and draw through 2 loops on hook) 3 times.

♡ **Rnd 1:** With **right** side facing, join thread with slip st in seam at underarm; ch 3, dc in same sp, 2 dc in end of each row across to next seam, tr in seam, 2 dc in end of each row across; join with slip st to first dc.

♡ **Rnds 2 and 3:** Ch 3, (work FPdc around next st, work BPdc around next st) around; join with slip st to first dc.

♡ **Rnd 4:** Ch 1, sc in same st, ch 2, (sc in next st, ch 2) around; join with slip st to first sc, finish off.

♡ Repeat for second Sleeve.

Design by Leana Moon.

Classy Mini Muffler

Welcome chilly weather with this classy mini muffler. Worked in shell stitches to create its familiar pineapple pattern, the toasty neck-warmer makes a chic accent. It's fast to finish, so you can make several to coordinate with all of your outerwear.

Finished Size: Approximately 5" x 32"
(Before beginning, see General Instructions, page 202.)

MATERIALS
Sport Weight Yarn, approximately:
1¼ ounces, (35 grams, 120 yards)
Crochet hook, size H (5.00 mm) **or** size needed for gauge

GAUGE: Rows 1-9 = 5"

PATTERN STITCHES
BEGINNING SHELL
Ch 3 **(counts as first dc, now and throughout),** (dc, ch 1, 2 dc) in same sp.

SHELL
(2 Dc, ch 1, 2 dc) in sp indicated.

PICOT
Ch 3, slip st in third ch from hook.

FIRST HALF
Ch 17 loosely.

♡ **Row 1:** Sc in second ch from hook, (ch 3, skip next 2 chs, sc in next ch) across: 5 ch-3 sps.

♡ **Row 2:** (Right side) Turn; slip st in first ch-3 sp, work beginning Shell, ch 1, skip next ch-3 sp, 6 tr in next ch-3 sp, ch 1, skip next ch-3 sp, work Shell in last ch-3 sp.

Note: Loop a short piece of yarn around any stitch to mark last row as **right** side.

♡ **Row 3:** Turn; slip st in first 2 dc and in next ch-1 sp, work beginning Shell, ch 1, sc in next tr, (ch 3, sc in next tr) 5 times, ch 1, work Shell in next Shell (ch-1 sp).

♡ **Row 4:** Turn; slip st in first 2 dc and in next ch-1 sp, work beginning Shell, ch 1, sc in next ch-3 sp, (ch 3, sc in next ch-3 sp) 4 times, ch 1, work Shell in next Shell.

♡ **Row 5:** Turn; slip st in first 2 dc and in next ch-1 sp, work beginning Shell, ch 2, sc in next ch-3 sp, (ch 3, sc in next ch-3 sp) 3 times, ch 2, work Shell in next Shell.

♡ **Row 6:** Turn; slip st in first 2 dc and in next ch-1 sp, work beginning Shell, ch 2, sc in next ch-3 sp, (ch 3, sc in next ch-3 sp) twice, ch 2, work Shell in next Shell.

♡ **Row 7:** Turn; slip st in first 2 dc and in next ch-1 sp, work beginning Shell, ch 3, (sc in next ch-3 sp, ch 3) twice, work Shell in next Shell.

♡ **Row 8:** Turn; slip st in first 2 dc and in next ch-1 sp, work beginning Shell, ch 4, skip next ch-3 sp, sc in next ch-3 sp, ch 4, work Shell in next Shell.

♡ **Row 9:** Turn; slip st in first 2 dc and in next ch-1 sp, work beginning Shell, ch 3, skip next 2 ch-4 sps, work Shell in next Shell.

♡ **Row 10:** Turn; slip st in first 2 dc and in next ch-1 sp, work beginning Shell, ch 1, 6 tr in next ch-3 sp, ch 1, work Shell in next Shell.

♡ **Rows 11-25:** Repeat Rows 3-10 once, then repeat Rows 3-9 once **more.**

♡ **Row 26:** Turn; slip st in first 2 dc and in next ch-1 sp, work beginning Shell, skip next ch-3 sp, work Shell in next Shell.

♡ **Row 27:** Turn; slip st in first 2 dc and in next ch-1 sp, ch 3, slip st in next Shell.

♡ **Row 28:** Turn; slip st in ch-3 sp, work beginning Shell, finish off.

SECOND HALF
♡ **Row 1:** With **right** side facing and working over beginning ch, join yarn with slip st in first ch-3 sp; work beginning Shell in same sp, ch 1, skip next ch-3 sp, 6 tr in next ch-3 sp, ch 1, skip next ch-3 sp, work Shell in last ch-3 sp.

♡ **Rows 2-24:**: Work same as First Half, Rows 3-10 twice, then repeat Rows 3-9 once **more.**

♡ **Rows 25-27:**: Work same as First Half, Rows 26-28.

EDGING
With **right** side facing, join yarn with slip st in first dc on either point; ch 1, sc in same st, work Picot, ★ skip next dc, sc in next ch-1 sp, work Picot 3 times, sc in same sp, work Picot, skip next dc, sc in next dc, work Picot; working in end of rows, (sc in top of next dc, work Picot) across to beginning ch-3 sp, (sc, work Picot) twice in ch-3 sp, (sc in top of next dc, work Picot) across; repeat from ★ once **more;** join with slip st to first sc, finish off.

Design by Carol L. Jensen.

Quick Q-Hook Afghan

Colorful ombre yarn brings a lovely mosaic look to this simple afghan. And because the wrap is crocheted with a Q-hook and two strands of yarn, it's oh-so quick to create. You'll be cuddling up in this cozy charmer in no time!

(Before beginning, see General Instructions, page 202.)
Finished Size: 46" x 61¹/₂ "
MATERIALS
Worsted Weight Yarn:
73 ounces, (2,070 grams, 4,235 yards)
Crochet hook, size Q (15.00 mm)

Afghan is worked holding two strands of yarn together.

GAUGE: In pattern, 8 sts and 8 rows = 4¹/₂"

Gauge Swatch: 5" square
Ch 10 **loosely**.
Work same as Afghan Body for 9 rows. Finish off.

AFGHAN BODY
Ch 80 **loosely**.

♡ **Row 1:** Sc in second ch from hook and in each ch across: 79 sc.
♡ **Row 2** (Right side)**:** Ch 1, turn; sc in first sc, (dc in next sc, sc in next sc) across.
Note: Loop a short piece of yarn around any stitch to mark Row 2 as **right** side.

♡ **Row 3:** Ch 1, turn; sc in first sc, (dc in next dc, sc in next sc) across.
♡ **Row 4:** Ch 1, turn; sc in Back Loop Only of each st across *(Fig. 29, page 203)*.
♡ **Rows 5-7:** Ch 1, turn; working in **both** loops, sc in first sc, (dc in next st, sc in next st) across.
Repeat Rows 4-7 until Afghan measures approximately 60" from beginning ch, ending by working Row 7; do **not** finish off.

EDGING
♡ **Rnd 1:** Ch 1, turn; sc evenly around Afghan working 3 sc in each corner; join with slip st to first sc.
♡ **Rnd 2:** Ch 1, sc in each sc around working 3 sc in center sc of each corner 3-sc group; join with slip st to first sc, finish off.
Holding 14 strands together, add fringe evenly across short edges of Afghan *(Figs. 32a-d, page 203)*.

Design by Alice Hyche.

Dramatic Dishcloths

These dramatic dishcloths will spice up any kitchen! Aunt Lydia's® "Denim" worsted weight cotton gives the tidy-up trio its soft, absorbent durability.

(Before beginning, see General Instructions, page 202.)

MATERIALS
Aunt Lydia's Denim Crochet Thread [400 yards per ball]:
Shells
Red - 75 yards
Flower
Black - 50 yards
Red - 45 yards
Basket Weave
Red - 35 yards
Black - 35 yards
Jellybean - 30 yards
Crochet hook, size G (4.00 mm)

SHELLS
♡ Ch 35.

♡ **Row 1** (Right side)**:** Sc in back ridge of second ch from hook and each ch across: 34 sc.

♡ **Row 2:** Ch 1, turn; sc in first 2 sc, ★ ch 2, skip next 2 sc, sc in next 2 sc; repeat from ★ across: 18 sc and 8 ch-2 sps.

♡ **Row 3:** Ch 3 **(counts as first dc, now and throughout)**, turn; 4 dc in next ch-2 sp and in each ch-2 sp across to last 2 sc, skip next sc, dc in last sc: 34 dc.

♡ **Row 4:** Ch 1, turn; sc in first 2 dc, ★ ch 2, skip next 2 dc, sc in next 2 dc; repeat from ★ across: 18 sc and 8 ch-2 sps.

♡ **Rows 5-24:** Repeat Rows 3 and 4, 10 times.

♡ **Row 25:** Ch 1, turn; sc in first 2 sc, (2 sc in next ch-2 sp, sc in next 2 sc) across; finish off.

FLOWER
♡ With Red, ch 6; join with slip st to form a ring.

♡ **Rnd 1** (Right side)**:** Ch 1, sc in ring, (ch 5, sc in ring) 7 times, ch 2, dc in first sc to form last ch-5 sp: 8 ch-5 sps.

Note: Mark last round as **right** side.

♡ **Rnd 2:** Ch 1, (sc, ch 3) twice in same sp and in each ch-5 sp around; join with slip st to first sc, finish off: 16 ch-3 sps.

♡ **Rnd 3:** With **right** side facing, join Black with slip st in first ch-3 sp; ch 3 **(counts as first dc, now and throughout)**, (2 dc, ch 1, 3 dc) in same sp, skip next ch-3 sp, ★ (3 dc, ch 1, 3 dc) in next ch-3 sp, skip next ch-3 sp; repeat from ★ around; join with slip st to first dc, finish off: 48 dc and 8 ch-1 sps.

♡ **Rnd 4:** With **right** side facing, join Red with slip st in any ch-1 sp; ch 3, (dc, ch 1, 2 dc) in same sp, dc in next 2 dc, skip next 2 dc, dc in next 2 dc, ★ (2 dc, ch 1, 2 dc) in next ch-1 sp, dc in next 2 dc, skip next 2 dc, dc in next 2 dc; repeat from ★ around; join with slip st to first dc, finish off: 64 dc and 8 ch-1 sps.

♡ **Rnd 5:** With **right** side facing, join Black with slip st in any ch-1 sp; ch 3, (dc, ch 1, 2 dc) in same sp, dc in next 3 dc, skip next 2 dc, dc in next 3 dc, ★ (2 dc, ch 1, 2 dc) in next ch-1 sp, dc in next 3 dc, skip next 2 dc, dc in next 3 dc; repeat from ★ around; join with slip st to first dc, finish off: 80 dc and 8 chs.

♡ **Rnd 6:** With **right** side facing and working in Back Loops Only, join Red with sc in any ch; 2 sc in same st, sc in next 2 dc, hdc in next dc, dc in next dc, skip next 2 dc, dc in next dc, hdc in next dc, sc in next 2 dc, ★ 3 sc in next ch, sc in next 2 dc, hdc in next dc, dc in next dc, skip next 2 dc, dc in next dc, hdc in next dc, sc in next 2 dc; repeat from ★ around; join with slip st to **both** loops of first sc, finish off: 88 sts.

♡ **Rnd 7:** With **right** side facing and working in both loops, join Black with sc in center sc of any 3-sc group; sc in next 10 sts, (2 sc in next sc, sc in next 10 sts) around, sc in same st as first sc; join with slip st to first sc, do **not** finish off: 96 sc.

To work treble crochet (abbreviated tr)**,** YO twice, insert hook in sc indicated, YO and pull up a loop, (YO and draw through 2 loops on hook) 3 times.

To work double treble crochet (abbreviated dtr)**,** YO 3 times, insert hook in sc indicated, YO and pull up a loop, (YO and draw through 2 loops on hook) 4 times.

♡ **Rnd 8:** Ch 1, sc in same st and in next 11 sc, ★ † skip next 2 sc, 3 dc in next sc, ch 1, skip next 2 sc, (tr, 2 dtr) in next sc, ch 1 **(corner made)**, (2 dtr, tr) in next sc, ch 1, skip next 2 sc, 3 dc in next sc, skip next 2 sc †, sc in next 12 sc; repeat from ★ 2 times **more**, then repeat from † to † once; join with slip st to first sc, finish off: 96 sts and 12 ch-1 sps.

♡ **Rnd 9:** With **right** side facing, join Red with sc in any corner ch-1 sp; 2 sc in same sp, sc in each st and in each ch-1 sp around working 3 sc in each corner ch-1 sp; join with slip st to first sc, do **not** finish off: 116 sc.

♡ **Rnd 10:** Ch 3, (dc, ch 1, dc) in next sc, ★ dc in each sc across to center sc of next corner 3-sc group, (dc, ch 1, dc) in center sc; repeat from ★ 2 times **more**, dc in each sc across; join with slip st to first dc, finish off: 120 dc and 4 ch-1 sps.

♡ **Rnd 11:** With **right** side facing, join Black with sc in any corner ch-1 sp; ch 3, sc in same sp, ★ † [skip next dc, (sc, ch 3, sc) in next dc] 14 times, skip next 2 dc †, (sc, ch 3, sc) in corner ch-1 sp; repeat from ★ 2 times **more**, then repeat from † to † once; join with slip st to first sc, finish off.

BASKET WEAVE
♡ With Black, ch 34, place marker in third ch from hook for st placement.

♡ **Row 1:** Dc in fourth ch from hook **(3 skipped chs count as first dc)** and in each ch across changing to Red in last dc: 32 dc.

Note: Carry color not being used **loosely** along edge of piece.

To work Front Post double crochet (abbreviated FPdc)**,** YO, insert hook from **front** to **back** around post of st indicated, YO and pull up a loop, (YO and draw through 2 loops on hook) twice.

To work Back Post double crochet (abbreviated BPdc)**,** YO, insert hook from **back** to **front** around post of st indicated, YO and pull up a loop, (YO and draw through 2 loops on hook) twice.

♡ **Row 2** (Right side)**:** Ch 2 **(counts as first hdc, now and throughout)**, turn; work FPdc around each of next 2 dc, (work BPdc around each of next 2 dc, work FPdc around each of next 2 dc) across to last dc, hdc in last dc changing to Jellybean.

Note: Mark last row as **right** side.

♡ **Row 3:** Ch 2, turn; work FPdc around each of next 2 FPdc, (work BPdc around each of next 2 BPdc, work FPdc around each of next 2 FPdc) across, hdc in last hdc changing to Black.

♡ **Row 4:** Ch 2, turn; work FPdc around each of next 2 FPdc, (work BPdc around each of next 2 BPdc, work FPdc around each of next 2 FPdc) across, hdc in last hdc changing to Red.

♡ **Row 5:** Ch 2, turn; work FPdc around each of next 2 FPdc, (work BPdc around each of next 2 BPdc, work FPdc around each of next 2 FPdc) across, hdc in last hdc changing to Jellybean.

♡ **Rows 6-19:** Repeat Rows 3-5, 4 times; then repeat Rows 3 and 4 once **more**, cut Black and Jellybean.

♡ **Edging:** Ch 1, turn; 3 sc in first hdc, sc in each st across to last hdc, 3 sc in last hdc; sc evenly across end of rows; working in free loops of beginning ch, 3 sc in marked ch, sc in each ch across to last ch, 3 sc in last ch; sc evenly across end of rows; join with slip st to first sc, finish off.

Designs by Mary Jane Protus.

grapes galore DOILY

Rich with texture, this exquisite doily celebrates the beauty of an abundant fall harvest. Dramatic clusters of "grapes" fan out from an intricate center motif.

(Before beginning, see General Instructions, page 202.)

Finished Size: 20" diameter

MATERIALS

South Maid Cotton Thread (size 10) [400 yards per ball]: Camel - 2 balls

Steel crochet hook, size 10 (1.30 mm) **or** size needed for gauge

GAUGE: Rnds 1-5 = 2³/₄"

♡ Ch 6; join with slip st to form a ring.

♡ **Rnd 1** (Right side)**:** Ch 3 **(counts as first dc, now and throughout)**, 19 dc in ring; join with slip st to first dc: 20 dc.

♡ **Rnd 2:** Ch 4 **(counts as first dc plus ch 1)**, (dc in next 2 dc, ch 1) around to last dc, dc in last dc; join with slip st to first dc: 20 dc and 10 ch-1 sps.

♡ **Rnd 3:** Ch 3, dc in same st, ch 2, dc in next dc, ★ 2 dc in next dc, ch 2, dc in next dc; repeat from ★ around; join with slip st to first dc: 30 dc and 10 ch-2 sps.

♡ **Rnd 4:** Ch 3, dc in next dc, ch 3, 2 dc in next dc, ★ dc in next 2 dc, ch 3, 2 dc in next dc; repeat from ★ around; join with slip st to first dc: 40 dc and 10 ch-3 sps.

To work treble crochet (abbreviated *tr*), YO twice, insert hook in st or sp indicated, YO and pull up a loop, (YO and draw through 2 loops on hook) 3 times.

To work beginning double treble Cluster (abbreviated *beginning dtr Cluster*) *(uses first 4 dc)*, ch 4, YO 3 times, insert hook in **next** dc, YO and pull up a loop, (YO and draw through 2 loops on hook) 3 times, skip next sp, ★ YO 3 times, insert hook in **next** dc, YO and pull up a loop, (YO and draw through 2 loops on hook) 3 times; repeat from ★ once **more**, YO and draw through all 3 loops on hook.

To work double treble Cluster (abbreviated *dtr Cluster*) *(uses next 4 dc)*, † YO 3 times, insert hook in **next** dc, YO and pull up a loop, (YO and draw through 2 loops on hook) 3 times †; repeat from † to † once **more**, skip next sp, repeat from † to † twice, YO and draw through all 5 loops on hook.

♡ **Rnd 5:** Work beginning dtr Cluster, ch 5, tr in same dc as last leg of beginning dtr Cluster, ★ ch 5, work dtr Cluster, ch 5, tr in same dc as last leg of dtr Cluster just made; repeat from

★ around, ch 2, dc in top of beginning dtr Cluster to form last ch-5 sp: 10 Clusters and 20 ch-5 sps.

♡ **Rnd 6:** Ch 4 **(counts as first tr)**, (tr, dc, sc) in same sp, (sc, dc, 3 tr, dc, sc) in next ch-5 sp and in each ch-5 sp around, (sc, dc, tr) in same sp as first tr; join with slip st to first tr: 140 sts.

♡ **Rnd 7:** Ch 1, sc in same st, (ch 6, sc in center tr of next 7-st group) around, ch 3, dc in first sc to form last ch-6 sp: 20 ch-6 sps.

♡ **Rnd 8:** Ch 3, dc in same sp, ch 5, (3 dc in next ch-6 sp, ch 5) around, dc in same sp as first dc; join with slip st to first dc: 60 dc and 20 ch-5 sps.

♡ **Rnd 9:** Ch 3, dc in same st and in next dc, ch 4, dc in next dc, ★ 2 dc in next dc, dc in next dc, ch 4, dc in next dc; repeat from ★ around; join with slip st to first dc: 80 dc and 20 ch-4 sps.

♡ **Rnd 10:** Ch 8 **(counts as first tr plus ch 4)**, work dtr Cluster, ★ ch 4, tr in same dc as last leg of dtr Cluster just made, ch 4, work dtr Cluster; repeat from ★ around working last leg of last dtr Cluster in same dc as first tr, ch 4; join with slip st to first tr: 20 dtr Clusters and 20 tr.

♡ **Rnd 11:** Ch 7 **(counts as first tr plus ch 3)**, tr in same st, ch 6, ★ skip next dtr Cluster, (tr, ch 3, tr) in next tr, ch 6; repeat from ★ around; join with slip st to first tr: 20 ch-3 sps.

To work 2-tr Cluster, ★ YO twice, insert hook in ch-3 sp indicated, YO and pull up a loop, (YO and draw through 2 loops on hook) twice; repeat from ★ once **more**, YO and draw through all 3 loops on hook.

To work 3-tr Cluster, ★ YO twice, insert hook in ch-3 sp indicated, YO and pull up a loop, (YO and draw through 2 loops on hook) twice; repeat from ★ 2 times **more**, YO and draw through all 4 loops on hook.

♡ **Rnd 12:** Slip st in first ch-3 sp, ch 3, work (2-tr Cluster, ch 3, 3-tr Cluster) in same sp, ★ † ch 5, skip next ch-6 sp, tr in next ch-3 sp, (ch 3, tr in same sp) 5 times, ch 5, skip next ch-6 sp †, work (3-tr Cluster, ch 3, 3-tr Cluster) in next ch-3 sp; repeat from ★ 8 times **more**, then repeat from † to † once; join with slip st to top of first 2-tr Cluster: 60 ch-3 sps and 20 ch-5 sps.

To work Popcorn, work 5 tr in ch-3 sp indicated, drop loop from hook, insert hook in first tr of 5-tr group, hook dropped loop and draw through st.

♡ **Rnd 13:** Slip st in first ch-3 sp, ch 3, work (2-tr Cluster, ch 3, 3-tr Cluster) in same sp, ★ † ch 4, skip next ch-5 sp, work Popcorn in next ch-3 sp, (ch 3, work Popcorn in next ch-3 sp) 4 times, ch 4, skip next ch-5 sp †, work (3-tr Cluster, ch 3, 3-tr Cluster) in next ch-3 sp; repeat from ★ 8 times **more**, then repeat from † to † once; join with slip st to top of first 2-tr Cluster: 50 Popcorns and 70 sps.

♡ **Rnd 14:** Slip st in first ch-3 sp, ch 3, work (2-tr Cluster, ch 3, 3-tr Cluster) in same sp, ★ † ch 4, skip next ch-4 sp, work Popcorn in next ch-3 sp, (ch 3, work Popcorn in next ch-3 sp) 3 times, ch 4, skip next ch-4 sp †, work (3-tr Cluster, ch 3, 3-tr Cluster) in next ch-3 sp; repeat from ★ 8 times **more**, then repeat from † to † once; join with slip st to top of first 2-tr Cluster.

♡ **Rnd 15:** Slip st in first ch-3 sp, ch 3, work 2-tr Cluster in same sp, (ch 3, work 3-tr Cluster in same sp) twice, ★ † ch 5, skip next ch-4 sp, work Popcorn in next ch-3 sp, (ch 3, work Popcorn in next ch-3 sp) twice, ch 5, skip next ch-4 sp †, work [3-tr Cluster, (ch 3, 3-tr Cluster) twice] in next ch-3 sp; repeat from ★ 8 times **more**, then repeat from † to † once; join with slip st to top of first 2-tr Cluster: 60 sps.

♡ **Rnd 16:** Slip st in first ch-3 sp, ch 3, work (2-tr Cluster, ch 3, 3-tr Cluster) in same sp, ★ † ch 11, slip st in seventh ch from hook to form a ring, ch 4, work (3-tr Cluster, ch 3, 3-tr Cluster) in next ch-3 sp, ch 5, skip next ch-5 sp, work Popcorn in next ch-3 sp, ch 3, work Popcorn in next ch-3 sp, ch 5, skip next ch-5 sp †, work (3-tr Cluster, ch 3, 3-tr

Cluster) in next ch-3 sp; repeat from ★ 8 times **more**, then repeat from † to † once; join with slip st to top of first 2-tr Cluster: 70 sps and 10 rings.

♡ **Rnd 17:** Slip st in first ch-3 sp, ch 3, work (2-tr Cluster, ch 3, 3-tr Cluster) in same sp, † ch 3, ★ skip next sp, (tr, ch 3) 6 times in next ring, skip next ch-4 sp, work (3-tr Cluster, ch 3, 3-tr Cluster) in next ch-3 sp, ch 6, skip next ch-5 sp, work Popcorn in next ch-3 sp, ch 6, skip next ch-5 sp †, (work 3-tr Cluster, ch 3) twice in next ch-3 sp; repeat from ★ 8 times **more**, then repeat from † to † once; join with slip st to top of first 2-tr Cluster: 120 sps.

♡ **Rnd 18:** Slip st in first ch-3 sp, ch 3, work (2-tr Cluster, ch 3, 3-tr Cluster) in same sp, ★ † ch 4, skip next ch-3 sp, work Popcorn in next ch-3 sp, (ch 3, work Popcorn in next ch-3 sp) 4 times, ch 4, skip next ch-3 sp, work (3-tr Cluster, ch 3, 3-tr Cluster) in next ch-3 sp, ch 5, skip next ch-6 sp, sc in next Popcorn, ch 5, skip next ch-6 sp †, work (3-tr Cluster, ch 3, 3-tr Cluster) in next ch-3 sp; repeat from ★ 8 times **more**, then repeat from † to † once; join with slip st to top of first 2-tr Cluster: 100 sps.

♡ **Rnd 19:** Slip st in first ch-3 sp, ch 3, work (2-tr Cluster, ch 3, 3-tr Cluster) in same sp, ★ † ch 4, skip next ch-4 sp, work Popcorn in next ch-3 sp, (ch 3, work Popcorn in next ch-3 sp) 3 times, ch 4, skip next ch-4 sp, work (3-tr Cluster, ch 3, 3-tr Cluster) in next ch-3 sp, ch 5, skip next ch-5 sp, sc in next sc, ch 5, skip next ch-5 sp †, work (3-tr Cluster, ch 3, 3-tr Cluster) in next ch-3 sp; repeat from ★ 8 times **more**, then repeat from † to † once; join with slip st to top of first 2-tr Cluster: 90 sps.

♡ **Rnd 20:** Slip st in first ch-3 sp, ch 3, work (2-tr Cluster, ch 3, 3-tr Cluster) in same sp, ★ † ch 5, skip next ch-4 sp, work Popcorn in next ch-3 sp, (ch 3, work Popcorn in next ch-3 sp) twice, ch 5, skip next ch-4 sp, work (3-tr Cluster, ch 3, 3-tr Cluster) in next ch-3 sp, ch 11, slip st in seventh ch from hook to form a ring, ch 4, skip next 2 ch-5 sps †, work (3-tr Cluster, ch 3, 3-tr Cluster) in next ch-3 sp; repeat from ★ 8 times **more**, then repeat from † to † once; join with slip st to top of first 2-tr Cluster: 80 sps and 10 rings.

♡ **Rnd 21:** Slip st in first ch-3 sp, ch 3, work (2-tr Cluster, ch 3, 3-tr Cluster) in same sp, ★ † ch 5, skip next ch-5 sp, work Popcorn in next ch-3 sp, ch 3, work Popcorn in next ch-3 sp, ch 5, skip next ch-5 sp, work (3-tr Cluster, ch 3, 3-tr Cluster) in next ch-3 sp, ch 4, skip next sp, 7 tr in next

ring, ch 4, skip next ch-4 sp †, work (3-tr Cluster, ch 3, 3-tr Cluster) in next ch-3 sp; repeat from ★ 8 times **more**, then repeat from † to † once; join with slip st to top of first 2-tr Cluster: 70 sps.

♡ **Rnd 22:** Slip st in first ch-3 sp, ch 3, work (2-tr Cluster, ch 3, 3-tr Cluster) in same sp, ★ † ch 5, skip next ch-5 sp, work Popcorn in next ch-3 sp, ch 5, skip next ch-5 sp, work (3-tr Cluster, ch 3, 3-tr Cluster) in next ch-3 sp, ch 4, skip next ch-4 sp, 2 tr in each of next 7 tr, ch 4, skip next ch-4 sp †, work (3-tr Cluster, ch 3, 3-tr Cluster) in next ch-3 sp; repeat from ★ 8 times **more**, then repeat from † to † once; join with slip st to top of first 2-tr Cluster: 60 sps.

♡ **Rnd 23:** Slip st in first ch-3 sp, ch 3, work (2-tr Cluster, ch 3, 3-tr Cluster) in same sp, ★ † ch 5, skip next ch-5 sp, sc in next Popcorn, ch 5, skip next ch-5 sp, work (3-tr Cluster, ch 3, 3-tr Cluster) in next ch-3 sp, ch 4, skip next ch-4 sp, tr in next tr, (ch 1, tr in next tr) 13 times, ch 4, skip next ch-4 sp †, work (3-tr Cluster, ch 3, 3-tr Cluster) in next ch-3 sp; repeat from ★ 8 times **more**, then repeat from † to † once; join with slip st to top of first 2-tr Cluster: 190 sps.

♡ **Rnd 24:** Slip st in first ch-3 sp, ch 3, work (2-tr Cluster, ch 3, 3-tr Cluster) in same sp, ★ † ch 4, skip next ch-5 sp, sc in next sc, ch 4, skip next ch-5 sp, work (3-tr Cluster, ch 3, 3-tr Cluster) in next ch-3 sp, ch 4, skip next ch-4 sp, tr in next tr, (ch 2, tr in next tr) 13 times, ch 4, skip next ch-4 sp †, work (3-tr Cluster, ch 3, 3-tr Cluster) in next ch-3 sp; repeat from ★ 8 times **more**, then repeat from † to † once; join with slip st to top of first 2-tr Cluster.

♡ **Rnd 25:** Slip st in first ch-3 sp, ch 3, work (2-tr Cluster, ch 3, 3-tr Cluster) in same sp, ★ † ch 1, skip next 2 ch-4 sps, work (3-tr Cluster, ch 3, 3-tr Cluster) in next ch-3 sp, ch 4, skip next ch-4 sp, tr in next tr, (ch 3, tr in next tr) 13 times, ch 4, skip next ch-4 sp †, work (3-tr Cluster, ch 3, 3-tr Cluster) in next ch-3 sp; repeat from ★ 8 times **more**, then repeat from † to † once; join with slip st to top of first 2-tr Cluster: 180 sps.

To work Picot, ch 4, slip st in top of last tr made.

♡ **Rnd 26:** Slip st in first ch-3 sp, ch 1, sc in same sp, ★ † (3 tr, work Picot, 2 tr) in next ch-1 sp, sc in next ch-3 sp, ch 4, (2 tr, work Picot, tr) in next ch-4 sp, [ch 3, sc in next ch-3 sp, ch 3, (2 tr, work Picot, tr) in next sp] 7 times, ch 4 †, sc in next ch-3 sp; repeat from ★ 8 times **more**, then repeat from † to † once; join with slip st to first sc, finish off.

Design by Margaret Rost.

Play-Pretty Cardigan

Crocheted with baby fingering weight yarn, this precious cardigan will keep a wee one warm. The button-up sweater features an irresistibly touchable waffle pattern, a variegated pastel yoke, and ribbed edgings on the neck, sleeves, and hem. It can be made in sizes 6, 12, or 18 months.

(Before beginning, see General Instructions, page 202.)

Finished Chest Measurements:
6 months - 21", **12 months** - 22",
18 months - 22¹/₂"

Size Note: Instructions are written for size 6 months with sizes 12 and 18 months in braces { }. Instructions will be easier to read if you circle all the numbers pertaining to your baby's size. If only one number is given, it applies to all sizes.

MATERIALS

Red Heart Baby Fingering Weight Yarn [1³/₄ ounces (270 yards) per skein (White) or 1¹/₂ ounces (230 yards) per skein (Hushabye)]:
White - 3{4-5} skeins
Hushabye - 1 skein
Crochet hooks, sizes B (2.25 mm) **and** C (2.75 mm) **or** sizes needed for gauge
³/₈" Buttons - 6
Yarn needle

GAUGE: With larger size hook, in pattern, (ch 2, tr) 4 times = 2" and 8 rows = 1³/₄"

RIBBING

♡ With White and smaller size hook, ch 12 **loosely.**

♡ **Row 1:** Sc in back ridge of second ch from hook and each ch across: 11 sc.

♡ **Row 2:** Ch 1, turn; sc in Back Loop Only of each sc across.

♡ Repeat Row 2 until 60{63-65} ribs **[120{126-130} rows]** are complete; do **not** finish off.

BODY

♡ Change to larger size hook.

♡ **Row 1** (Right side)**:** Ch 1, work 121{127-130} sc evenly spaced across end of rows.

Note: Mark last row as **right** side.

To work treble crochet (abbreviated tr), YO twice, insert hook in st indicated, YO and pull up a loop, (YO and draw through 2 loops on hook) 3 times.

♡ **Row 2:** Ch 6 (counts as first tr plus ch 2, now and throughout)**,** turn; skip next 2 sc, tr in next sc, ★ ch 2, skip next 2 sc, tr in next sc; repeat from ★ across: 40{42-43} ch-2 sps.

To work tr Cluster, ★ YO twice, insert hook in st or sp indicated, YO and pull up a loop, (YO and draw through 2 loops on hook) twice; repeat from ★ once **more,** YO and draw through all 3 loops on hook.

♡ **Row 3:** Ch 1, turn; sc in first tr, ★ working **behind** next ch-2 sp, work tr Cluster in each of next 2 skipped sc on row **below,** sc in next tr; repeat from ★ across: 80{84-86} tr Clusters.

♡ **Row 4:** Ch 6, turn; skip next 2 sts, tr in next sc, ★ ch 2, skip next 2 sts, tr in next sc; repeat from ★ across: 40{42-43} ch-2 sps.

♡ **Row 5:** Ch 1, turn; sc in first tr, ★ working **behind** next ch-2 sp, work 2 tr Clusters in ch-2 sp **below,** sc in next tr; repeat from ★ across: 80{84-86} tr Clusters.

♡ **Rows 6 thru 27{29-31}:** Repeat Rows 4 and 5, 11{12-13} times; do **not** finish off.

LEFT FRONT

♡ **Row 1:** Ch 6, turn; skip next 2 sts, tr in next sc, ★ ch 2, skip next 2 sts, tr in next sc; repeat from ★ 6{7-7} times **more,** leave remaining 96{99-102} sts unworked: 8{9-9} ch-2 sps.

♡ **Row 2:** Ch 1, turn; sc in first tr, ★ working **behind** next ch-2 sp, work 2 tr Clusters in ch-2 sp **below,** sc in next tr; repeat from ★ across: 16{18-18} tr Clusters.

♡ **Row 3:** Ch 6, turn; skip next 2 sts, tr in next sc, ★ ch 2, skip next 2 sts, tr in next sc; repeat from ★ across: 8{9-9} ch-2 sps.

♡ **Row 4:** Ch 1, turn; sc in first tr, ★ working **behind** next ch-2 sp, work 2 tr Clusters in ch-2 sp **below,** sc in next tr; repeat from ★ across: 16{18-18} tr Clusters.

♡ **Row 5:** Ch 6, turn; skip next 2 sts, tr in next sc, ★ ch 2, skip next 2 sts, tr in next sc; repeat from ★ across changing to Hushabye in last tr.

♡ **Row 6:** Ch 1, turn; sc in first tr, ★ working **behind** next ch-2 sp, work tr Cluster in each of next 2 tr Clusters two rows **below,** sc in next tr; repeat from ★ across changing to White in last sc.

♡ **Rows 7 thru 11{13-15}:** Repeat Rows 5 and 6, 2{3-4} times; then repeat Row 5 once **more.**

♡ **Row 12{14-16}:** Ch 1, turn; sc in first tr, ★ working **behind** next ch-2 sp, work tr Cluster in each of next 2 tr Clusters two rows **below,** sc in next tr; repeat from ★ across; finish off.

NECK SHAPING

♡ **Row 1:** With **wrong** side facing and larger size hook, skip first 3{6-6} sts and join White with sc in next sc; ch 3, skip next 2 sts, tr in next sc, ★ ch 2, skip next 2 sts, tr in next sc; repeat from ★ across changing to Hushabye in last tr: 6 ch-2 sps and one ch-3 sp.

To work dc Cluster, ★ YO, insert hook in st indicated, YO and pull up a loop, YO and draw through 2 loops on hook; repeat from ★ once **more,** YO and draw through all 3 loops on hook.

♡ **Row 2:** Ch 1, turn; sc in first tr, ★ working **behind** next ch-2 sp, work tr Cluster in each of next 2 tr Clusters two rows **below,** sc in next tr; repeat from ★ 5 times **more,** working **behind** next ch-3 sp, work tr Cluster in next tr Cluster two rows **below,** work dc Cluster in next tr Cluster two rows **below,** slip st in last sc; finish off: 14 Clusters.

♡ **Row 3:** With **wrong** side facing and larger size hook, skip first 3 sts and join White with sc in next sc; ch 3, skip next 2 sts, tr in next sc, ★ ch 2, skip next 2 sts, tr in next sc; repeat from ★ across changing to Hushabye in last tr: 5 ch-2 sps and one ch-3 sp.

♡ **Row 4:** Ch 1, turn; sc in first tr, ★ working **behind** next ch-2 sp, work tr Cluster in each of next 2 tr Clusters two rows **below,** sc in next tr; repeat from ★ 4 times **more,** working **behind** next ch-3 sp, work tr Cluster in next tr Cluster two rows **below,** work dc Cluster in next tr Cluster two rows **below,** slip st in last sc; finish off: 12 Clusters.

♡ **Row 5:** With **wrong** side facing and larger size hook, skip first 3 sts and join White with slip st in next sc; ch 6, skip next 2 sts, tr in next sc, ★ ch 2, skip next 2 sts, tr in next sc; repeat from ★ across changing to Hushabye in last tr: 5 ch-2 sps.

♡ **Row 6:** Ch 1, turn; sc in first tr, ★ working **behind** next ch-2 sp, work tr Cluster in each of next 2 tr Clusters two rows **below,** sc in next tr; repeat from ★ across; finish off: 10 tr Clusters.

BACK

♡ **Row 1:** With **wrong** side facing and larger size hook, skip next 8 sts from Left Front and join White with slip st in next sc; ch 6, skip next 2 sts, tr in next sc, ★ ch 2, skip next 2 sts, tr in next sc; repeat from ★ 16{16-17} times **more,** leave remaining 33{36-36} sts unworked: 18{18-19} ch-2 sps.

♡ **Row 2:** Ch 1, turn; sc in first tr, ★ working **behind** next ch-2 sp, work 2 tr Clusters in ch-2 sp **below,** sc in next tr; repeat from ★ across: 36{36-38} tr Clusters.

♡ **Row 3:** Ch 6, turn; skip next 2 sts, tr in next sc, ★ ch 2, skip next 2 sts, tr in next sc; repeat from ★ across: 18{18-19} ch-2 sps.

♡ **Rows 4 thru 18{20-22}:** Repeat Rows 2 and 3, 7{8-9} times; then repeat Row 2 once **more;** finish off.

RIGHT FRONT

♡ **Row 1:** With **wrong** side facing and larger size hook, skip next 8 sts from Back and join White with slip st in next sc; ch 6, skip next 2 sts, tr in next sc, ★ ch 2, skip next 2 sts, tr in next sc; repeat from ★ across: 8{9-9} ch-2 sps.

♡ **Row 2:** Ch 1, turn; sc in first tr, ★ working **behind** next ch-2 sp, work 2 tr Clusters in ch-2 sp **below,** sc in next tr; repeat from ★ across: 16{18-18} tr Clusters.

♡ **Row 3:** Ch 6, turn; skip next 2 sts, tr in next sc, ★ ch 2, skip next 2 sts, tr in next sc; repeat from ★ across: 8{9-9} ch-2 sps.

♡ **Row 4:** Ch 1, turn; sc in first tr, ★ working **behind** next ch-2 sp, work 2 tr Clusters in ch-2 sp **below,** sc in next tr; repeat from ★ across: 16{18-18} tr Clusters.

♡ **Row 5:** Ch 6, turn; skip next 2 sts, tr in next sc, ★ ch 2, skip next 2 sts, tr in next sc; repeat from ★ across changing to Hushabye in last tr.

♡ **Row 6:** Ch 1, turn; sc in first tr, ★ working **behind** next ch-2 sp, work tr Cluster in each of next 2 tr Clusters two rows **below,** sc in next tr; repeat from ★ across changing to White in last sc.

♡ **Rows 7 thru 12{14-16}:** Repeat Rows 5 and 6, 3{4-5} times; do **not** finish off.

NECK SHAPING

♡ **Row 1:** Ch 6, turn; skip next 2 sts, tr in next sc, ★ ch 2, skip next 2 sts, tr in next sc; repeat from ★ 4 times **more,** ch 3, skip next 2 sts, sc in next sc changing to Hushabye, leave remaining 3{6-6} sts unworked: 6 ch-2 sps and one ch-3 sp.

♡ **Row 2:** Turn; slip st in first sc, working **behind** next ch-3 sp, work dc Cluster in next tr Cluster two rows **below,** work tr Cluster in next tr Cluster two rows **below,** sc in next tr, ★ working **behind** next ch-2 sp, work tr Cluster in each of next 2 tr Clusters two rows **below,** sc in next tr; repeat from ★ across changing to White in last sc: 14 Clusters.

♡ **Row 3:** Ch 6, turn; skip next 2 sts, tr in next sc, ★ ch 2, skip next 2 sts, tr in next sc; repeat from ★ 3 times **more,** ch 3, skip next 2 sts, sc in next sc changing to Hushabye, leave remaining 3 sts unworked: 5 ch-2 sps and one ch-3 sp.

♡ **Row 4:** Turn; slip st in first sc, working **behind** next ch-3 sp, work dc Cluster in next tr Cluster two rows **below**, work tr Cluster in next tr Cluster two rows **below**, sc in next tr, ★ working **behind** next ch-2 sp, work tr Cluster in each of next 2 tr Clusters two rows **below**, sc in next tr; repeat from ★ across changing to White in last sc: 12 Clusters.

♡ **Row 5:** Ch 6, turn; skip next 2 sts, tr in next sc, ★ ch 2, skip next 2 sts, tr in next sc; repeat from ★ 3 times **more** changing to Hushabye in last tr, leave remaining 3 sts unworked: 5 ch-2 sps.

♡ **Row 6:** Ch 1, turn; sc in first tr, ★ working **behind** next ch-2 sp, work tr Cluster in each of next 2 tr Clusters two rows **below**, sc in next tr; repeat from ★ across; finish off: 10 tr Clusters.

SLEEVE (Make 2)
RIBBING
♡ With White and smaller size hook, ch 19 **loosely.**

♡ **Row 1:** Sc in back ridge of second ch from hook and each ch across: 18 sc.

♡ **Row 2:** Ch 1, turn; sc in Back Loop Only of each sc across.

♡ Repeat Row 2 until 17{20-20} ribs [{34-40-40} rows] are complete; do **not** finish off.

BODY
♡ Change to larger size hook.

♡ **Row 1** (Right side)**:** Ch 1, sc in end of each row across: 34{40-40} sc.

Note: Mark last row as **right** side.

♡ **Row 2:** Ch 6, turn; skip next 2 sc, tr in next sc, ★ ch 2, skip next 2 sc, tr in next sc; repeat from ★ across: 11 {13-13} ch-2 sps.

♡ **Row 3:** Ch 1, turn; sc in first tr, ★ working **behind** next ch-2 sp, work tr Cluster in each of next 2 skipped sc on row **below**, sc in next tr; repeat from ★ across: 22{26-26} tr Clusters.

♡ **Row 4** (Increase row)**:** Ch 6, turn; tr in same st, ch 2, ★ skip next 2 sts, tr in next sc, ch 2; repeat from ★ across to last 3 sts, skip next 2 sts, (tr, ch 2, tr) in last sc: 13{15-15} ch-2 sps.

♡ **Row 5:** Ch 1, turn; sc in first tr, working **behind** next ch-2 sp, work 2 tr Clusters in first sc on row **below**, sc in next tr, ★ working **behind** next ch-2 sp, work 2 tr Clusters in ch-2 sp **below**, sc in next tr; repeat from ★ across to last ch-2 sp, working **behind** last ch-2 sp, work 2 tr Clusters in last sc on row **below**, sc in last tr: 26{30-30} tr Clusters.

♡ **Row 6:** Ch 6, turn; skip next 2 sts, tr in next sc, ★ ch 2, skip next 2 sts, tr in next sc; repeat from ★ across: 13 {15-15} ch-2 sps.

♡ **Row 7:** Ch 1, turn; sc in first tr, ★ working **behind** next ch-2 sp, work 2 tr Clusters in ch-2 sp **below**, sc in next tr; repeat from ★ across: 26{30-30} tr Clusters.

♡ **Row 8:** Ch 6, turn; skip next 2 sts, tr in next sc, ★ ch 2, skip next 2 sts, tr in next sc; repeat from ★ across: 13 {15-15} ch-2 sps.

♡ **Row 9:** Ch 1, turn; sc in first tr, ★ working **behind** next ch-2 sp, work 2 tr Clusters in ch-2 sp **below**, sc in next tr; repeat from ★ across: 26{30-30} tr Clusters.

♡ **Row 10** (Increase row)**:** Ch 6, turn; tr in same st, ch 2, ★ skip next 2 sts, tr in next sc, ch 2; repeat from ★ across to last 3 sts, skip next 2 sts, (tr, ch 2, tr) in last sc: 15{17-17} ch-2 sps.

♡ **Row 11:** Ch 1, turn; sc in first tr, working **behind** next ch-2 sp, work 2 tr Clusters in first sc on row **below**, sc in next tr, ★ working **behind** next ch-2 sp, work 2 tr Clusters in ch-2 sp **below**, sc in next tr; repeat from ★ across to last ch-2 sp, working **behind** last ch-2 sp, work 2 tr Clusters in last sc on row **below**, sc in last tr: 30{34-34} tr Clusters.

♡ **Rows 12 thru 25{29-33}:** Repeat Rows 6-11, 2{2-3} times; then repeat Rows 6 and 7, 1{3-2} time(s) **more**; finish off: 38{42-46} tr Clusters.

FINISHING
♡ Sew shoulder seams.

♡ Sew underarm seam of each Sleeve.

♡ Sew each Sleeve to Cardigan, matching center of last row on Sleeve to shoulder seam and underarm seam to center of skipped stitches at side of Cardigan.

NECK RIBBING
♡ **Foundation Row:** With **right** side facing and smaller size hook, join White with sc in top right corner of Right Front; work 59{63-67} sc evenly spaced across entire neck edge: 60{64-68} sc.

♡ **Row 1:** Ch 10 **loosely,** turn; sc in back ridge of second ch from hook and each ch across, sc in first 2 sc on Foundation Row: 11 sc.

♡ **Row 2:** Turn; skip first 2 sc, sc in Back Loop Only of each sc across: 9 sc.

♡ **Row 3:** Ch 1, turn; sc in Back Loop Only of each sc across, sc in **both** loops of next 2 sc on Foundation Row: 11 sc.

♡ Repeat Rows 2 and 3 across, ending by working Row 2; finish off.

BUTTONHOLE BAND
Note: Work Buttonhole Band on Right Front for girl's Cardigan and on Left Front for boy's Cardigan.

♡ **Foundation Row:** With **right** side facing and smaller size hook, join White with sc in right corner of Front; work 74{84-84} sc evenly spaced across edge of Front: 75{85-85} sc.

♡ **Row 1:** Ch 9 **loosely,** turn; sc in back ridge of second ch from hook and each ch across, sc in first 2 sc on Foundation Row: 10 sc.

♡ **Row 2:** Turn; skip first 2 sc, sc in Back Loop Only of each sc across: 8 sc.

♡ **Row 3** (Buttonhole row)**:** Ch 1, turn; sc in Back Loop Only of first 3 sc, ch 2, skip next 2 sc, sc in Back Loop Only of next 3 sc and in **both** loops of next 2 sc on Foundation Row: 8 sc and 2 chs.

♡ **Row 4:** Turn; skip first 2 sc, sc in Back Loop Only of next 3 sc, sc in next 2 chs and in Back Loop Only of each sc across: 8 sc.

♡ **Row 5:** Ch 1, turn; sc in Back Loop Only of each sc across, sc in **both** loops of next 2 sc on Foundation Row: 10 sc.

♡ **Row 6:** Turn; skip first 2 sc, sc in Back Loop Only of each sc across: 8 sc.

♡ **Rows 7 thru 16{18-18}:** Repeat Rows 5 and 6, 5{6-6} times.

♡ **Row 17{19-19}** (Buttonhole row)**:** Ch 1, turn; sc in Back Loop Only of first 3 sc, ch 2, skip next 2 sc, sc in Back Loop Only of next 3 sc and in **both** loops of next 2 sc on Foundation Row: 8 sc and 2 chs.

♡ **Row 18{20-20}:** Turn; skip first 2 sc, sc in Back Loop Only of next 3 sc, sc in next 2 chs and in Back Loop Only of each sc across: 8 sc.

♡ **Rows 19{21-21} thru 74 {84-84}:** Repeat Rows 5 thru 18{20-20}, 4 times.

♡ **Row 75{85-85}:** Ch 1, turn; sc in Back Loop Only of each sc across, slip st in **both** loops of last sc on Foundation Row; finish off.

BUTTON BAND
♡ **Foundation Row:** With **right** side facing and smaller size hook, join White with sc in right corner of Front; work 74{84-84} sc evenly spaced across edge of Front: 75{85-85} sc.

♡ **Row 1:** Ch 9 **loosely,** turn; sc in back ridge of second ch from hook and each ch across, sc in first 2 sc on Foundation Row: 10 sc.

♡ **Row 2:** Turn; skip first 2 sc, sc in Back Loop Only of each sc across: 8 sc.

♡ **Row 3:** Ch 1, turn; sc in Back Loop Only of each sc across, sc in **both** loops of next 2 sc on Foundation Row: 10 sc.

♡ **Rows 4 thru 74{84-84}:** Repeat Rows 2 and 3, 35{40-40} times; then repeat Row 2 once **more.**

♡ **Row 75{85-85}:** Ch 1, turn; sc in Back Loop Only of each sc across, slip st in **both** loops of last sc on Foundation Row; finish off.

♡ Add buttons.

Design by Christina Romo.

Pretty Eyeglass Pouch

In the blink of an eye, you can fashion this pretty pouch to protect your glasses! The elegant design features dainty roses, which are crocheted separately and then sewn on, and a drawstring closure.

(Before beginning, see General Instructions, page 202.)

Finished Size: 3 1/2" x 7 1/2"

MATERIALS

J. & P. Coats Cotton Thread (size 10) [225 yards per ball (White) or 150 yards per ball (Mint Green and Orchid Pink)]: White - 1 ball; Mint Green - 1 ball; Orchid Pink - 1 ball
Steel crochet hook, size 5 (1.90 mm) **or** size needed for gauge
Tapestry needle
2 - 7" Squares of fabric for lining
Sewing needle and thread
GAUGE: (5 dc, sc) 3 times = 2 1/4"
Rows 1-8 = 1 7/8"

POUCH
FRONT
♥ With White, ch 26.

♥ **Row 1:** Sc in second ch from hook and in each ch across: 25 sc.

♥ **Row 2** (Right side)**:** Ch 3 **(counts as first dc, now and throughout)**, turn; 2 dc in same st, skip next 2 sc, sc in next sc, ★ skip next 2 sc, 5 dc in next sc, skip next 2 sc, sc in next sc; repeat from ★ across to last 3 sc, skip next 2 sc, 3 dc in last sc: 21 dc and 4 sc.

Note: Mark last row as **right** side.

♥ **Row 3:** Ch 1, turn; sc in first dc, ★ 5 dc in next sc, skip next 2 dc, sc in next dc; repeat from ★ across: 20 dc and 5 sc.

♥ **Row 4:** Ch 3, turn; 2 dc in same st, skip next 2 dc, sc in next dc, ★ 5 dc in next sc, skip next 2 dc, sc in next dc; repeat from ★ across to last 3 sts, skip next 2 dc, 3 dc in last sc: 21 dc and 4 sc.

♥ **Rows 5-27:** Repeat Rows 3 and 4, 11 times; then repeat Row 3 once **more**.

♥ **Edging:** Ch 1, turn; 2 sc in first sc, sc in each st across to last sc, 3 sc in last sc; work 52 sc evenly spaced across end of rows; working in free loops of beginning ch, 3 sc in ch at base of first sc, sc in each ch across to last ch, 3 sc in last ch; work 52 sc evenly spaced across end of rows, sc in same st as first sc; join with slip st to first sc, finish off: 162 sc.

BACK
♥ Work same as Front except do **not** finish off.

JOINING
♥ **Row 1:** Ch 1, turn; with **wrong** sides together, Front towards you, and working in **both** loops of each st on **both** pieces, sc in same st and in each sc across to center sc of next corner 3-sc group, ★ 2 sc in center sc, sc in each sc across to center sc of next corner 3-sc group; repeat from ★ once **more**, sc in center sc, leave remaining 25 sc unworked (opening).

♥ **Row 2:** Ch 1, do **not** turn; working from **left** to **right**, work reverse sc **(Figs. 31a-d, page 203)** in each sc across; finish off.

TRIM
♥ **Rnd 1** (Eyelet rnd)**:** With **right** side facing and working in unworked sc of Edging, join White with slip st in one end of Row 1 on Joining; ch 5, dc in next sc, † ch 2, (skip next sc, dc in next sc, ch 2) 12 times †, dc in end of Row 1 on Joining, repeat from † to † once,

skip last sc; join with slip st to third ch of beginning ch-5: 27 sts and 27 ch-2 sps.

♥ **Rnd 2:** Ch 1, 2 sc in same st, ★ † 2 sc in next ch-2 sp, (sc in next dc, 2 sc in next ch-2 sp) 8 times †, 2 sc in next dc; repeat from ★ once **more**, then repeat from † to † once; join with slip st to first sc: 84 sc.

♥ **Rnd 3:** Ch 1, sc in same st, skip next 3 sc, 5 dc in next sc, skip next 2 sc, ★ sc in next sc, skip next 3 sc, 5 dc in next sc, skip next 2 sc; repeat from ★ around; join with slip st to first sc, finish off.

DRAWSTRING
♥ With Orchid Pink, ch 125, slip st in second ch from hook and in each ch across; finish off and knot each end.

♥ Weave Drawstring through Eyelet rnd and knot together 1" from ends.

ROSEBUD (Make 3)
♥ With Orchid Pink and leaving a long end for sewing, ch 15.

♥ **Row 1:** Sc in sixth ch from hook, ★ ch 3, skip next 2 chs, sc in next ch; repeat from ★ across: 4 sps.

♥ **Row 2** (Right side)**:** Ch 1, turn; (sc, 4 hdc, sc) in each sp across; finish off.

Note: Mark last row as **right** side.

♥ **Row 3:** With **right** side facing, join White with slip st in first sc; slip st in each st across; finish off.

♥ Thread tapestry needle with long end. With **right** side facing and using photo as a guide, roll Rosebud tightly and sew through all thicknesses at base of Rosebud to secure; do **not** cut end.

LEAF (Make 3)
To work treble crochet (abbreviated tr), YO twice, insert hook in st indicated, YO and pull up a loop, (YO and draw through 2 loops on hook) 3 times.

To work Picot, ch 3, slip st in top of last tr made.

♥ With Mint Green, ch 5, in fifth ch from hook work (3 tr, Picot, 2 tr, ch 4, slip st); finish off leaving a long end for sewing.

♥ Using photo as a guide for placement, sew Rosebuds and Leaves to Pouch.

LINING
♥ For inner lining, fold one fabric square in half. With **right** sides together, using a 1/4" seam allowance, sew lining along side and bottom edges; trim seam allowances. Press open edge of lining 1/4" to wrong side. Repeat with second fabric square for outer lining; turn outer lining right side out and press. Matching wrong sides and seams, place inner lining inside outer lining and whipstitch linings together along pressed edges. Slip lining into Pouch and sew to Edging.

Design by Nanette M. Seale.

Heartwarming Wrap for Baby

Rows of tiny hearts, fashioned with a unique cluster stitch, perfectly reflect a parent's love on this darling throw. It's sure to make baby's trip home from the hospital a memorable one. Finished with a lacy ruffle and satin ribbon, the afghan looks pretty in pink — or any color!

(Before beginning, see General Instructions, page 202.)

Finished Size: 33" x 43"

MATERIALS

Sport Weight Yarn: 17 ounces, (480 grams, 1,715 yards)
Crochet hook, size F (3.75 mm) **or** size needed for gauge
¹/₂" Ribbon - 6 yards
GAUGE: In pattern,
16 dc = 4"; 10 rows = 4¹/₄"

AFGHAN BODY

Ch 107 **loosely.**

♡ **Row 1** (Eyelet row)**:** Dc in eighth ch from hook, ★ ch 2, skip next 2 chs, dc in next ch; repeat from ★ across: 34 sps.

♡ **Row 2:** Ch 5 **(counts as first dc plus ch 2, now and throughout),** turn; dc in next dc, (2 dc in next ch-2 sp, dc in next dc) across to beginning ch, ch 2, skip next 2 chs, dc in next ch: 99 dc.

To work Double Cluster, YO, insert hook from **front** to **back** around post of dc **below** last dc worked *(Fig. 28, page 203),* † YO and pull up a loop, YO and draw through 2 loops on hook, YO, insert hook from **front** to **back** around **same** dc, YO and pull up a loop, YO and draw through 2 loops on hook †, YO, skip next dc, insert hook from **front** to **back** around post of next dc, repeat from † to † once, YO and draw through all 5 loops on hook.

♡ **Row 3** (Right side)**:** Ch 5, turn; dc in next 2 dc, work Double Cluster, ★ dc in same dc and in next 2 dc, work Double Cluster; repeat from ★ across to last 2 dc, dc in same dc and in next dc, ch 2, dc in last dc: 24 Double Clusters.

♡ **Row 4:** Ch 5, turn; dc in next 2 dc, dc in each Double Cluster and in each dc across to last dc, ch 2, dc in last dc: 99 dc.

♡ **Rows 5-83:** Repeat Rows 3 and 4, 39 times; then repeat Row 3 once **more.**

♡ **Row 84** (Eyelet row)**:** Ch 5, turn; dc in next dc, ch 2, ★ skip next 2 sts, dc in next st, ch 2; repeat from ★ across to last dc, dc in last dc; do **not** finish off: 34 sps.

EDGING

♡ **Rnd 1:** Ch 1, turn; (sc, ch 5) 3 times in first corner sp, † (sc, ch 5) twice in each sp across to next corner sp, (sc, ch 5) 6 times in corner sp, (sc, ch 5) twice in next sp, (sc in next sp, ch 5) across to next corner sp †, (sc, ch 5) 6 times in corner sp, repeat from † to † once, sc in first corner sp, (ch 5, sc in same sp) twice, ch 2, dc in first sc to form last ch-5 sp: 318 ch-5 sps.

♡ **Rnd 2:** Ch 1, sc in same sp, (ch 5, sc in next ch-5 sp) around, ch 2, dc in first sc to form last ch-5 sp.

To work Puff St, ★ YO, insert hook in sp indicated, YO and pull up a loop even with loop on hook; repeat from ★ 3 times **more,** YO and draw through all 9 loops on hook *(Fig. 1).*

Fig 1

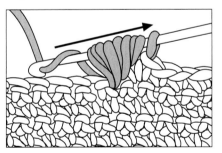

♡ **Rnd 3:** Ch 1, sc in same sp, ch 5, sc in next ch-5 sp, ch 5, work Puff St in next ch-5 sp, ★ ch 5, (sc in next ch-5 sp, ch 5) twice, work Puff St in next ch-5 sp; repeat from ★ around, ch 2, dc in first sc to form last ch-5 sp: 106 Puff Sts.

♡ **Rnd 4:** Ch 1, sc in same sp, ch 5, work Puff St in next ch-5 sp, ch 5, ★ (sc in next ch-5 sp, ch 5) twice, work Puff St in next ch-5 sp, ch 5; repeat from ★ around to last ch-5 sp, sc in last ch-5 sp, ch 2, dc in first sc to form last ch-5 sp.

♡ **Rnd 5:** Ch 1, work Puff St in same sp, (ch 5, sc in next ch-5 sp) twice, ★ ch 5, work Puff St in next ch-5 sp, (ch 5, sc in next ch-5 sp) twice; repeat from ★ around, ch 2, dc in top of first Puff St to form last ch-5 sp.

♡ **Rnds 6 and 7:** Repeat Rnds 3 and 4.

♡ **Rnd 8:** Ch 1, sc in same sp, ch 5, sc in third ch from hook, ch 2, ★ sc in next ch-5 sp, ch 5, sc in third ch from hook, ch 2; repeat from ★ around; join with slip st to first sc, finish off.

Weave ribbon through each Eyelet row, leaving a 10" length at each end. Weave ribbon through ch-2 sps on remaining two sides, leaving a 10" length at each end. Tie ends in a bow at each corner.

Design by Terry Kimbrough.

Blushing Lace Blanket

It'll be love at first sight when you see this lacy wrap draped over a chair or sofa! We crocheted ours in blushing pink, but the dreamy design will look fabulous in any color you choose.

(Before beginning, see General Instructions, page 202.)

Finished Size: 53^1/$_2$" x 75^1/$_2$"

MATERIALS
Red Heart Worsted Weight Yarn [8 ounces (452 yards) per skein]:
Rose Pink - 6 skeins
Crochet hook, size I (5.50 mm) **or** size needed for gauge

GAUGE: In pattern, 2 repeats = 3^3/$_4$"; Rows 1-5 = 3^1/$_2$"

♡ Ch 139 **loosely**, place marker in third ch from hook for st placement.

♡ **Row 1** (Right side)**:** (Dc, ch 3, dc) in fifth ch from hook **(4 skipped chs count as first dc plus one skipped ch)**, ★ ch 1, skip next 2 chs, dc in next ch, ch 1, skip next 2 chs, (dc, ch 3, dc) in next ch; repeat from ★ across to last 2 chs, skip next ch, dc in last ch: 70 dc and 23 ch-3 sps.

♡ **Row 2:** Ch 1, turn; sc in first dc, ★ 5 dc in next ch-3 sp, skip next dc, sc in next dc; repeat from ★ across: 115 dc and 24 sc. ***To work treble crochet*** (abbreviated tr), YO twice, insert hook in st indicated, YO and pull up a loop, (YO and draw through 2 loops on hook) 3 times.

♡ **Row 3:** Ch 3 **(counts as first dc, now and throughout)**, turn; skip next 2 dc, (dc, ch 3, dc) in next dc, ★ skip next 2 dc, working **over** next sc on previous row, work 3 tr in dc one row **below** sc, skip next 2 dc, (dc, ch 3, dc) in next dc; repeat from ★ across to last 3 sts, skip next 2 dc, dc in last sc: 22 3-tr groups and 23 ch-3 sps.

♡ **Row 4:** Ch 4 **(counts as first dc plus ch 1, now and throughout)**, turn; dc in center ch of next ch-3, ch 1, ★ skip next dc and next tr, (dc, ch 3, dc) in next tr, ch 1, dc in center ch of next ch-3, ch 1; repeat from ★ across to last 2 dc, skip next dc, dc in last dc: 69 dc and 22 ch-3 sps.

♡ **Row 5:** Ch 3, turn; (dc, ch 3, dc) in next dc, ★ ch 1, dc in center ch of next ch-3, ch 1, skip next dc, (dc, ch 3, dc) in next dc; repeat from ★ across to last dc, dc in last dc: 70 dc and 23 ch-3 sps.

♡ **Row 6:** Ch 1, turn; sc in first dc, ★ 5 dc in next ch-3 sp, skip next dc, sc in next dc; repeat from ★ across: 115 dc and 24 sc.

♡ **Row 7:** Ch 3, turn; skip next 2 dc, (dc, ch 3, dc) in next dc, ★ skip next 2 dc, working **over** next sc on previous row, work 3 tr in dc one row **below** sc, skip next 2 dc, (dc, ch 3, dc) in next dc; repeat from ★ across to last 3 sts, skip next 2 dc, dc in last sc: 22 3-tr groups and 23 ch-3 sps.

♡ **Rows 8-99:** Repeat Rows 4-7, 23 times; do **not** finish off.

EDGING

♡ **Rnd 1:** Ch 2 **(counts as first hdc, now and throughout)**, turn; hdc in same st, skip next dc, hdc in next 3 chs, ★ skip next dc, hdc in next 3 tr, skip next dc, hdc in next 3 chs; repeat from ★ across to last 2 dc, skip next dc, 3 hdc in last dc; † working in end of rows, 3 hdc in first row, hdc in next row, (3 hdc in each of next 3 rows, hdc in next row) across to last row, 3 hdc in last row †; working in free loops of beginning ch, 3 hdc in marked ch, hdc in each ch across to last ch, 3 hdc in last ch, repeat from † to † once, hdc in same st as first hdc; join with slip st to first hdc: 776 hdc.

♡ **Rnds 2 and 3:** Ch 2, turn; working in Back Loops Only, hdc in same st, ★ hdc in next hdc and in each hdc across to center hdc of next corner 3-hdc group, 3 hdc in center hdc; repeat from ★ 2 times **more**, hdc in next hdc and in each hdc across, hdc in same st as first hdc; join with slip st to first hdc: 792 hdc.

♡ **Rnd 4:** Ch 3, turn; working in both loops, 2 dc in same st, ★ † ch 1, skip next hdc, (dc in next hdc, ch 1, skip next hdc) across to center hdc of next corner 3-hdc group †, (3 dc, ch 1, 3 dc) in corner hdc; repeat from ★ 2 times **more**, then repeat from † to † once, 3 dc in same st as first dc, sc in first dc to form last ch-1 sp: 416 dc and 400 ch-1 sps.

♡ **Rnd 5:** Ch 3, turn; 2 dc in same sp, ★ † ch 1, skip next 3 dc, (dc in next dc, ch 1) across to within 3 dc of next corner ch-1 sp, skip next 3 dc †, (3 dc, ch 2, 3 dc) in corner ch-1 sp; repeat from ★ 2 times **more**, then repeat from † to † once, 3 dc in same sp as first dc, hdc in first dc to form last ch-2 sp.

♡ **Rnd 6:** Ch 2, turn; hdc in same sp, hdc in next dc and in each dc and each ch across to corner ch-2 sp, ★ 3 hdc in corner ch-2 sp, hdc in next dc and in each dc and each ch across to next corner ch-3 sp; repeat from ★ 2 times **more**, hdc in same sp as first hdc; join with slip st to first hdc: 824 hdc.

♡ **Rnd 7:** Ch 2, turn; working in Back Loops Only, hdc in same st, ★ hdc in next hdc and in each hdc across to center hdc of next corner 3-hdc group, 3 hdc in center hdc; repeat from ★ 2 times **more**, hdc in next hdc and in each hdc across, hdc in same st as first hdc; join with slip st to first hdc: 832 hdc.

♡ **Rnd 8:** Ch 2, turn; working in Back Loops Only, 2 hdc in same st, † hdc in next hdc and in each hdc across to center hdc of next corner 3-hdc group, 5 hdc in corner hdc, skip next hdc, hdc in next hdc and in each hdc across to center hdc of next corner 3-hdc group, 5 hdc in center hdc, repeat from † to † once, 2 hdc in same st as first hdc; join with slip st to first hdc: 846 hdc.

To work Picot, ch 3, sc in third ch from hook.

♡ **Rnd 9:** Ch 2, do **not** turn; 4 hdc in same st, work Picot, ★ † (skip next 2 hdc, sc in next hdc, work Picot) across to next corner 5-hdc group, skip next 2 hdc †, 5 hdc in center hdc, work Picot; repeat from ★ 2 times **more**, then repeat from † to † once; join with slip st to first hdc, finish off.

Design by Barbara Shaffer.

Cabled Cardigan

You'll look unforgettable in this rich red raglan cardigan. Our knit sensation is a stylish fashion for work or play. The easy instructions are written for sizes 32 to 48 and include a wide cable band along the neckline and pockets on the front.

Please read General Instructions, page 203, before beginning.

INSTRUCTIONS

Size: **32 36 40 44 48**
Chest Measurement: 32" 36" 40" 44" 48"
Finished Chest
  Measurement: 37" 41" 45" 50" 54"

Size Note: Instructions are written with sizes 32 and 36 in the first set of braces { } and with sizes 40, 44, and 48 in the second set of braces. Instructions will be easier to read if you circle all the numbers pertaining to your size.

MATERIALS
Worsted Weight Yarn:
{18-20} {23-26-28} ounces,
[{510-570} {650-740-800} grams,
{1,130-1,255}{1,445-1,635-1,760}yards]
Straight knitting needles, sizes 7 (4.50 mm) **and** 10 (6.00 mm) **or** sizes needed for gauge
Markers
Cable needle
Stitch holders - 2
Yarn needle
Sewing needle and thread (optional)
1½"w Grosgrain ribbon - 2½yards (optional)

GAUGE: With large size needles,
in Stockinette Stitch,
16 sts and 22 rows = 4"
DO NOT HESITATE TO CHANGE NEEDLE SIZE TO OBTAIN CORRECT GAUGE.

STITCH GUIDE
KNIT 2 TOGETHER (abbreviated K2 tog)
Insert the right needle into the **front** of the first two stitches on the left needle as if to **knit (Fig. 1)**, then **knit** them together.

Fig. 1

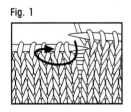

PURL 2 TOGETHER (abbreviated P2 tog)
Insert the right needle into the **front** of the first two stitches on the left needle as if to **purl (Fig. 2)**, then **purl** them together.

Fig. 2

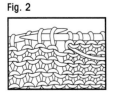

SLIP 1, KNIT 1, PASS SLIPPED STITCH OVER (abbreviated slip 1, K1, PSSO)
Slip one stitch as if to **knit**. Knit the next stitch. With the left needle, bring the slipped stitch over the knit stitch **(Fig. 3)** and off the needle.

Fig. 3

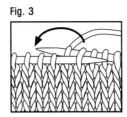

INCREASES
Knit into the **front** and into the **back** of the next stitch.

MARKERS
As a convenience to you, we have used markers to help distinguish the beginning of a pattern. Place markers as instructed. You may use purchased markers or tie a length of contrasting color yarn around the needle. When you reach a marker on each row, slip it from the left needle to the right needle; remove it when no longer needed.

ZEROS
To consolidate the length of an involved pattern, Zeros are sometimes used so that all sizes can be combined. For example, increase every {0-10}{10-10-8} rows, means size 32 would do nothing, and sizes 36, 40 and 44 would increase every 10 rows and size 48 would increase every 8 rows.

WEAVING SEAMS
With the **right** side of both pieces facing you and the edges even, sew through both sides once to secure the seam. Insert the needle under the bar **between** the first and second stitches on the row and pull the yarn through **(Fig. 4)**. Insert the needle under the next bar on the second side. Repeat from side to side, being careful to match rows. If the edges are different lengths, it may be necessary to insert the needle under two bars at one edge.

Fig. 4

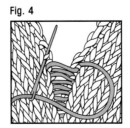

BACK
RIBBING
With small size needles, cast on {76-84} {92-102-110} sts **loosely**.
Work in K1, P1 ribbing for approximately 1".
BODY
Change to large size needles.
Work in Stockinette Stitch until Back measures approximately {16-16} {17-17-17}" from cast on edge or desired length to underarm, ending by working a **purl** row.
RAGLAN SHAPING
Rows 1 and 2: Bind off {4-5} {8-10-12} sts at the beginning of next 2 rows, work across: {68-74} {76-82-86} sts.
Row 3: K1, slip 1 as if to **purl**, knit across to last 2 sts, slip 1 as if to **purl**, K1.
Row 4: Purl across.
Row 5 (Decrease row): K1, slip 1 as if to **knit**, K1, PSSO, knit across to last 3 sts, K2 tog, K1: {66-72} {74-80-84} sts.
Row 6: Purl across.
Row 7: K1, slip 1 as if to **purl**, knit across to last 2 sts, slip 1 as if to **purl**, K1.
Row 8: Purl across.
Row 9 (Decrease row): K1, slip 1 as if to **knit**, K1, PSSO, knit across to last 3 sts, K2 tog, K1: {64-70} {72-78-82} sts.
Repeat Rows 6-9, {3-2} {2-3-3} times; then repeat Rows 8 and 9, {17-20} {21-22-24} times **more**.
Bind off remaining {24-26} {26-28-28} sts **loosely**.

POCKET LINING (Make 2)
With large size needles, cast on {27-27} {27-29-29} sts **loosely**.
Work in Stockinette Stitch for approximately 7", ending by working a **purl** row.
Decrease Row: Slip 1 as if to **knit**, K1, PSSO, knit across to last 2 sts, K2 tog: {25-25} {25-27-27} sts. Slip sts onto st holder; cut yarn.

LEFT FRONT
RIBBING
With small size needles, cast on{38-42} {46-50-54} sts **loosely**.
Work in K1, P1 ribbing for approximately 1" increasing 4 sts evenly spaced across last row: {42-46} {50-54-58} sts.
BODY
Change to large size needles.
Row 1 (Right side): Knit across to last 10 sts, place marker, P1, K8, P1 (Cable Band).
Row 2: K1, P8, K1, purl across.
Row 3: Knit across to marker, P1, K8, P1.
Row 4: K1, P8, K1, purl across.
Rows 5 and 6: Repeat Rows 3 and 4.

Continued on page 66.

KNIT

Row 7: Knit across to marker, P1, slip next 4 sts onto cable needle and hold in **back** of work, K4 from left needle, K4 from cable needle, P1.

Row 8: K1, P8, K1, purl across.

Rows 9-14: Repeat Rows 3 and 4, 3 times.

Repeat Rows 7-14 for pattern until Left Front measures approximately 7" from cast on edge, ending by working a **wrong** side row.

POCKET PLACEMENT

Note: Maintain established pattern for Cable Band throughout.

Row 1: Knit {3-7} {11-13-17} sts, P1, (K1, P1) {12-12} {12-13-13} times, K4, work across.

Row 2: K1, P8, K1, P4, K1, (P1, K1) {12-12} {12-13-13} times, purl across.

Rows 3-6: Repeat Rows 1 and 2, twice.

Row 7: Knit {3-7} {11-13-17} sts, bind off next {25-25} {25-27-27} sts in established ribbing, K3, work across: {17-21} {25-27-31} sts.

Row 8: K1, P8, K1, P4, slip sts from first Pocket Lining st holder onto left needle, purl across: {42-46} {50-54-58} sts.

Work even until Left Front measures same as Back to Raglan Shaping, ending by working a **wrong** side row.

RAGLAN AND NECK SHAPING

Row 1: Bind off {4-5} {8-10-12} sts, knit across to marker, work across: {38-41} {42-44-46} sts.

Row 2: K1, P8, K1, purl across.

Row 3: K1, slip 1 as if to **purl**, knit across to marker, work across.

Row 4: K1, P8, K1, purl across.

Row 5 (Decrease row): K1, slip 1 as if to **knit**, K1, PSSO, knit across to within 2 sts of marker, K2 tog, work across: {36-39} {40-42-44} sts.

Repeat Rows 2-5, {4-3} {3-4-4} times: {28-33} {34-34-36} sts.

Continue to decrease one stitch at armhole edge in same manner, every other row, {16-19} {20-21-23} times AND AT THE SAME TIME decrease one stitch at neck edge, every fourth row, {1-3} {3-2-2} time(s) **more**, ending by working a **wrong** side row: 11 sts.

Next Row: Removing marker, P2 tog, tie a short piece of yarn around st just worked, work across: 10 sts.

Work even until Cable Band measures approximately {5-5¼} {5¼-6-6}" from marked st.

Bind off remaining 10 sts.

RIGHT FRONT
RIBBING

With small size needles, cast on {38-42} {46-50-54} sts **loosely**.

Work in K1, P1 ribbing for approximately 1" increasing 4 sts evenly spaced across last row: {42-46} {50-54-58} sts.

BODY

Change to large size needles.

Row 1 (Right side): P1, K8, P1 (Cable Band), place marker, knit across.

Row 2: Purl across to marker, K1, P8, K1.

Row 3: P1, K8, P1, knit across.

Row 4: Purl across to marker, K1, P8, K1.

Rows 5 and 6: Repeat Rows 3 and 4.

Row 7: P1, slip next 4 sts onto cable needle and hold in **front** of work, K4 from left needle, K4 from cable needle, P1, knit across.

Row 8: Purl across to marker, K1, P8, K1.

Rows 9-14: Repeat Rows 3 and 4, 3 times.

Repeat Rows 7-14 for pattern until Right Front measures approximately 7" from cast on edge, ending by working a **wrong** side row.

POCKET PLACEMENT

Note: Maintain established pattern for Cable Band throughout.

Row 1: Work across to marker, K4, P1, (K1, P1) {12-12} {12-13-13} times, knit across.

Row 2: Purl {3-7} {11-13-17} sts, K1, (P1, K1) {12-12} {12-13-13} times, P4, K1, P8, K1.

Rows 3-6: Repeat Rows 1 and 2, twice.

Row 7: Work across to marker, K4, bind off next {25-25} {25-27-27} sts in established ribbing, knit across: {17-21} {25-27-31} sts.

Row 8: Purl across to bound off sts, slip sts from Pocket Lining st holder onto left needle, purl across to marker, K1, P8, K1: {42-46} {50-54-58} sts.

Work even until Right Front measures same as Back to Raglan Shaping, ending by working a **right** side row.

RAGLAN AND NECK SHAPING

Row 1: Bind off {4-5} {8-10-12} sts, purl across to marker, K1, P8, K1: {38-41} {42-44-46} sts.

Row 2: Work across to marker, knit across to last 2 sts, slip 1 as if to **purl**, K1.

Row 3: Purl across to marker, K1, P8, K1.

Row 4 (Decrease row): Work across to marker, slip 1 as if to **knit**, K1, PSSO, knit across to last 3 sts, K2 tog, K1: {36-39} {40-42-44} sts.

Row 5: Purl across to marker, K1, P8, K1.

Row 6: Work across to marker, knit across to last 2 sts, slip 1 as if to **purl**, K1.

Row 7: Purl across to marker, K1, P8, K1.

Row 8 (Decrease row): Work across to marker, slip 1 as if to **knit**, K1, PSSO, knit across to last 3 sts, K2 tog, K1: {34-37} {38-40-42} sts.

Repeat Rows 5-8, {3-2} {2-3-3} times: {28-33} {34-34-36} sts.

Continue to decrease one stitch at armhole edge in same manner, every other row, {16-19} {20-21-23} times AND AT THE SAME TIME decrease one stitch at neck edge, every fourth row, {1-3} {3-2-2} times **more**, ending by working a **wrong** side row: 11 sts.

Next Row: Work across to within one st of marker, removing marker, P2 tog, tie a short piece of yarn around st just worked: 10 sts. Work even until Cable Band measures approximately {5-5¼} {5¼-6-6}" from marked st.

Bind off remaining 10 sts.

SLEEVE (Make 2)
RIBBING

With small size needles, cast on {36-38} {40-42-44} sts **loosely**.

Work in K1, P1 ribbing for approximately 1", increasing {6-6} {6-8-8} sts evenly spaced across last row: {42-44} {46-50-52} sts.

BODY

Change to large size needles.

Work in Stockinette Stitch, increasing one stitch at **each** edge, every {10-8} {8-8-6} rows, {7-2} {6-7-1} time(s); then increase every {0-10} {10-10-8} rows, {0-6} {3-2-9} times: {56-60} {64-68-72} sts.

Work even until Sleeve measures approximately {17¼-17¾} {18¼-18¾-19¼}" from cast on edge or desired length to underarm, ending by working a **purl** row.

RAGLAN SHAPING

Rows 1 and 2: Bind off {4-5} {8-10-12} sts at the beginning of next 2 rows, work across: {48-50} {48-48-48} sts.

Row 3: K1, slip 1 as if to **purl**, knit across to last 2 sts, slip 1 as if to **purl**, K1.

Row 4: Purl across.

Row 5 (Decrease row): K1, slip 1 as if to **knit**, K1, PSSO, knit across to last 3 sts, K2 tog, K1: {46-48} {46-46-46} sts.

Row 6: Purl across.

Row 7: K1, slip 1 as if to **purl**, knit across to last 2 sts, slip 1 as if to **purl**, K1.

Row 8: Purl across.

Row 9 (Decrease row): K1, slip 1 as if to **knit**, K1, PSSO, knit across to last 3 sts, K2 tog, K1: {44-46} {44-44-44} sts.

Repeat Rows 6-9, {5-5} {7-11-13} times; then repeat Rows 8 and 9, {13-14} {11-6-4} times **more**. Bind off remaining {8-8} {8-10-10} sts **loosely**.

FINISHING

Weave raglan seams.

Weave underarm and side in one continuous seam.

Sew Cable Bands together.

Sew Band to Back neck edge.

Sew Pocket Linings in place.

If desired, grosgrain ribbon may be sewn to back of Cable Band for added stability.

Design by Darla Sims.

KNIT

Precious Sweater

The perfect playground companion on a chilly day, this adorable knitted sweater offers warmth and style! Fashioned with classic cables in your choice of three children's sizes, our little pullover is sure to become a winter wardrobe favorite.

Please read General Instructions, page 203, before beginning.

INSTRUCTIONS

Size: 2 4 6

Finished Chest
Measurement: 25" 27" 29"

Size Note: Instructions are written for size 2, with sizes 4 and 6 in braces { }. Instructions will be easier to read if you circle all the numbers pertaining to your size.

MATERIALS

Sport Weight Yarn:
  8{9-10} ounces,
  [230{260-280} grams,
  685{770-857} yards]
Straight knitting needles, sizes 3 (3.25 mm) **and** 5 (3.75 mm) **or** sizes needed for gauge

16" Circular knitting needle, size 3 (3.25 mm) **or** size needed for gauge
Cable needle
Stitch holders - 2
Markers
Yarn needle

GAUGE: With large size needles, in Stockinette Stitch, 24 sts and 32 rows = 4"
  DO NOT HESITATE TO CHANGE NEEDLE SIZE TO OBTAIN CORRECT GAUGE.

STITCH GUIDE
INCREASES
Increases are made by working into the front **and** into the back of the same st.
PURL 2 TOGETHER (abbreviated P2 tog)
Insert the right needle into the **front** of the first two sts on the left needle as if to **purl**, then **purl** them together.

PURL 2 TOGETHER THROUGH THE BACK LOOP (abbreviated P2 tog tbl)
Insert the right needle into the **back** of both sts from **back** to **front** (Fig. 1), then **purl** them together.

Fig. 1

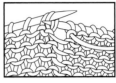

KNIT 2 TOGETHER (abbreviated K2 tog)
Insert the right needle into the **front** of the first two sts on the left needle as if to **knit**, then **knit** them together.
SLIP, SLIP, KNIT (abbreviated SSK)
With yarn in back of work, separately slip two sts as if to **knit**. Insert the **left** needle into the **front** of both slipped sts and knit them together.
BACK CABLE (abbreviated BC)
Slip next 2 sts onto cable needle and hold in **back** of work, K2 from left needle, K2 from cable needle.
FRONT CABLE (abbreviated FC)
Slip next 2 sts onto cable needle and hold in **front** of work, K2 from left needle, K2 from cable needle.
PICKING UP STITCHES
When instructed to pick up stitches, insert the needle from the **front** to the **back** under two strands at the edge of the worked piece **(Fig. 2)**. Put the yarn around the needle as if to **knit**, then bring the needle with the yarn back through the stitch to the right side, resulting in a stitch on the needle.
Repeat this along the edge, picking up the required number of stitches.
A crochet hook may be helpful to pull yarn through.

Fig. 2

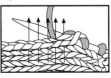

KNIT

Continued on page 68.

BACK
RIBBING
With small size needles, cast on 76{82-88} sts **loosely**.

Work in K1, P1 ribbing for 1³/₄" increasing one st at end of last row: 77{83-89} sts.

BODY
Change to large size needles.

Row 1 (Right side)**:** Knit across.

Row 2: Purl across.

Row 3: K2, P1, (K5, P1) across to last 2 sts, K2.

Row 4: (P1, K1) twice, P3, ★ K1, P1, K1, P3; repeat from ★ across to last 4 sts, (K1, P1) twice.

Row 5: K4, P1, K1, P1, ★ K3, P1, K1, P1; repeat from ★ across to last 4 sts, K4.

Row 6: P5, (K1, P5) across.

Row 7: Knit across.

Row 8: Purl across.

Rows 9-11: Knit across.

Row 12: P2, K1, (P5, K1) across to last 2 sts, P2.

Rows 13 and 14: Repeat Rows 11 and 12.

Rows 15-17: Knit across.

Repeat Rows 2-17 until Back measures approximately 8¹/₂{9¹/₂-10¹/₂}" from cast on edge, ending by working Row 8 or Row 14.

YOKE
Rows 1-4: Knit across increasing one st at end of Row 4: 78{84-90} sts.

Row 5: K 11{12-14}, P1, K1, P1, K2, BC, P1, K1, P1, ★ K 10{12-13}, P1, K1, P1, K2, BC, P1, K1, P1; repeat from ★ once **more**, K 11{12-14}.

Row 6: P 12{13-15}, K1, P8, K1, ★ P 12{14-15), K1, P8, K1; repeat from ★ once **more**, P 12{13-15}.

Row 7: K 11{12-14}, P1, K1, P1, FC, K2, P1, K1, P1, ★ K 10{12-13}, P1, K1, P1, FC, K2, P1, K1, P1; repeat from ★ once **more**, K 11{12-14}.

Row 8: Repeat Row 6.

Repeat Rows 5-8 until Back measures approximately 14{15¹/₂-17}" from cast on edge, ending by working a **wrong** side row. Bind off 25{28-31} sts, work across next 27 sts maintaining established pattern, bind off last 25{28-31} sts; slip remaining 28 sts onto st holder; cut yarn.

FRONT
Work same as Back until Front measures approximately 12{13¹/₂-14³/₄}" from cast on edge, ending by working a **wrong** side row.

NECK SHAPING
Note: Both sides of Neck are worked at the same time, using a separate yarn for each side. Maintain established pattern throughout.

Row 1: Work across 28{31-34} sts, K2 tog, slip next 18 sts onto st holder; with second yarn, SSK, work across: 29{32-35} sts **each** side.

Row 2 (Decrease row)**:** Work across to within 2 sts of neck edge, P2 tog tbl **(Fig. 1, page 67)**; with second yarn, P2 tog, work across: 28{31-34} sts **each** side.

Row 3 (Decrease row)**:** Work across to within 2 sts of neck edge, K2 tog; with second yarn, SSK, work across: 27{30-33} sts **each** side.

Row 4: Work across; with second yarn, work across.

Rows 5-7: Repeat Rows 3 and 4 once, then repeat Row 3 once **more**: 25{28-31} sts **each** side.

Work even until Front measures same as Back, ending by working a **wrong** side row. Bind off remaining sts.

Sew shoulder seams.

SLEEVE
With **right** side facing and using large size needles, pick up 66{72-78} sts evenly spaced across Front and Back Yokes **(Fig. 2, page 67)**.

Row 1: P7{10-13}, K1, P8, K1, ★ P 11, K1, P8, K1; repeat from ★ once **more**, P7{10-13}.

Row 2: K6{9-12}, P1, K1, P1, FC, K2, P1, K1, P1, ★ K9, P1, K1, P1, FC, K2, P1, K1, P1; repeat from ★ once **more**, K6{9-12}.

Row 3: Repeat Row 1.

Row 4: K6{9-12}, P1, K1, P1, K2, BC, P1, K1, P1, ★ K9, P1, K1, P1, K2, BC, P1, K1, P1; repeat from ★ once **more**, K6{9-12}.

Rows 5-9: Repeat Rows 1-4 once, then repeat Row 1 once **more**.

Row 10 (Decrease row)**:** K1, SSK, K3{6-9}, P1, K1, P1, FC, K2, P1, K1, P1, ★ K9, P1, K1, P1, FC, K2, P1, K1, P1; repeat from ★ once **more**, K3{6-9}, K2 tog, K1: 64{70-76} sts.

Row 11: P6{9-12}, K1, P8, K1, ★ P 11, K1, P8, K1; repeat from ★ once **more**, P6{9-12}.

Row 12: K5{8-11}, P1, K1, P1, K2, BC, P1, K1, P1, ★ K9, P1, K1, P1, K2, BC, P1, K1, P1; repeat from ★ once **more**, K5{8-11}.

Row 13: Repeat Row 11.

Row 14: K5{8-11}, P1, K1, P1, FC, K2, P1, K1, P1, ★ K9, P1, K1, P1, FC, K2, P1, K1, P1; repeat from ★ once **more**, K5{8-11}.

Rows 15-17: Repeat Rows 11-13.

Row 18 (Decrease row)**:** K1, SSK, K2{5-8}, P1, K1, P1, FC, K2, P1, K1, P1, ★ K9, P1, K1, P1, FC, K2, P1, K1, P1; repeat from ★ once **more**, K2{5-8}, K2 tog, K1: 62{68-74} sts.

Rows 19: P5{8-11}, K1, P8 ,K1 ,★ P11,K1, P8, K1; repeat from ★ once **more,** P5{8-11}.

Row 20: K4{7-10}, P1, K1, P1, K2, BC, P1, K1, P1, ★ K9, P1, K1, P1, K2, BC, P1, K1, P1; repeat from ★ once **more,** K4{7-10}.

Row 21: Repeat row 19.

Rows 22-25: Knit across.

Row 26 (Decrease row)**:** K1, SSK, knit across to last 3 sts, K2 tog, K1: 60{66-72} sts.

Row 27: Purl across.

Row 28: K6, (P1, K5) across.

Row 29: P4, K1, P1, ★ K1, P3, K1, P1; repeat from ★ across.

Row 30: K2, ★ P1, K1, P1, K3; repeat from ★ across to last 4 sts, (P1, K1) twice.

Row 31: P2, K1, (P5, K1) across to last 3 sts, P3.

Row 32: Knit across.

Row 33: Purl across.

Row 34 (Decrease row)**:** K1, SSK, knit across to last 3 sts, K2 tog, K1: 58{64-70} sts.

Rows 35 and 36: Knit across.

Row 37: P4, (K1, P5) across.

Row 38: Knit across.

Row 39: P4, (K1, P5) across.

Rows 40 and 41: Knit across.

Row 42 (Decrease row)**:** K1, SSK, knit across to last 3 sts, K2 tog, K1: 56{62-68} sts.

Working in pattern, continue to decrease one stitch at **each** edge in same manner, every eighth row, 3{5-6} times **more:** 50{52-56} sts.

Work even until Sleeve measures approximately 8{8³/₄-9³/₄}", ending by working a **wrong** side row.

RIBBING
Change to small size needles.

Row 1: Work in K1, P1 ribbing across decreasing 14{12-12} sts evenly spaced: 36{40-44} sts.

Work in K1, P1 ribbing for 1¹/₂", ending by working a **wrong** side row.

Bind off all sts **loosely** in ribbing.

Repeat for second Sleeve.

FINISHING
Sew underarm and side in one continuous seam.

NECK BAND
With **right** side facing and using circular needle, knit 28 sts from Back st holder, pick up 14 sts along left neck edge, slip 18 sts from Front st holder onto empty needle and knit across, pick up 14 sts along right neck edge, place marker to indicate beginning of round: 74 sts.

Work in K1, P1 ribbing for 2".

Bind off all sts **very loosely** in ribbing.

Fold Neck Band in half to wrong side of sweater.

Sew loosely in place along base of ribbing.

Design by Joan Beebe.

KNIT

COZY HAND MITTS

Fingerless hand mitts are all the rage! They're quick and easy to knit, and they keep hands warm while allowing freer movement than traditional gloves or mittens.

Please read General Instructions, page 203, before beginning.

Finished Size: 6¹/₂" (16.5 cm) around by 6" (15 cm) long

MATERIALS

Worsted Weight Yarn:
  80 yards (73 meters)
Straight knitting needles, size 8 (5 mm)
  or size needed for gauge
Yarn needle

GAUGE: In Stockinette Stitch,
  18 stitches and
  24 rows = 4" (10 cm)

Gauge Swatch: 4" (10 cm) square
Cast on 18 stitches.
Row 1 (Right side): Knit each stitch across.
Row 2: Purl each stitch across.
Rows 3-24: Repeat Rows 1 and 2, 11 times.
Bind off all stitches in knit.

MITT (Make 2)
WRIST RIBBING
Leaving a long end for sewing, cast on 32 stitches **loosely.**

Row 1: (Knit 2, purl 2) across. Repeat Row 1 until the ribbing measures 2" (5 cm).

BODY
Work in Stockinette Stitch (knit one row, purl one row) until the piece measures 4" (10 cm) from the cast on edge, ending by working a **purl** row.

PALM RIBBING
Row 1: (Knit 2, purl 2) across.

Repeat Row 1 until the ribbing measures 2" (5 cm).

Bind off all stitches in ribbing, leaving a long end for sewing.

FINISHING
Thread the yarn needle with the first long end. Fold the Mitt with the **right** side facing you and the edges lined up. Weave the Wrist Ribbing and the side of the Body for the first 2¹/₂" as follows: Sew through **both** sides once to secure the seam. Insert the needle under the bar between the first and second stitches on the row and pull the yarn through **(Fig. 1)**. Insert the needle under the next bar on the second side. Repeat from side to side, being careful to line up the rows and pulling the seam closed as you work. Weave in the yarn end. Thread the yarn needle with the second yarn end. Weave the Palm Ribbing and the side of Body for the last 2¹/₄", leaving a 1¹/₄" opening for your thumb. Weave in the yarn end.

Fig. 1

DASHING DOG COAT

The Dog Coat is fun and fashionable for dogs of any size. On your next walk, you can really show off your knitting talent as your favorite pooch wears the colorful coat in style!

Please read General Instructions, page 203, before beginning.

Size:	Sm	Med	Lg	X-Lg
Finished Measurement:	12"	14"	16"	18"

(from neck to base of tail)

Size Note: Instructions are written for size Small, with sizes Medium, Large, and X-Large in braces { }. Instructions will be easier to read if you circle all the numbers pertaining to your dog's size. If only one number is given, it applies to all sizes.

MATERIALS

Worsted Weight Yarn:
3{4-5-6} ounces,
[90{110-140-170} grams,
170{225-285-340} yards]
Straight knitting needles, size 7 (4.50 mm) **or** size needed for gauge
Stitch holder
Markers - 2
$3/4$" Buttons - 2
Yarn needle

GAUGE: In pattern, 20 sts and 26 rows = 4"

Extra skills needed: Knit Increases (page 65), using markers (page 65), K2 tog (Knit 2 together, Fig. 1, page 65), slip 1, K1, PSSO (Slip 1, knit 1, pass slipped stitch over, Fig. 3, page 65), picking up stitches (Fig. 2, page 67), and YO (Yarn overs, Figs. 1a-d, page 75).

BODY

Cast on 40{44-52-56} sts.

Row 1: Knit across.

Rows 2-7: K1, increase, knit across to last 2 sts, increase, K1: 52{56-64-68} sts.

Row 8 (Right side): K6, place marker, knit across to last 6 sts, place marker, K6.

Note: Loop a short piece of yarn around any stitch to mark Row 8 as **right** side.

Rows 9 and 10: Knit across to first marker, (P2, K2) across to next marker, knit across.

Rows 11 and 12: Knit across to first marker, (K2, P2) across to next marker, knit across.

Repeat Rows 9-12 for pattern until Body measures approximately 11{13-15-17}" from cast on edge, ending by working a **wrong** side row.

NECK SHAPING

Note: Both sides of the Neck are worked at the same time, using separate yarn for each side. This guarantees that both sides will be the same length. **Maintain established pattern throughout.**

Row 1: Work across 18{18-20-22} sts, slip next 16{20-24-24} sts onto st holder; with second yarn, work across: 18{18-20-22} sts **each** side.

Row 2 (Decrease row): Work across to within 2 sts of Neck edge, K2 tog; with second yarn, slip 1 as if to **knit**, K1, PSSO, work across: 17{17-19-21} sts **each** side.

Rows 3 and 4: Repeat Row 2: 15{15-17-19} sts **each** side.

Continue to decrease one stitch at **each** Neck edge, every other row, 3{3-4-5} times: 12{12-13-14} sts **each** side.

Work even until Coat measures approximately 14{16$1/2$-18$1/2$-21}" from cast on edge, ending by working a **wrong** side row.

Bind off all sts.

FINISHING
NECKBAND

With **right** side facing, pick up 18{22-22-24} sts along right Neck edge, slip 16{20-24-24} sts from st holder onto empty needle and knit across, pick up 18{22-22-24} sts along left Neck edge: 52{64-68-72} sts.

Knit 8 rows.

Bind off all sts in knit.

BAND

With **right** side facing and beginning 5$1/2${6$1/2$-7$1/2$-8$1/2$}" down from left bound off edge, pick up 10 sts evenly spaced across 2".

Knit every row until Coat fits snugly around Dog's chest.

Next Row (Buttonhole row): K2, YO (buttonhole), K2 tog, K2, K2 tog, YO (buttonhole), K2.

Knit 3 rows.

Bind off all sts in knit.

Sew end of Right Neck to end of Left Neck.

Weave in yarn ends.

Sew Buttons to Body, opposite Band.

Design by Evie Rosen.

KNIT

Easy Dishcloths

Thirsty dishcloths are handy kitchen helpers, and they're quick to knit! These are perfect beginner projects and can be taken with you wherever you go, since they require only a small amount of cotton yarn to make each one.

Please read General Instructions, page 203, before beginning.

BLUE DISHCLOTH

Finished Size: Approximately 10" square

MATERIALS
100% Cotton Worsted Weight Yarn: 95 yards
Straight knitting needles, size 8 (5.00 mm)
Yarn needle

Cast on 46 sts.

Rows 1-4: Knit across.

Row 5 (Right side): K9, P2, (K6, P2) 4 times, K3.

Row 6: K3, P1, K2, (P6, K2) 4 times, P5, K3.

Row 7: K7, P2, (K6, P2) 4 times, K5.

Row 8: K3, P3, K2, (P6, K2) 4 times, P3, K3.

Row 9: K5, P2, (K6, P2) 4 times, K7.

Row 10: K3, P5, K2, (P6, K2) 4 times, P1, K3.

Row 11: K3, purl across to last 3 sts, K3.

Rows 12-16: Repeat Rows 6-10.

Row 17: K3, P2, (K6, P2) 4 times, K9.

Row 18: Knit across.

Rows 19-73: Repeat Rows 5-18, 3 times; then repeat Rows 5-17 once **more**.

Rows 74-77: Knit across.

Bind off all sts in **knit**.

Weave in yarn ends.

Design by Linda Luder

VARIEGATED DISHCLOTH

Finished Size: Approximately 10" square

MATERIALS
100% Cotton Worsted Weight Yarn: 125 yards
Straight knitting needles, size 7 (4.50 mm)
Yarn needle

Cast on 51 sts.

Row 1: K1, ★ P1, K1; repeat from ★ across.

Repeat Row 1 for Seed Stitch until Dishcloth measures approximately 10" from cast on edge.

Bind off all sts in **pattern**.

Weave in yarn ends.

Design by Eunice Svinicki.

Please read General Instructions, page 203, before beginning.

PEACEFUL AFGHAN

Finished Size: 45" x 60"

MATERIALS

Worsted Weight Yarn:
39 ounces, (1,110 grams, 2,455 yards)
29" Circular knitting needles, size 17 (12.75 mm) **or** size needed for gauge
Cable needle

Note: Afghan is worked holding two strands of yarn together.

GAUGE: In Stockinette Stitch, 9 sts and 12 rows = 4"

STITCH GUIDE

CABLE (uses 6 sts)
Slip next 2 stitches onto cable needle and hold in **back** of work, K1 from left needle, K2 from cable needle, slip next stitch onto cable needle and hold in **front** of work, K2 from left needle, K1 from cable needle.

Quick to knit using two strands of yarn, this classic cabled afghan is a handsome choice for a quiet spot. It makes a fine gift, too.

Cast on 116 sts.

Rows 1-5: Knit across.

Row 6 (Right side): K5, P1, K6, P1, ★ work Cable, P1, K6, P1; repeat from ★ across to last 5 sts, K5.

Row 7: K6, P6, (K1, P6) across to last 6 sts, K6.

Row 8: K5, P1, K6, P1, ★ work Cable, P1, K6, P1; repeat from ★ across to last 5 sts, K5.

Row 9: K6, P6, (K1, P6) across to last 6 sts, K6.

Row 10: K5, P1, K6, P1, ★ work Cable, P1, K6, P1; repeat from ★ across to last 5 sts, K5.

Row 11: K6, P6, (K1, P6) across to last 6 sts, K6.

Row 12: K5, P1, work Cable, P1, ★ K6, P1, work Cable, P1; repeat from ★ across to last 5 sts, K5.

Row 13: K6, P6, (K1, P6) across to last 6 sts, K6.

Row 14: K5, P1, work Cable, P1, ★ K6, P1, work Cable, P1; repeat from ★ across to last 5 sts, K5.

Row 15: K6, P6, (K1, P6) across to last 6 sts, K6.

Row 16: K5, P1, work Cable, P1, ★ K6, P1, work Cable, P1; repeat from ★ across to last 5 sts, K5.

Row 17: K6, P6, (K1, P6) across to last 6 sts, K6.

Repeat Rows 6-17 for pattern until Afghan measures approximately 58" from cast on edge, ending by working Row 10.

Last 5 Rows: Knit across.

Bind off all sts.

Design by Anita Lewis.

sweet and simple baby wrap

Need a shower gift in a hurry? With its simplistic styling, this sleepytime afghan works up in a jiffy! A lattice-look fringe lends a decorative finish.

Baby Thymes
Nursery
Fragrance
Mist

CRADLE
AND AL
Everything
Welcoming
New Baby

Please read General Instructions, page 203, before beginning.

Finished Size: 32" x 42"

MATERIALS

Sport Weight Yarn:
    13 ounces, (370 grams, 1,635 yards)
    29" Circular knitting needle, size 6 (4.00 mm)
      or size needed for gauge
    Crochet hook for fringe

GAUGE: In pattern, 18 sts and 24 rows = 4"

See Yarn Overs, below, before beginning.

YARN OVERS

**After a knit stitch,
before a knit stitch**

Bring the yarn forward **between** the needles, then back **over** the top of the right hand needle, so that it is now in position to knit the next stitch (**Fig.1a**).

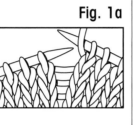

Fig. 1a

**After a purl stitch,
before a purl stitch**

Take yarn **over** the right hand needle to the back, then forward **under** it, so that it is now in position to purl the next stitch (**Fig. 1b**).

Fig. 1b

**After a knit stitch,
before a purl stitch**

Bring yarn forward **between** the needles, then back **over** the top of the right hand needle and forward **between** the needles again, so that it is now in position to purl the next stitch (**Fig. 1c**).

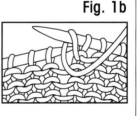

Fig. 1c

**After a purl stitch,
before a knit stitch**

Take yarn **over** right hand needle to the back, so that it is now in position to knit the next stitch (**Fig. 1d**).

Fig. 1d

AFGHAN

Cast on 146 sts.
Rows 1-6: Purl across.
Row 7 (Right side): P4, ★ YO, K2 tog (**Fig. 1, page 65**); repeat from ★ across to last 4 sts, P4.

Row 8: Purl across.
Row 9: P4, (K2 tog, YO) across to last 4 sts, P4.
Rows 10-12: Purl across.
Row 13: P4, (YO, K2 tog) across to last 4 sts, P4.
Repeat Rows 8-13 for pattern until Afghan measures approximately 41" from cast on edge, ending by working Row 9.
Last 6 Rows: Purl across.
Bind off all sts in **purl**.
Holding seven 18" lengths of yarn together, add fringe evenly across short edges of Afghan through Step 3 (**see Fringe, below**).

FRINGE

After completing Step(s) specified in individual instructions, lay Afghan flat on a hard surface and trim the ends.

Cut a piece of cardboard 8" wide and half as long as specified in individual instructions for strands. Wind the yarn **loosely** and **evenly** around the cardboard lengthwise until the card is filled, then cut across one end; repeat as needed.

Step 1: Hold together as many strands of yarn as specified for the finished fringe; fold in half. With **wrong** side facing and using a crochet hook, draw the folded end up through a stitch and pull the loose ends through the folded end (**Fig. 2a**); draw the knot up **tightly** (**Fig. 2b**). Repeat spacing as desired.

Step 2: Divide each group in half and knot together with half of next group (**Fig. 2c**).

Step 3: Separate each group in same manner and knot again (**Fig. 2d**).

Fig. 2a

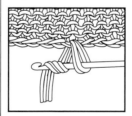

Fig. 2b

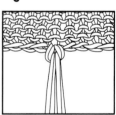

Fig. 2c

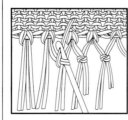

Fig. 2d

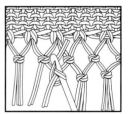

Design by Jean Lampe.

KNIT

Roman Stripe Quilt

This striking pattern is often called Sunshine and Shadows when pieced in solid fabrics rather than prints. We selected a variety of rustic plaids for a homespun look and used black for the solid triangles to blend the tones beautifully. To create the striped sections with ease, we rotary cut strip-pieced sets using an angle-cutting ruler.

SKILL LEVEL: 1 2 3 4 5
BLOCK SIZE: 7" x 7"
QUILT SIZE: 78" x 92"

YARDAGE REQUIREMENTS

Yardage is based on 45"w fabric.

- 4⁵/₈ yds of black plaid
- 2³/₄ yds **total** of assorted plaids
- 2¹/₈ yds of red plaid
- 1⁷/₈ yds of black solid
  7¹/₄ yds for backing
  1 yd for binding
  90" x 108" batting

You will also need:

  Companion Angle™ Rotary Cutting Ruler
    (made by EZ International)

CUTTING OUT THE PIECES

All measurements include a ¹/₄" seam allowance.

1.   **From black plaid:**
   - Cut 2 lengthwise strips 12¹/₄" x 82" for **top/bottom outer borders**.
   - Cut 2 lengthwise strips 12¹/₄" x 72" for **side outer borders**.

2. **From assorted plaids:**
   - Cut a total of 44 **strips** 1³/₄"w.

3. **From red plaid:**
   - Cut 2 lengthwise strips 2³/₄" x 67" for **side inner borders**.
   - Cut 2 lengthwise strips 2³/₄" x 58" for **top/bottom inner borders**.

4. **From black solid:**
   - Cut 7 strips 7⁷/₈"w. From these strips, cut 32 squares 7⁷/₈" x 7⁷/₈". Cut squares once diagonally to make 64 **triangles** (you will need 63 and have 1 left over).

square (cut 32)   **triangle** (cut 64)

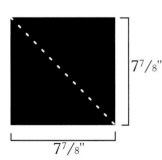   

7⁷/₈"

7⁷/₈"

ASSEMBLING THE QUILT TOP

Follow **Piecing and Pressing***, page 205, to make quilt top.*

1. Sew 4 **strips** together in random color order to make **Strip Set**. Make 11 **Strip Sets**.

Strip Set (make 11)

2. Aligning top and bottom edges of ruler with long edges of strip set, use Companion Angle ruler to cut 63 **Unit 1's** from **Strip Sets**, turning ruler 180° after each cut (**Fig. 1**).

Fig. 1

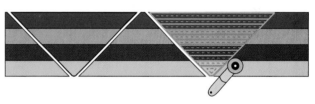

Unit 1 (make 63)

3. Sew 1 **Unit 1** and 1 **triangle** together to make **Block**. Make 63 **Blocks**.

Block (make 63)

4. Sew 7 **Blocks** together to make **Row**. Make 9 **Rows**.

Row (make 9)

5. Referring to **Quilt Top Diagram**, sew **Rows** together to make center section of quilt top.
6. Follow **Adding Squared Borders**, page 206, to sew **side**, then **top** and **bottom inner borders** to center section. Add **side**, then **top** and **bottom outer borders** to complete **Quilt Top**.

COMPLETING THE QUILT

1. Follow **Quilting**, page 205, to mark, layer, and quilt, using **Quilting Diagram** as a suggestion. Our quilt is machine quilted.
2. Cut a 34" square of binding fabric. Follow **Binding**, page 207, to bind quilt using $2^1/2$"w bias binding with mitered corners.

MAKING CONTINUOUS BIAS STRIP BINDING

1. Cut a square from binding fabric the size indicated in the project instructions. Cut square in half diagonally to make 2 triangles.
2. With right sides together and using a $^1/_4$" seam allowance, sew triangles together **(Fig. 1)**; press seam allowance open.

Fig. 1

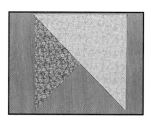

3. On wrong side of fabric, draw lines the width of the binding as specified in the project instructions, usually $2^1/2$" **(Fig. 2)**. Cut off any remaining fabric less than this width.

Fig. 2

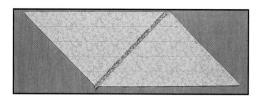

4. With right sides inside, bring short edges together to form a tube; match raw edges so that first drawn line of top section meets second drawn line of bottom section **(Fig. 3)**.

Fig. 3

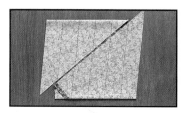

5. Carefully pin edges together by inserting pins through drawn lines at the point where drawn lines intersect, making sure the pins go through intersections on both sides. Using $^1/_4$" seam allowance, sew edges together. Press seam allowances open.
6. To cut continuous strip, begin cutting along first drawn line. Continue cutting along drawn line around tube.
7. Trim ends of bias strip square.
8. Matching wrong sides and raw edges, press bias strip in half lengthwise to complete binding.

Quilting Diagram

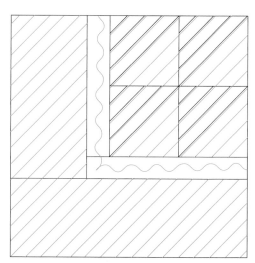

Quilt Top Diagram

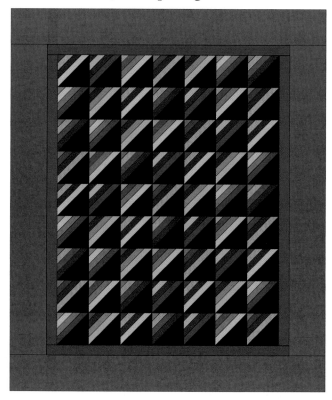

Spring Bouquet Quilt

Most people won't notice at first glance, but this floral print quilt has a secret. The pieces for the easy blocks were cut and sewn without any curves — it's the rounded quilting pattern that fools the eye!

SPRING BOUQUET QUILT

SKILL LEVEL: 1 2 3 4 5
BLOCK SIZE: 12" x 12"
QUILT SIZE: 85" x 97"

YARDAGE REQUIREMENTS

Yardage is based on 45"w fabric.

- $5^1/4$ yds of large floral print
- $3^5/8$ yds of small floral print
- $1^3/4$ yds of white print
- $1^3/4$ yds of green print
  $7^3/4$ yds for backing
  1 yd for binding
  120" x 120" batting

You will also need:
Companion Angle™ Rotary Cutting Ruler
(made by EZ International)

CUTTING OUT THE PIECES

All measurements include a $^1/4$" seam allowance.

1. **From large floral print:**
   - Cut 8 selvage-to-selvage strips 9"w. From these strips, cut 32 **squares** 9" x 9".
   - Cut 2 lengthwise strips $6^1/2$" x 100" for **side borders**.
   - Cut 2 lengthwise strips $6^1/2$" x 76" for **top/bottom borders**.
   - From remaining fabric, cut 10 additional **squares** 9" x 9".

2. **From small floral print:**
   - Cut 42 selvage-to-selvage **strips** $2^3/4$"w.

3. **From white print:**
   - Cut 21 selvage-to-selvage **strips** $2^1/2$"w.

4. **From green print:**
   - Cut 21 selvage-to-selvage **strips** $2^1/2$"w.

ASSEMBLING THE QUILT TOP

*Follow **Piecing and Pressing**, page 206, to make quilt top.*

1. Assemble **strips** to make 21 **Strip Set A's** and 21 **Strip Set B's**.

Strip Set A (make 21)

Strip Set B (make 21)

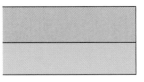

2. Line up 9" sewing line (dashed line) on Companion Angle™ ruler ($4^3/4$" from top of ruler) with bottom edge of **Strip Set A** (**Fig. 1**). Cut on both sides of ruler to make **Unit 1**. Make 84 **Unit 1's**. Repeat with **Strip Set B's** to make 84 **Unit 2's**.

Fig. 1

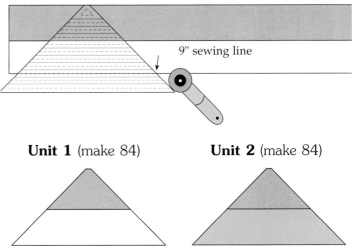

9" sewing line

Unit 1 (make 84)   **Unit 2** (make 84)

3. Assemble 4 **Unit 1's** and 1 **square** to make **Block A**. Make 21 **Block A's**. Assemble 4 **Unit 2's** and 1 **square** to make **Block B**. Make 21 **Block B's**.

Block A (make 21)

Block B (make 21)

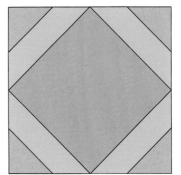

4. Assemble 3 **Block A's** and 3 **Block B's** to make **Row**. Make 7 **Rows**.

Row (make 7)

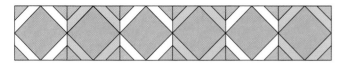

5. Referring to **Quilt Top Diagram**, assemble **Rows** to make center section of quilt top.
6. Follow **Adding Squared Borders**, page 206, to attach **top**, **bottom**, then **side borders** to center section to complete **Quilt Top**.

COMPLETING THE QUILT
1. Follow **Quilting**, page 205, to mark, layer, and quilt, using **Quilting Diagram** as a suggestion. Our quilt is hand quilted using **Quilting Pattern**, page 89.
2. Cut a 32" square of binding fabric. Follow **Binding**, page 207, to bind quilt using $2^1/_2$"w bias binding with mitered corners.

Quilting Diagram

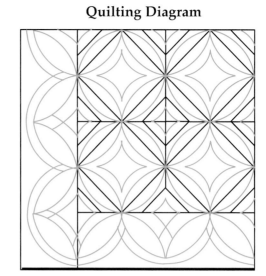

Quilt Top Diagram

QUILTING

Cuddly Crib Quilt

Updated with time-saving techniques, the age-old craft of quilting is a perfect way to welcome a brand-new baby into the family. For quick appliqués, we fused on the hearts, flowers, and leaves and machine stitched the edges with clear nylon thread, so there's no need to change thread colors. We stencil-painted the vines and strip-pieced the checkerboard rows.

This versatile pattern can be fashioned in many different color combinations. Our bright version makes the following substitutions from the original soft pink quilt instructions: white-on-white print for the white fabric listed; yellow check for the yellow solid; green stripe for the green check; and purple check, stripe, and dot prints for the three pink prints.

QUILT SIZE: 41" x 51"

YARDAGE REQUIREMENTS

Yardage is based on 45"w fabric.

☐ 1³/₄ yds of white solid
☐ ³/₈ yd of pale yellow solid
▨ ¹/₂ yd of green check
▨ ¹/₄ yd of light pink print
▨ ¹/₄ yd of medium pink print
▨ ¹/₄ yd of dark pink print
　 2³/₄ yds for backing
　 ³/₄ yd for binding
　 48" x 60" batting

You will also need:
　 paper-backed fusible web
　 transparent monofilament thread for appliqué
　 plastic template material
　 craft knife
　 green fabric paint
　 stencil brush

CUTTING OUT THE PIECES

All measurements include a ¹/₄" seam allowance.

1. **From white solid:** ☐
   - Cut 2 **strips** 2¹/₂"w.
   - Cut 2 **side outer borders** 6¹/₂" x 36¹/₂".
   - Cut 2 **top/bottom outer borders** 6¹/₂" x 26¹/₂".
   - Cut 2 **panels** 9¹/₂" x 26¹/₂".

2. **From pale yellow solid:** ☐
   - Cut 4 **strips** 2¹/₂"w.

3. **From green check:** ▨
   - Cut 1 strip 1¹/₄"w. From this strip, cut **4 border pieces** 1¹/₄" x 6¹/₂".
   - Cut 2 **top/bottom inner borders** 1¹/₄" x 40".
   - Cut **2 side inner borders** 1¹/₄" x 36¹/₂".

4. **From 3 pink prints:** ◩
   - Cut 2 **strips** 2¹/₂"w from **each** fabric.

ASSEMBLING THE QUILT TOP

*Follow **Piecing and Pressing,** page 205, to make quilt top.*

1. (**Note:** Measurements for stencil placement on **Quilt Top Diagram** do not include seam allowances.) Referring to **Quilt Top Diagram,** page 84, use **Stem Stencil** pattern, page 84, and follow **Stenciling**, page 204, to stencil stems on outer borders. Stencil stems on panels, using only 2 segments of stem stencil for each design area.

2. Use patterns and follow **Making Appliqués,** page 127, to cut 32 **leaves** and 4 **flower bases** from green check, 4 **flower petals** from light pink print, 10 **hearts** from medium pink print, and 8 **flower petals** from dark pink print. Follow **Invisible Appliqué,** page 206, to stitch appliqués to **panels** and **outer borders.**

3. Sew pale yellow and dark pink print **strips** together to make **Strip Set A**. Make 2 **Strip Set A's**. Cut across **Strip Set A's** at 2¹/₂" intervals to make 29 **Unit 1's**. Repeat with light pink print, medium pink print, and white **strips** to make 2 **Strip Set B's** and 22 **Unit 2's**.

Strip Set A (make 2)　　　**Unit 1** (make 29)

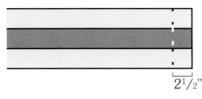
2¹/₂"

Strip Set B (make 2)　　　**Unit 2** (make 22)

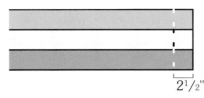
2¹/₂"

4. Sew 7 **Unit 1's** and 6 **Unit 2's** together to make **Row**. Make 3 **Rows.**

Row (make 3)

5. Sew 2 **Unit 1's** and 1 **Unit 2** together to make **Border Square**. Make 4 **Border Squares.**

Border Square (make 4)

6. Referring to **Quilt Top Diagram**, page 84, sew **Rows** and **panels** together to make center section of quilt top.

7. Sew **side inner borders,** then **side outer borders** to center section.

8. Sew 2 **Border Squares,** 2 **border pieces,** and 1 **top/bottom outer border** together to make **Border Unit**. Make 2 **Border Units.**

9. Sew **top/bottom inner borders,** then **Border Units** to center section to complete **Quilt Top.**

COMPLETING THE QUILT

1. Follow **Quilting**, page 205, to mark, layer, and quilt, using **Quilting Diagram** as a suggestion.
2. Follow **Binding**, page 207, to bind quilt using 4"w straight-grain binding with mitered corners.

Quilting Diagram

Quilt Top Diagram

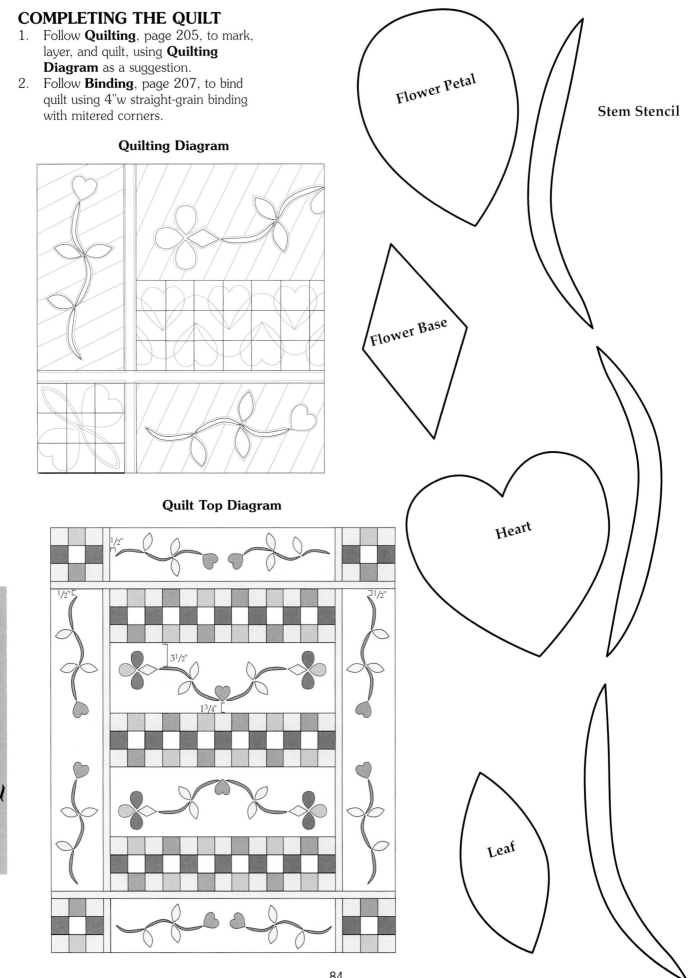

Flower Petal

Stem Stencil

Flower Base

Heart

Leaf

84

Flower Basket Wall Hanging

As pretty as they are practical, baskets have always inspired quiltmakers. Not until the Civil War era, however, did basket designs emerge in pieced patchwork blocks rather than appliqué. Edged with a scrapwork border, this wall hanging blooms to life with appliquéd blossoms cut from print fabrics and a fresh combination of floral and grid quilting.

FLOWER BASKET WALL HANGING

SKILL LEVEL: 1 2 3 4 5
SIZE: 23" x 23"

YARDAGE REQUIREMENTS

Yardage is based on 45"w fabric.

☐ $^3/_8$ yd of white print

☐ $^1/_4$ yd of floral with blue background

☐   1 fat quarter (18" x 22" piece) each of green print, pink print, pink check, large yellow print, small yellow print, and floral with white background

■ $^1/_4$ yd of green check for border
floral scraps for appliqués
1 yd for backing and hanging sleeve
$^1/_2$ yd for binding
27" x 27" batting

You will also need:
paper-backed fusible web
transparent monofilament thread for appliqué

CUTTING OUT THE PIECES

All measurements include a $^1/_4$" seam allowance.

1. **From white print:** ☐
   - Cut 2 **rectangles** 4" x 7$^1/_2$".
   - Cut 1 **square** 4" x 4".
   - Cut 1 square 4$^3/_8$" x 4$^3/_8$". Cut square once diagonally to make 2 **medium triangles**. (You will need 1 and have 1 left over.)
   - Cut 2 squares 8$^1/_4$" x 8$^1/_4$". Cut each square once diagonally to make 4 **large triangles**.
   - Cut 1 square 4$^3/_4$" x 4$^3/_4$". Cut square twice diagonally to make 4 **small triangles**. (You will need 2 and have 2 left over.)

2. **From floral with blue background:** ☐
   - Cut 1 strip 3$^1/_2$"w. From this strip, cut 4 **rectangles** 3$^1/_2$" x 4$^3/_8$" and 4 **squares** 3$^1/_2$" x 3$^1/_2$".

3. **From green print:**
   - Cut 1 square 4$^3/_8$" x 4$^3/_8$". Cut square once diagonally to make 2 **medium triangles.**
   - Cut 4 **squares** 3$^1/_2$" x 3$^1/_2$".

4. **From pink print:** ■
   - Cut 3 **squares** 3$^1/_2$" x 3$^1/_2$".

5. **From pink check:** ■
   - Cut 4 **squares** 3$^1/_2$" x 3$^1/_2$".

6. **From large yellow print:** ■
   - Cut 2 **rectangles** 2$^1/_4$" x 7".
   - Cut 2 **squares** 3$^1/_2$" x 3$^1/_2$".

7. **From small yellow print:** ☐
   - Cut 2 **rectangles** 2$^1/_4$" x 7".
   - Cut 1 **square** 3$^1/_2$" x 3$^1/_2$".

8. **From floral with white background:** ☐
   - Cut 2 **squares** 3$^1/_2$" x 3$^1/_2$".

9. **From green check:** ■
   - Cut 2 **top/bottom inner borders** 1" x 15$^3/_8$".
   - Cut 2 **side borders** 1" x 16$^3/_8$".

ASSEMBLING THE WALL HANGING TOP

*Follow **Piecing and Pressing**, page 205, to make wall hanging top.*

1. Sew 2 **medium triangles** together to make 1 **triangle-square.**

triangle-square (make 1)

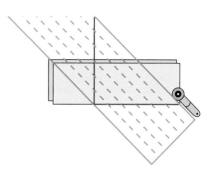

2. To cut parallelograms, refer to **Fig. 1** and place 2 large yellow print **rectangles** right sides together on mat. Align the 45° marking on the rotary cutting ruler (shown in pink) along lower right edge of rectangles. Cut along right side of ruler to cut 1 end of both rectangles at a 45° angle.

Fig. 1

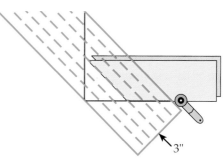

3. Turn cut rectangles 180° on mat and align the 45° marking on the rotary cutting ruler along lower left edge of rectangles. Align the previously cut 45° edge at the 3" marking on the ruler. Cut rectangles as shown in **Fig. 2** to cut 1 **parallelogram** from each rectangle.

Fig. 2

4. Using small yellow print **rectangles**, repeat Steps 2 and 3 to cut 1 **parallelogram** from each rectangle.

QUILTING

5. (**Note:** When stitching set-in seams, start at the outer point and sew toward where the corner will form; stop 1/4" from corner and backstitch, then clip threads. To sew an adjacent seam, pivot the triangle or square to match raw edges of next diamond; start at the corner and take 2 or 3 stitches, then backstitch, making sure not to backstitch into the previous seam allowance. Stitching forward, continue to outer point.) Using set-in seams, sew parallelograms together to make 1 **Unit 1a** and 1 **Unit 1b**. Sew **Unit 1a** and **Unit 1b** together to make **Unit 2**.

Unit 1a (make 1) **Unit 1b** (make 1)

Unit 2 (make 1)

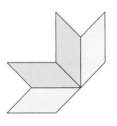

6. Using set-in seams, sew 2 **triangles** and **Unit 2** together to make **Unit 3**; then sew 1 **square** and **Unit 3** together to make **Unit 4**.

Unit 3 (make 1) **Unit 4** (make 1)

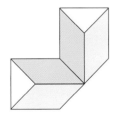
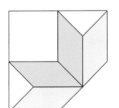

7. Sew **Unit 4** and 1 **triangle** together to make **Unit 5**.

Unit 5 (make 1)

8. Sew **Unit 5** and 1 **small rectangle** together to make **Unit 6.**

Unit 6 (make 1)

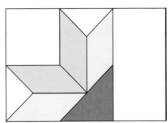

9. Sew 1 **small rectangle** and 1 **triangle-square** together to make **Unit 7**.

Unit 7 (make 1)

10. Sew **Unit 6** and **Unit 7** together to make **Block**.

Block (make 1)

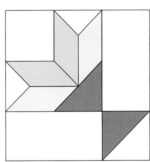

11. Referring to **Wall Hanging Top Diagram**, page 88, sew **triangles** and **Block** together to make center section of wall hanging top.

12. Referring to **Wall Hanging Top Diagram**, sew **top, bottom**, then **side inner borders** to center section.

13. With floral with blue background rectangle placed at center of border, sew 4 **squares** and 1 **rectangle** together to make 1 **Top Pieced Border** and 1 **Bottom Pieced Border**.

Top Pieced Border (make 1)

Bottom Pieced Border (make 1)

QUILTING

14. With floral with blue background rectangle placed at center of border, sew 6 **squares** and 1 **rectangle** together to make 1 **Right Pieced Border** and 1 **Left Pieced Border.**

Right Side Pieced Border (make 1)

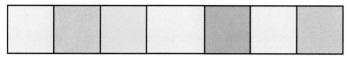

Left Side Pieced Border (make 1)

15. Sew **Top, Bottom, Right,** then **Left Pieced Borders** to center section of wall hanging top.

16. For appliqués, fuse web to wrong side of floral scraps. Cut desired motifs from fabric. Remove paper backing. Referring to photo, follow **Invisible Appliqué,** page 206, to appliqué motifs to wall hanging top.

COMPLETING THE WALL HANGING

1. Follow **Quilting,** page 205, to mark, layer, and quilt using **Quilting Diagram** as a suggestion. Our wall hanging is hand quilted using the Flower Quilting Pattern, page 89.

2. Follow **Making a Hanging Sleeve,** below, to attach hanging sleeve to wall hanging.

3. Cut an 18" square of binding fabric. Follow **Binding,** page 207, to bind wall hanging using 2 1/2"w bias binding with mitered corners.

MAKING A HANGING SLEEVE

Attaching a hanging sleeve to the back of your wall hanging before the binding is added allows you to display your completed project on a wall.

1. Measure the width of the wall hanging top and subtract 1". Cut a piece of fabric 7"w by the determined measurement.

2. Press short edges of fabric piece 1/4" to wrong side; press edges 1/4" to wrong side again and machine stitch in place.

3. Matching wrong sides, fold piece in half lengthwise to form a tube.

4. Follow project instructions to sew binding to wall hanging top and to trim backing and batting. Before blindstitching binding to backing, match raw edges and stitch hanging sleeve to center top edge on back of wall hanging.

5. Finish binding wall hanging, treating the hanging sleeve as part of the backing.

6. Blindstitch bottom of hanging sleeve to backing, taking care not to stitch through to front of wall hanging.

7. Insert dowel or slat into hanging sleeve.

Quilting Diagram

Wall Hanging Top Diagram

QUILTING

Flower Quilting Pattern

1/4 Quilting Pattern

SPRING BOUQUET QUILT
(Continued from page 81.)

← placement guides

QUILTING

Floral Fantasy Topiaries

For a special occasion or for no reason at all, show someone how much you care with one of these gorgeous topiaries! They're so easy to create, you'll want to make all three. Just take a foam ball or topiary form and cover it with miniature rosebuds, leaves, or moss and a swirl of flowers. Pretty ribbons, twining ivy, or a cluster of flowers are lovely trims. Present our friendly floral gift in a purchased decorative container or create your own by painting a plain clay pot.

FLORALS

LEAF-COVERED TOPIARY TREE

You will need a 4"h clay pot; pink acrylic spray paint; metallic gold acrylic paint; small sponge piece; a 4" dia. plastic foam ball; floral foam to fit in pot; a twig for trunk; sheet moss; silk leaves to cover ball (we used approx. 65 rose leaves); assorted silk flowers with leaves; $7/8$ yd of $1^1/2$"w ribbon; a $1^3/4$" x 4" piece of heavy ivory paper, metallic gold paint pen with fine point, and a dark pink felt-tip pen with medium point for gift card; wire cutters; paper towels; hot glue gun; and glue sticks.

1. Allowing to dry after each coat, spray paint pot pink.
2. To sponge-paint pot, dip dampened sponge piece into gold acrylic paint; remove excess paint on a paper towel. Using a light stamping motion, use sponge piece to paint pot as desired. Allow to dry.
3. For topiary form, hot glue floral foam into pot to $1/2$" from rim. Hot glue sheet moss over foam, covering foam completely. For trunk, cut twig to 4" longer than desired finished height of trunk. Insert 1 end of twig 2" into foam ball; insert remaining end 2" into center of foam in pot. Use hot glue to secure trunk if necessary.
4. Use wire cutters to remove leaves from stems. Working from bottom to top of topiary ball and overlapping leaves, glue leaves to ball, covering ball completely.
5. Glue center of ribbon to top of topiary; trim ends.
6. Glue flowers and leaves to top of topiary over ribbon.

7. For gift card, use a ruler and gold paint pen to draw a border $1/4$" from edges of ivory paper piece. Allow to dry. Use pink pen to write message on card. Use a small dot of hot glue to secure card to tree.

ROSE TOPIARY TREE

You will need a purchased decorative container (we used a 5" dia. x $3^1/2$"h metal bucket); a topiary form with a 5" dia. foam ball top and base to fit in container; floral foam to fill remainder of container to $1/2$" from rim (if needed); sheet moss; small silk roses to cover ball (we used approx. one hundred thirty-five $3/4$" dia. roses); silk ivy; $2/3$ yd of 1"w wired ribbon; a $1^3/4$" x 4" piece of heavy ivory paper, metallic gold paint pen with fine point, and a dark pink felt-tip pen with medium point for gift card; wire cutters; hot glue gun; and glue sticks.

1. Glue base of topiary form into container. If necessary, use pieces of floral foam to fill remainder of container to $1/2$" from rim; glue to secure. Glue sheet moss over foam, covering foam completely.
2. Use wire cutters to remove roses from stems. Glue roses to foam ball, covering ball completely.
3. Cut a length of ivy same length as trunk plus 4". Insert 1" of 1 end of ivy into foam ball near trunk; wind ivy around trunk. Insert remaining end of ivy into foam in pot near trunk, trimming to fit if necessary.
4. Tie ribbon into a bow; trim ends. Glue bow to trunk below foam ball.
5. For gift card, follow Step 7 of Leaf-Covered Topiary Tree instructions.

FLORAL SWAG TOPIARY TREE

You will need a $4^1/4$"h clay pot; metallic gold acrylic spray paint; metallic gold acrylic paint; small sponge piece; a 9"h plastic foam cone; floral foam to fit in pot; a twig for trunk; sheet moss; dried crushed herbs and craft glue (optional); 24" long silk floral swag; three $1^1/2$ yd lengths of $1/16$"w satin ribbon; a $1^3/4$" x 4" piece of heavy ivory paper, metallic gold paint pen with fine point, and a dark pink felt-tip pen with medium point for gift card; paper towels; hot glue gun; and glue sticks.

1. Allowing to dry after each coat, spray paint pot gold.
2. To sponge-paint pot, use liquid acrylic paint and follow Step 2 of Leaf-Covered Topiary Tree instructions.
3. For topiary form, use cone instead of ball and follow Step 3 of Leaf-Covered Topiary Tree instructions.
4. To cover cone with moss or herbs, hot glue sheet moss to cone, trimming to fit as necessary, or spread a thin layer of craft glue over cone and roll in herbs; allow to dry.
5. Beginning with 1 end of swag at top of cone and winding around cone to bottom edge, hot glue floral swag to cone, trimming to fit if necessary.
6. Tie ribbons together into a bow; trim ends. Hot glue bow to top of cone.
7. For gift card, follow Step 7 of Leaf-Covered Topiary Tree instructions.

Birdbath Cascade

You will need a birdbath with base, cream and rust acrylic paint, paintbrushes, plastic foam ring to fit in birdbath, sheet moss, floral pins, decorative container to fit in center of foam ring, floral foam, and dried florals (we used bear grass, millet, ammobium, nigella, and white sierra bud).

Refer to Painting Techniques, page 204, before beginning project. Allow paint to dry after each application.

1. Paint birdbath and base cream; *Dry Brush* with rust paint.

2. Cover foam ring with moss; secure with floral pins. Center ring in birdbath. Fill container with floral foam; place in center of ring.

3. Arrange bear grass around rim of container. Working toward center, add millet, then ammobium, nigella, and sierra bud.

Dried grasses and flowers serenely cascade from this antiqued birdbath.

Season's Greetings Wreath

Used in ancient Greece and Rome to bestow glory and tribute on men of honor, wreaths of bay leaves are especially symbolic adornments for celebrating the birth of Christ. A store-bought bay wreath gives you a head start on this festive decoration.

With a purchased bay leaf wreath, a hot glue gun, glue sticks, and an assortment of decorations that can be found at your local craft store, this wreath can be completed in minutes. Our decorations include dried pomegranates, stems of artificial berries, assorted pinecones, nuts, and sprigs of evergreen, which are all hot glued in place on the wreath. We used a black fabric marking pen with medium point to write our holiday messages on purchased wooden heart cutouts and then used a stencil brush to lightly stamp the edges of the hearts with brown paint to give them a natural finish. A raffia bow hot glued in place completes this cheerful wreath.

Pinecone Bouquet

You'll give your home a vibrant splash of color with this basketful of "fresh-cut" flowers! The perky blossoms are crafted by painting trimmed pinecones, attaching them to wire "stems," and adding silk greenery for a long-lasting arrangement.

Loblolly, Ponderosa, and Jeffrey cones are all approximately $2^1/_2$" to 6" long and oval-shaped, with thin scales that are flat on top. Shortleaf and Austrian are similar to the preceding cones but smaller, ranging in size from $1^1/_2$" to $2^1/_2$" long. Any of these cones can be used for making the flowers in this project.

Note: Loblolly and Shortleaf pinecones were used for this project. Mature, freshly fallen cones work best. These will be open and ready to use. If your cones have dust or cobwebs on them, clean lightly using a soft brush. Allow paint to dry between each coat.

You will need assorted sizes of pinecones (we used 20); basket approx. 13"h (including handle) with 5"dia. base; limb trimmers; wire cutters; safety goggles; gloss-finish clear acrylic spray sealer; spray paint (white, yellow, pink, lavender, and blue); acrylic paint (yellow, orange, and green); paintbrush; twenty-one 18" lengths of 18 gauge floral wire; green floral tape; floral foam; sheet moss; assorted silk greenery (we used bear grass, yellow-tint baby's breath, and variegated eucalyptus); 1 yd $2^1/_4$"w yellow gingham wire-edge ribbon; $^3/_4$ yd each of $^1/_8$"w blue and $^1/_8$"w purple satin ribbon; $1^1/_2$ yds $^1/_4$"w pink satin ribbon; sharp awl; thick potholder; hot glue gun; and hot glue sticks.

1. Using limb trimmers, cut off top $^1/_3$ to $^1/_2$ of cone; discard top (Fig. 1).

Fig. 1

2. For flower center, use wire cutters to trim scales from the top end $^1/_2$" to $^3/_4$" down (Fig. 2). Trim closely, rounding the edges.

Fig. 2

3. Using awl, make hole in bottom of flower (Fig. 3) .

Fig. 3

4. Hot glue wire in hole on bottom of flower. Allow glue to cool, holding wire in place (Fig. 4).

Fig. 4

5. Spray flower with sealer; spray with white spray paint.
6. Spray flower petals desired color.
7. Using paintbrush, paint center of flower with yellow or orange acrylic paint. Paint base of flower with green acrylic paint.
8. Wrap stem with floral tape.
9. Cut floral foam to fit in basket; glue to secure. Cover foam with moss.
10. Cut stems of flowers in varying lengths from 6"-12". Insert stems into foam, placing longer stems in center of arrangement and shorter stems around edge.
11. Cut stems of silk greenery in varying lengths from 6"-12". Insert stems into foam, placing longer stems in center of arrangement and shorter stems around edge.
12. Tie wire-edge ribbon in a bow. Use remaining wire length to attach bow to basket handle.
13. Cut pink ribbon in half. Holding all satin ribbon lengths together, tie in a bow. Hot glue satin ribbon bow to center of yellow gingham bow. Trim ribbon ends as desired.

Design by Theresa Morgan.

Lovely Lavender

A *weathered clay pot* *makes an elegant base* *for a dramatic lavender* *topiary. The beribboned* *arrangement is assembled* *using a cardboard* *tube covered with* *preserved leaves.*

You will need a hot glue gun, $5/8$" dia. turned wooden knobs, 5"h terra cotta flowerpot, green and white acrylic paint, floral foam, 9" length of wrapping paper tube, dried lavender bunch, preserved galax leaves, white marble chips, and $1^1/2$"w wired ribbon.

Refer to Painting Techniques, page 204, before beginning project. Allow paint to dry after each application.

1. Glue knobs around rim of pot.

2. Paint pot green. For color wash, mix equal parts of water and white paint; apply to pot. *Spatter Paint* pot with white.

3. Cut floral foam to fit in pot; glue in place. Cut a 3" deep hole in center of foam to fit wrapping paper tube. Place tube in foam; place lavender in tube.

4. Beginning at top and overlapping as needed to cover tube completely, glue leaves to tube.

5. Cover foam surface with marble chips. Tie ribbon into a bow around leaves; notch ribbon ends.

Summer Roses Wreath

The romantic beauty of flowers is captured in a grapevine wreath abloom with silk roses, hydrangeas, snapdragons, and other naturals from the garden.

You will need a large grapevine wreath, artificial silk and dried florals (we used 12 medium roses, 4 large roses, 6 hydrangeas, 3 snapdragons, 12 Queen Anne's lace, 12 maidenhair fern, and three sprigs of purple berries), and a hot glue gun.

1. Arrange roses, snapdragons, and other large items evenly on wreath and glue in place.

2. Glue remaining florals, cut into smaller sections as necessary, in place to fill in remainder of wreath.

Blossoming Accents

A picture frame and a clock covered with dried ammobium blossoms are lovely additions to any décor. Meanwhile, larkspur and sierra bud are the focal point of an eye-catching topiary, arrayed with beautiful nigella flowers and standing tall in a simple clay pot.

DECORATED FRAME

You will need a wooden picture frame, ivory spray paint, hot glue gun, and dried florals (we used ammobium flowers).

1. Paint frame.

2. Use hot glue to attach small bunches of flowers to cover frame as desired.

LAYERED TOPIARY

You will need a 6" dia. terra cotta flowerpot, hot glue gun, floral foam, sheet moss, dried larkspur, sierra bud, ammobium, and nigella, and floral wire.

1. Trim larkspur stems to 17" long; trim sierra bud stems to 9" to 12" long. Place several stems of larkspur together. Arrange sierra around larkspur; wrap tightly with floral wire.

2. Place wired bundle in pot; use pieces of foam to tightly fill pot around bundle. Cover foam surface with moss.

3. Remove stems from nigella and ammobium. Glue two rows of nigella flower heads over wire. Glue clusters of ammobium around rim of flowerpot.

FLORAL CLOCK

You will need a clock in a ready-to-finish wooden frame with base, white primer, crackle medium, ivory and green acrylic paint, satin finish varnish, hot glue gun, dried ammobium and sierra bud flowers, and dried fern fronds.

1. Remove clock from frame; apply primer to frame and base.

2. Using green for basecoat and ivory for top coat, follow manufacturer's instructions to apply crackle finish to base only. Apply varnish; allow to dry.

3. Glue small bunches dried flowers in place to cover surface of clock frame. Trim with fern fronds and additional dried flowers.

4. Replace clock in frame.

Clay Pot Creations

Plain flower pots really blossom when you dress them up to hold gifts, treats, hobby supplies, plants, and other fun items. With ordinary clay pots, a little paint or glue, and a few odds and ends from your craft closet, you'll be turning out clever painted pots in no time!

PAINTING

CLAY POT TECHNIQUES

PAINTING

PREPARING YOUR CLAY POT
- Erase any pencil markings.
- Sand off rough edges using fine-grit sandpaper.
- Remove any dust from clay pot using a damp cloth.

TRANSFERRING PATTERNS
1. Trace each pattern onto tracing paper.
2. Position pattern on pot. Insert a piece of transfer paper between pot and tracing paper.
3. Draw over pattern with dull pencil.

MAKING CUTOUTS
1. Trace patterns onto tracing paper.
2. Cut out patterns.
3. Use patterns to cut pieces from paper or fabric.

DECOUPAGE
1. Coat the pot and the back of the cutout with decoupage glue.
2. Place cutout in position on pot and brush on another layer of decoupage glue.
3. While still wet, use your finger to smooth over cutout, getting any excess glue from underneath cutout.
4. If you get air bubbles in cutout, prick them with a straight pin and smooth over them again with decoupage glue.

PAINTING
- You may need several coats of paint to get complete coverage.
- Most mistakes can be lightly sanded off.

SPONGE PAINTING
1. Wet sponge piece; squeeze out excess water.
2. Squeeze out a puddle of paint onto paper plate.
3. Dip sponge piece in paint; do not saturate. Blot sponge piece on paper towel.
4. Lightly press sponge piece on desired area of project.

PAINTING DOTS
1. Dip the handle end of paintbrush into paint.
2. Touch handle to desired area. The size of the dot is determined by the size of the handle.

SHADING
1. Dampen brush with water; dip one corner of brush into a darker paint.
2. Stroke brush on wax paper a few times to blend.
3. Apply paint along outline of an area using one stroke.

FINISHING YOUR CLAY POT
- Seal your clay pot using brush-on sealer, spray sealer, or decoupage glue. You may use either matte or glossy finish.
- If you plan on using your clay pot as a planter, use a liner or protect the inside of the clay pot with several coats of sealer.

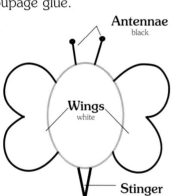

Antennae
black

Wings
white

Stinger
black

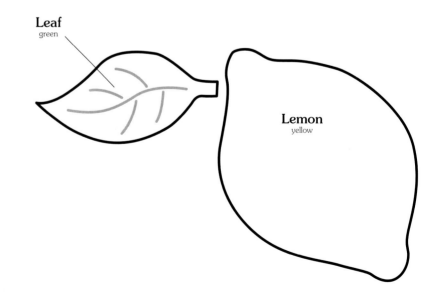

Leaf
green

Lemon
yellow

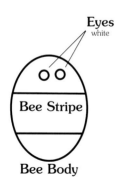

Eyes
white

Bee Stripe

Bee Body

LEMONS
(Photo, page 99)

SUPPLIES
6½" dia. clay pot; acrylic paints — blue, white, yellow, green, and gold; paintbrushes; construction paper — yellow and green; tracing paper; sponge pieces; red jumbo rickrack; decoupage glue; and craft glue.

INSTRUCTIONS
For further information, please read Clay Pot Techniques, page 100.

1. Paint pot blue; sponge paint using white paint. Paint rim yellow.
2. Use lemon and leaf patterns, page 100, to make cutouts from construction paper.
3. Using grey area on pattern as a guide, paint accents on leaves using green paint. Sponge paint bottom edge of lemons using gold paint.
4. Decoupage cutouts onto pot. Seal pot using decoupage glue.
5. Glue rickrack around rim using craft glue.

CHERRIES
(Photo, page 99)

SUPPLIES
4½" dia. clay pot; acrylic paints — yellow, white, blue, red, light green, dark green, and black; paintbrushes; tracing paper; transfer paper; red polymer clay; glue gun; dull pencil; and sealer.

INSTRUCTIONS
For further information, please read Clay Pot Techniques, page 100.

1. Paint pot yellow and rim white. Paint blue stripes on rim.
2. Transfer stem and leaf pattern to pot. Paint stem and leaf.
3. For each cherry, roll out a ¾" ball of clay. Place ball over cherry pattern; flatten ball to fit pattern. Remove from pattern. Bake clay pieces following manufacturer's instructions. Glue cherries to pot.
4. Paint red dots on background.
5. Seal pot.

BEEHIVE
(Photo, page 99)

SUPPLIES
6½" dia. clay pot; 6½" dia. clay saucer; acrylic paints — light gold, white, tan, gold, and black; paintbrushes; toothbrush; tracing paper; transfer paper; polymer clay — black and yellow; 1" wooden ball; 4-ply jute; glue gun; dull pencil; and sealer.

INSTRUCTIONS
For further information, please read Clay Pot Techniques, page 100.

1. Paint pot light gold and rim white. Paint ½"w black checks on rim. Paint wooden ball black.
2. Transfer honeycomb pattern, below, to pot as many times as desired. Paint honeycomb outline tan. Shade inside of honeycombs using gold paint.
3. Transfer antennae, wings, and stinger patterns, page 100, to pot. Paint designs. Paint black dots on ends of antennae. Spatter paint pot and rim using gold paint.
4. For each bee body, roll out a ¾" ball of black clay. Place ball over bee body pattern, page 100; flatten ball to fit pattern. Remove from pattern. For stripe, roll out a ¼" long x ¾" dia. tube of yellow clay. Place tube over bee stripe pattern; flatten tube to fit pattern. Remove from pattern. Press yellow stripe onto black bee body. Bake clay pieces following manufacturer's instructions. Paint eyes on bees.
5. Glue bees to pot over painted wings.
6. Seal pot.
7. For lid, glue jute to bottom of saucer by coiling from the outside edge towards the center.
8. Glue ball to top of lid.

Designs by Holly Witt.

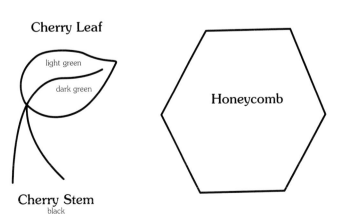

Cherry Leaf

light green

dark green

Honeycomb

Cherry Stem

black

Cherry

PAINTING

Beautiful Bucket Planter

PAINTING

You don't need a green thumb to make a weather-beaten bucket blossom into a pretty planter. Just gather up some paint, a few finials, and an ivy stencil. You'll soon have a charming cachepot guaranteed to make any plant beautiful!

You will need sandpaper; metal bucket; tack cloth; brush-on primer; paintbrushes; desired colors of acrylic paint, including green; stencil brush; ivy stencil; drill and bits; three 3" dia. wooden turnings for feet; three 1" long wood screws; and clear acrylic spray sealer.
Refer to Painting Techniques, page 204, before beginning project. Allow primer, paint, and sealer to dry after each application.

1. Sand bucket; wipe with tack cloth.
2. Apply primer to outside of bucket. Paint sections on bucket desired basecoat colors; paint feet.
3. *Stencil* green ivy around center of bucket. Paint stripes and diamond outlines around bucket; use end of paintbrush handle to paint dots for berries among ivy leaves.
4. Drill three evenly spaced holes in bottom of bucket to attach feet. Working from inside, use screws to attach feet to bottom of bucket.
5. Apply two to three coats of sealer to planter.

decoupaged rooster chest

Use narrow masking tape to help paint the plaid design on this little chest; then decoupage the rooster panels from wallpaper.

You will need a wooden chest; black, off-white, and red acrylic paints; crackle medium; #1 and #4 script liner brushes; paintbrushes; $3/4$"w painter's masking tape; wallpaper rooster panels; decoupage glue; primer; sealer; and any additional supplies from Step 1.

1. Read and follow Preparing to Paint, page 109.
2. Mask off rectangular area on top of chest. To make curved corners, use a compass to draw a portion of a circle on tape, then use a craft knife to gently cut and remove tape along curved line. Paint chest black; let dry and remove tape. Paint drawers and previously masked area on top off-white.
3. Refer to manufacturer's instructions to apply crackle medium to sides of chest; let dry.
4. Brush red paint on crackled areas.
5. Mark center of each side of chest top and drawers. Center a strip of tape vertically between these marks. Apply second strip of tape along either side of center tape strip, butting edges together without overlapping. Continue working out to the sides of the surface. Leaving the center stripe off-white, remove every other strip of tape and paint red; let dry and remove remainder of tape. Repeat to create horizontal stripes.
6. Draw a light pencil line through center of each vertical and horizontal red stripe. Use #4 brush to paint every other pencil line black and remaining pencil lines off-white.
7. Draw a light pencil line through center of each horizontal and vertical off-white stripe. Use #1 brush to paint every other pencil line red and remaining pencil lines black.
8. Cut out rooster panels from wallpaper; découpage to drawers.
9. Allowing to dry between coats, apply several coats of water-based varnish or polyurethane sealer to chest.

PAINTING

Man's Best Friend

Your best friend in the canine world deserves to be honored with his or her photo in a special display. This fun frame is especially easy to paint.

MATERIALS:

5 ¹/₂" x 7 ¹/₄" Frame with
  4 ⁵/₈" x 3" opening
Krylon® Crystal Clear
KOH-I-NOOR Rapidograph® Pen
  .25 tip, Black ink
Transfer paper

DecoArt™ Americana® Acrylic Paint:

Hauser Medium Green
Black Forest Green
Antique White
Lamp Black
Raw Sienna
Grey Sky

Loew-Cornell® Paintbrushes:

Series: 7550 Size ¹/₂" Wash
Series: 7300 Size 12 Shader
Series: 7000 Sizes 1, 3 Round

INSTRUCTIONS:

1. Remove the plastic from the window opening.

2. Paint the frame Hauser Medium Green. Shade around the window opening and edges with Black Forest Green.

3. Transfer the pattern onto the frame.

4. Paint the bones Antique White, shaded with Raw Sienna.

5. Paint the paws and letters Lamp Black.

6. Do the line work with the Rapidograph pen.

7. Paint your dog's name in the bone.

8. Spray with two to three very light coats of Krylon spray. Let dry between coats. Light coats are very important so that the ink doesn't bleed.

9. Return the plastic to the window opening and insert your best friend's photo.

Design by Carolyn Stearns.

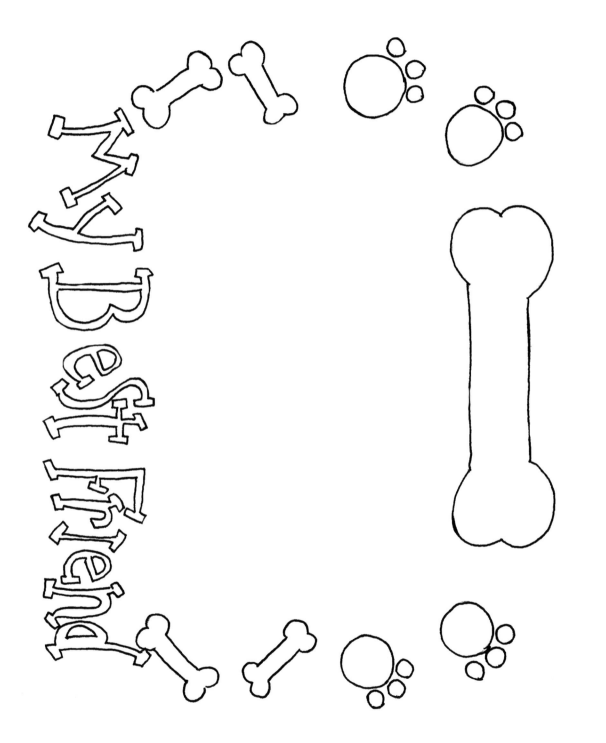

My Best Friend

MAGICAL GARDEN PADDED CHEST

Providing extra seating for visitors, this padded chest is also a handy place to store playthings and other treasures.

SUPPLIES

You will need a wooden toy box with removable seat; primer; antique white latex paint; non-toxic brush-on sealer; dark yellow, light pink, pink, blue, light green, and green acrylic paint; tracing paper; transfer paper; black permanent fine-point marker; fabric to cover seat; and a staple gun.

INSTRUCTIONS

1. Remove seat from toy box. Read Preparing to Paint, page 109.
2. Prepare box for painting. Paint box antique white. Paint edge of lid with light pink and pink stripes. Paint bottom edge of box blue. Paint details on bottom edge dark yellow.

3. Reducing or enlarging on photocopier if necessary, trace flower patterns, page 107, onto tracing paper. For each flower, position tracing paper on chest, slide transfer paper underneath, and use a dull pencil or stylus to trace over design. Paint designs according to patterns. Use marker to outline designs.
4. Apply sealer to toy box.
5. To cover seat, measure width and length of seat. Cut a piece of fabric 8" larger than determined measurements. Staple edges of fabric to back of seat, smoothing fabric over front. Reattach seat to toy chest.

Flowers

rosy repose

Trimmed in al fresco shades of pink and green, this
glorious chair simply demands attention. Create your own
with a bit of paint and a favorite floral fabric.

*You will need a wooden chair with
removable seat; light green, pink,
dark pink, white, dark green, and
light tan acrylic paints; fabric for seat;
batting; staple gun; paintbrushes;
primer; sealer; and any additional
supplies listed in Step 1.*

1. Read Choosing Your Chair,
Preparing to Paint, Painting Your
Chair, Painting Details, and
Covering a Seat, page 109.

2. Prepare chair for painting.
Referring to photo for color
placement, paint chair light green,
dark pink, and light tan. Paint dark
green dots on seat support.

3. Use dark pink paint to paint
comma strokes on chair back and
top front of legs. Highlight top of
comma strokes using white paint.

4. Refer to photo and lightly mark
placement of roses on chair back.
For each rose, paint a dark pink
$^3/_4$" long x $^1/_2$" wide oval. Thin pink
paint using water. Use thinned
paint to paint a second oval over
dark pink oval; add a white dot to
upper center of oval. Use light
green paint to add two comma
strokes to bottom of rose for leaves.

5. Apply sealer to chair.

6. Cover seat.

Design by Diana Cates.

Choosing Your Chair

If you can't find the exact chair pictured you can still paint the project. Just use the instructions as a general guideline to create your own unique chair.

Preparing to Paint

For safety's sake, carefully follow all manufacturers' instructions and warnings when using any cleaning, stripping, painting, or finishing product. For children's chairs, use non-toxic paints, primers, and sealers that are recommended for that purpose.

You may need household cleaner, oil soap, sponges, soft cloths, old paintbrush, toothbrush, paint/varnish stripper, wood putty, putty knife, wire brush, assorted grit or gauge sandpaper or steel wool, tack cloth, and items for repairing chair (hammer, screwdriver, drill, nails, screws, clamps, wood glue).

Preparation is the key. Before you paint, your goal is to have the chair in working condition, clean, and ready to accept paint.

1. Clean chair. Remove seat, if needed. Remove dirt, dust, and surface grime by cleaning it with a non-abrasive cleaner such as oil soap.
2. Prepare surface. The type of finish currently on your chair determines preparations.
   Unfinished wood — Use fine-grit sandpaper to lightly sand entire surface.
   Stained or stained and sealed surface — Use fine-grit sandpaper to lightly sand entire surface.
   Painted surfaces in good condition — Use fine-grit sandpaper to lightly sand entire surface.
   Painted surfaces in poor condition — Knock off any peeling or chipping paint with a wire brush. Smooth rough areas with medium-grit sandpaper, then go over entire chair lightly with fine-grit paper.
   Painted surface with multiple paint layers — If your chair has many paint layers or the surface is lumpy or shows heavy brush strokes, your best option may be to strip the chair back to bare wood using a paint stripper. After stripping chair, make sure you lightly sand the entire surface.

3. Make repairs and remove hardware.
4. Wipe down chair using a tack cloth to remove dust.

Painting Your Chair

You may need low-tack painter's masking tape, kraft paper, primer, paint, and paintbrushes.

1. Mask off any area you don't wish to paint. Use masking tape and kraft paper as needed.
2. Apply a primer to your prepared surface before painting. Your paint will go on more smoothly and it will adhere better to your surface.
3. In most cases, you will need to paint the entire chair a single background color before you add decorative details. Apply paint using a paintbrush designed for the type of paint you are using, or you may use spray paint. Both types of paint may require more than one coat for even coverage.

Once the background color is dry, follow project instructions to paint details.

Painting Details

Dots — Dip the handle end of a paintbrush into paint. Touch end of paintbrush to surface.

Comma Strokes — Dip liner paintbrush into paint. Touch tip of paintbrush to surface, allowing brush hairs to spread out. Pull paintbrush toward you, lifting brush gradually as you pull to create the tail of the stroke (Fig. 1). For left or right comma strokes, pull the paintbrush to the left or right when you are creating the tail of the stroke (Fig. 2).

Fig. 1   **Fig. 2**

Covering a Seat

You will need fabric to cover seat, batting and/or upholstery foam, and staple gun.

1. Remove seat from chair. Draw around seat on wrong side of fabric. Cut out fabric 4" outside drawn line.
2. If using batting, cut batting same size as fabric. Layer batting, then fabric on seat. Fold fabric at corners diagonally over batting to fit seat corners. Alternating sides and pulling taut, staple edges of fabric to bottom of seat. Trim as necessary.
3. If using upholstery foam, cut foam same shape as seat. Wrap batting around foam to soften edges of foam piece. Layer foam, then fabric on seat. Wrap fabric around seat and staple edges to bottom of seat. Trim excess fabric.
4. Reattach seat to chair.

Dragonflies Candle

Hand-painted candles are a gorgeous accent for any room, and this whimsical garden scene is no exception. Friends are sure to admire your painting skills — and don't be surprised if you get a few hints for gifts!

1. To prepare candle surface, buff with nylon hose.

2. Sponge sides of candle with White + candle painting medium. Reducing or enlarging on a photocopier to fit your candle, trace pattern onto tracing paper. Tape transfer paper, then pattern, to candle. Trace over design with a stylus or ballpoint pen.

3. Stipple Hauser Light Green around base of candle with scruffy brush. Use flat brush to paint fence posts Burnt Sienna. Shade fence posts with Asphaltum.

4. Paint birdhouses Golden Straw. Shade birdhouses with Burnt Sienna. Use #5 round brush to paint Asphaltum comma strokes for roof. Add detailing to front of birdhouses with Asphaltum. Use #3 round brush to paint birdhouse poles and perches with Asphaltum. Bounce brush slightly as you paint line to give a "bumpy" look. Paint dragonfly bodies in same manner with Asphaltum.

5. Use #5 round brush to paint Salem Blue teardrop strokes for dragonfly wings. Let dry, then add Golden Straw dots.

Note: Painted candles are for decorative use only.

*Design by
Julie G. McGuffee.*

DecoArt™ Americana® Paints:

Alizarin Crimson
Asphaltum
Avocado
Baby Blue
Burnt Sienna
Golden Straw
Hauser Light Green
Plum
Raspberry
Salem Blue
Summer Lilac
Wedgewood Blue
White

Supplies:

#3 Round Brush
#5 Round Brush
#8 Flat Brush
10/0 Liner Brush
DecoArt™ Candle Painting Medium
Transfer Paper

PAINTING

Pink Blossoms Bowl

Supplies :

Glass Bowl
Delta CeramDecor™ Air-Dry PermEnamel™ Paints:
Fuchsia
Cotton Candy Pink
Crocus Yellow
Ultra White
True Green
Hunter Green
Delta PermEnamel™ Surface Conditioner
Delta PermEnamel™ Clear Gloss Glaze
Tracing Paper
Tape

Paintbrushes :

#3 round
#10 flat

Delicate blossoms practically dance across this sparkling glass bowl. Use this exquisite bauble as a creative candy dish or an enchanting votive holder. Or create several in a variety of colors to scatter throughout the house!

Directions :

1 Prepare glass with Surface Conditioner. Trace pattern onto tracing paper and slip inside the glass bowl. Tape into place where you want design painted.

2 Using your #3 round brush loaded with Fuchsia and tipped with Cotton Candy Pink, stroke on blossoms. Pull your strokes from the outside toward the center.

3 Using the same brush, pat Crocus Yellow in for the centers. While still wet, add a dot of Ultra White to the lower left hand side of center.

4 Leaves and strokes are painted using a #3 round brush loaded with True Green and Hunter Green.

5 Using Fuchsia for the three outside dots and Crocus Yellow for the center dot, dot flowers around rest of bowl with the wooden end of the brush.

6 Paint rim of bowl with Fuchsia. Using the #10 flat brush double-loaded with Cotton Candy Pink and Fuchsia, add stripes around the bottom rim of bowl.

7 When dry, apply Gloss Glaze over the painted areas only. Allow to dry.

Design by Dorris Sorensen.

From my Garden of Painting Tips...

When banding the rim or edge of a bowl or any other object, try using a piece of cosmetic sponge. Dip the flat edge of the sponge into the paint, place on the rim, and very lightly drag it around the edge. The amount of pressure you apply to the sponge will determine how much paint is applied. The sponge will glide easily around the edge and give a smooth even coat.

Natural Array

A garden hand rake makes an innovative photo display (below) for pictures of loved ones, while additional photographs are enclosed in frames easily decorated with twigs and dried sisal leaves.

DECORATED FRAMES

You will need wooden picture frames, ivory spray paint, hot glue gun, and dried florals (we used sisal leaves, twigs, ammobium flowers, and raffia).

1. Paint frames.

2. Use hot glue to attach small bunches of flowers, leaves, or twigs (tied with raffia) to cover each frame as desired.

RAKE PHOTO KEEPER

You will need a 4" dia. terra cotta pot, hand rake with flat tines, floral foam, excelsior, raffia, mini spring-type wooden clothespins, and acrylic paint to match rake handle.

1. Place rake handle in pot; use pieces of foam to tightly fill pot around handle. Cover foam surface with excelsior.

2. Tie raffia into a bow around rake.

3. Paint clothespins; allow to dry. Use clothespins to attach photos to rake tines.

MEMORY KEEPING

Lacy Wedding Album

Preserve every cherished photo of that special day with this gorgeous wedding album. White fabric, lace, ribbon, and roses transform a plain album into a stunning gift the bride and groom will treasure forever.

Lacy Wedding Album

(Shown on page 113)

You will need a 9½" x 11½" *photo album with a* 2½" *spine, 1 yd of* 45"w *white fabric, 1" thick batting (one* 21½" x 11½" *piece and one* 8" x 10" *piece), two 9" x 11" pieces of poster board, 8" x 10" pre-cut mat with a* 4½" x 6½" *oval opening,* 1½ *yds of* ¼" *braided trim, 38" length of* 1"w *flat lace, 32" length of* 1½"w *flat lace,* 2¼ *yds of* ³⁄₈"w *white satin ribbon, 20" length of* 1½"w *white organza ribbon, assorted ribbon roses, and clear-drying craft glue.*

Covering Album

1. Remove pages from album and lay open on work surface.
2. Cut two 3" x 11½" strips of fabric. Glue one long edge of fabric strip ¼" under one side of rings. Repeat with remaining fabric strip and other side of rings; allow glue to dry.
3. With album closed, glue 21½" x 11½" piece of batting to outside of album.
4. Cut a 24½" x 14½" piece of fabric. Open album. With batting side down, center album on wrong side of fabric.
5. Referring to Fig. 1, turn fabric at bottom edge of album ¼" to wrong side for 4" in center. Glue folded fabric under spine of album. Repeat for top edge of album.

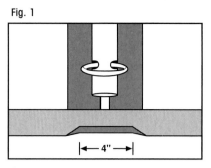

Fig. 1

|← 4" →|

6. Being sure fabric on front of album is smooth and taut, glue fabric to inside of album at **center only** of each side edge. Allow glue to dry. Glue fabric to remaining inside edges of album.
7. Glue fabric to corners on inside of album, folding, pleating, and trimming as necessary.
8. Cut two 11" x 13" pieces of fabric. Center one piece of poster board on wrong side of one piece of fabric. Fold fabric edges to back of poster board; glue in place, check frequently to be sure fabric is smooth and taut. Allow glue to dry. Glue fabric corners to back of poster board, folding and pleating as necessary. Allow glue to dry. Repeat for remaining poster board and fabric piece.
9. Glue back of one covered poster board to inside front of album approx. ¼" from top, bottom, and sides; repeat to glue remaining covered poster board to inside back of album. Allow glue to dry.

Making Covered Mat

1. Aligning edges, place mat on top of an 8" x 10" piece of batting. Draw along oval opening of mat on batting; cut along drawn line. Glue batting to front of mat.
2. Cut one 9½" x 11½" piece of fabric. With batting side down, center mat on wrong side of fabric. (**Note**: Do **not** cut out opening in fabric.) Glue fabric edges to back of mat, checking frequently to be sure fabric is smooth and taut. Allow glue to dry. Glue fabric corners to back of mat, folding and pleating as necessary. Allow glue to dry.
3. Cut out fabric inside mat opening to within 1" of mat. At ½" intervals clip into edges of fabric to within ⅛" of mat. Fold fabric to back of mat, making additional clips in fabric as necessary. Glue in place, checking frequently to be sure fabric is smooth and taut. Allow glue to dry.
4. Beginning at bottom edge, glue 15" length of ¼" braided trim around oval opening of covered mat.
5. Beginning at bottom left corner, refer to photo and glue a 38" length of 1"w flat lace to covered mat around outside edge. Centering on lace, glue a 38" length of white satin ribbon to covered mat around outside edge. Glue remaining 38" length of ¼" braided trim on top of ribbon.
6. Referring to photo and mitering corners, glue a 32" length of 1½"w flat lace to top of covered mat.
7. Tie organza ribbon in a bow. Tie two 10" lengths of white satin ribbon in bows. Refer to photo and glue bows and ribbon roses to bottom center of mat opening.
8. Leaving top edge open to insert photo, center and glue covered mat to album front.

*P*hotographs are meant to be shared, and a decorative photo album makes a great gift for your mother, sister, or friend. Anyone will enjoy displaying treasured snapshots in this special book.

Fancy Photo Keeper

WHAT TO BUY
10" x 11³/₄" photo album, ³/₄ yd. of border fabric with one wide border and one narrow border, ¹/₃ yd. of batting, and a flower charm

THINGS YOU HAVE AT HOME
Lightweight cardboard and a hot glue gun

FABRIC-COVERED PHOTO ALBUM
1. Measure width and height of open album; cut a piece of batting the determined measurement. Glue batting to outside of closed album.

2. Cut two 3"w fabric strips the height of the album. Glue one long edge of one fabric strip ¹/₄" under each side of binder hardware. Glue remaining edges of fabric strips to album.

3. Positioning wide border design on front of album, place open album batting side down on wrong side of fabric. Draw around album. Cut fabric 2" outside drawn line.

4. Center open album on wrong side of fabric piece. Glue corners of fabric over corners of album. Glue all edges of fabric to inside of album, trimming to fit around hardware.

5. Cutting ¹/₂" outside each edge of narrow border, cut a 13¹/₂" length from fabric for album trim. Press each long edge ¹/₂" to wrong side. Place trim on album; glue ends to inside of album. Pinching trim to gather slightly, glue charm over trim.

6. To cover inside of album, cut two 9¹/₂" x 11" pieces of cardboard. Cut two fabric pieces 1" larger on all sides than cardboard. Center one cardboard piece on wrong side of each fabric piece. Glue edges of fabric to cardboard. Glue wrong side of one cardboard piece to inside of each side of album.

YOU'RE ON "CANDIED" CAMERA!

*S*mile! You're on "candied" camera! A collage of candy wrappers and stickers, accented with bright paint, makes it easy for a young shutterbug to create a one-of-a-kind photo album cover.

WHAT TO BUY
5" x 7" photo album, pink dimensional paint, and $^{3}/_{4}$"h gold alphabet stickers

THINGS YOU HAVE AT HOME
Assorted candy wrappers, denatured alcohol, rubber cement, spray acrylic sealer, decorative-edge craft scissors, corrugated cardboard, black permanent medium-tip marker, and a hot glue gun

FUN PHOTO ALBUM

1. Clean back of candy wrappers with alcohol. Cut wrappers into desired shapes; use rubber cement to glue wrapper shapes to album front. Spray album front with acrylic sealer; allow to dry.

2. Referring to *Painting Techniques* (pg. 204), use paint to outline edges of wrappers; allow to dry.

3. Use craft scissors to cut a 1$^{1}/_{4}$" x 4" strip of cardboard. Use stickers to spell out "PHOTOS" on one side of cardboard strip. Use marker to outline each letter. Paint edges of cardboard strip; allow to dry.

4. Glue cardboard strip onto front of photo album.

Envelope
Soft and Sweet
(Continued from page 117)

Soft & Sweet

*O*ne of Baby's outgrown rompers makes a sweet cover for a small photo album. Special cutouts and edgings dress up the pages.

SUPPLIES

Small, square album; cardboard for inside front and back covers; pastel, white, and striped papers; Press 'N Punch™ Paper Punch (teddy bear and heart); fine black marker; Clouds Paper Edger; Mini Scallop Paper Edger; small pink rickrack; and a baby romper.

COVER

Cover a small album with a favorite romper that your child has outgrown (or use a new one). (See instructions for covering an album, page 115.)

PAGES

1. Mount photos on pastel background papers. Cut edges with Mini Scallop Paper Edger. Mount these on striped background paper and glue to pages.
2. Using the patterns, cut baby clothes out of pastel papers. Use a paper punch for the decorative polka-dots and a teddy bear and heart punch for the shirts. Glue rickrack across page for a clothesline and glue clothes underneath.

HOLLY'S HINTS

• You may have an exceptionally beautiful page design that you are proud of and want to share with everyone. Display this in a clear acrylic frame. You may always return that page to your photo album and display a new page at any time.

3. Cut edge of pages with Clouds Paper Edger and punch out holes to make edge look like lace.
4. Envelope: Use pattern, page 116, and Mini Scallop Edger to cut out shape of envelope. Glue envelope together, glue to page, and place a lock of baby's hair inside. Decorate envelope with the teddy bear that you punched out from the shirt.

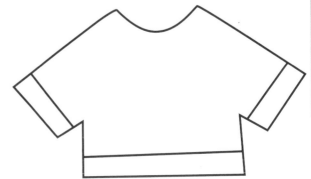

MEMORY KEEPING

Back To Nature

Pressed flowers and other souvenirs from a camping trip or hike can add wonderful touches to your scrapbooking.

HOLLY'S HINTS

• *If you are not sure that the decorative items you are using are acid-free (for example, florals, leaves, and souvenirs) use a color copy of your photo with the item. Or you may seal the items with decoupage medium.*

SUPPLIES

Album journal with ivory colored cover, ivory and brown papers, color copies of photos, pressed flowers and ferns, rectangular templates, and matte finish decoupage medium.

COVER

Put a drop of glue on the back of each pressed fern and flower and position on cover. Brush several coats of decoupage medium over ferns and flowers. Allow each layer to dry before applying a new coat. Several light coats are better than one heavy one.

PAGES

1. Take a favorite photo and enlarge it on a color copier to fill the entire page.

2. Mount a color copy of your original smaller photo on an ivory colored paper and cut out, leaving a ¼" edge around it. Glue to center of page.

3. Glue a small pressed fern to one corner of your color copied photo. Carefully brush decoupage medium over fern to encase it. Let dry, then apply another coat.

AND MORE PAGES

1. Nature subjects look more natural on ivory. Mount your photos on brown paper and glue to ivory page.

2. Glue pressed ferns around one corner of photo to frame it. Brush decoupage medium carefully over the fern as before.

3. Add any memorabilia to remind you of your special event or trip.

MEMORY KEEPING

Crazy Quilt Family Album

Printed papers or photocopies of fabrics are fun to use in patchwork patterns on albums and pages. Pinking scissors help create the look of rickrack.

SUPPLIES

White 7" x 10" album, assorted buttons, red rickrack, red paper, fine black marker, printed papers or color photocopies of fabrics, small rectangle of poster board, and Pinking Paper Edgers.

COVER

1. Make a color copy of red and blue fabrics on acid-free paper or use the printed papers available in craft stores. Cut the papers in an irregular crazy quilt pattern and glue to album cover.
2. Cut a small rectangle of white poster board to fit onto the center of your album cover. Hand letter your family's name and stitch marks with a black marker. Glue red rickrack around edge of poster board and glue on buttons.
3. Glue poster board rectangle to center of album cover.

HOLLY'S HINTS

- Use the same color scheme and design elements for your cover and inside pages to create continuity throughout your album. This makes your album easy to browse through and your photos remain the primary focus.
- It can be risky to letter on the album page. Instead, letter on a separate piece of paper, cut out, and glue under photo.

PAGES

1. Cut irregular crazy quilt shapes from the same papers used on cover. Fit them together and glue into place.
2. Cut photos 1/4" smaller than these paper quilt shapes. Glue photos onto paper shapes.
3. Make your own rickrack out of paper using the pinking scissors and glue on top of page. Hand write your special memories alongside photos with a black marker.

AND MORE PAGES

1. For another page, use the same fabric-printed paper and cut out a rectangular background for a single photo that you may want to "spotlight."
2. Cut more red "paper rickrack" and glue to top and bottom of rectangle. Add stitch marks with black marker.
3. Cut a border of printed paper to fit along bottom of your page. Cut the top edge of this border with the pinking scissors and glue.

MEMORY KEEPING

Catnap Cuddle-Ups

Whether curled among the bed pillows or on the windowsill, our momma cat and her three lovable kittens will add a cozy touch to your home. The napping felines are easy to sew in coordinating colors, and they all have a button accent at the base of their tails.

Instructions on page 127

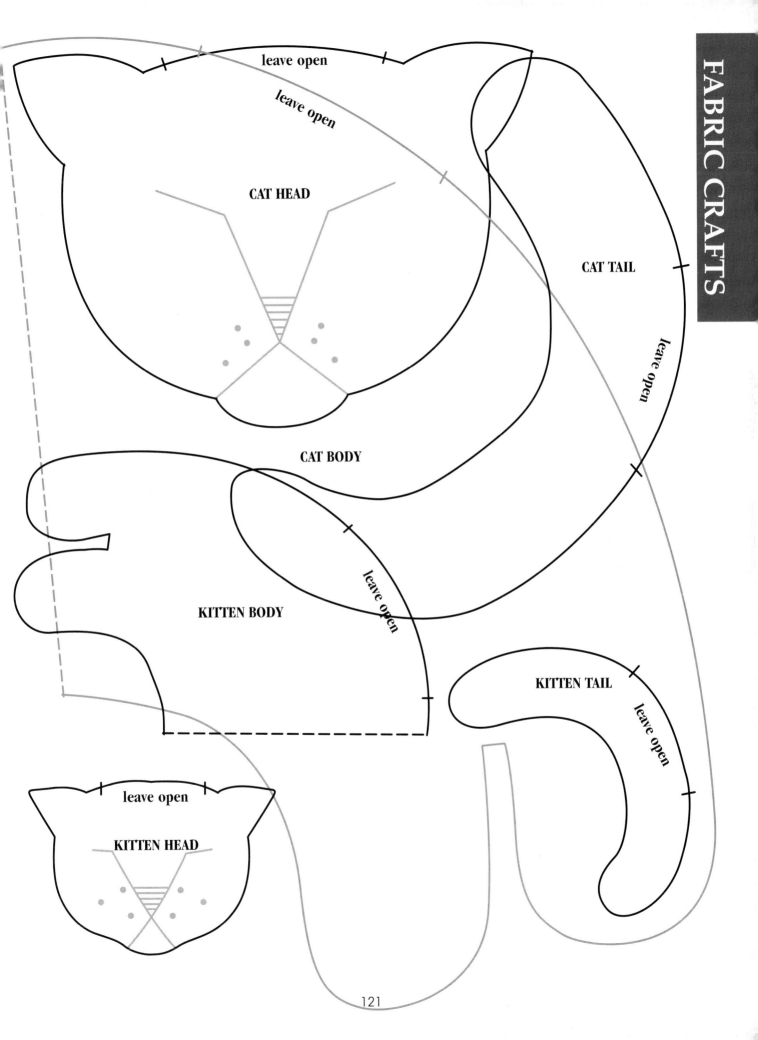

leave open

leave open

CAT HEAD

CAT TAIL

leave open

CAT BODY

leave open

KITTEN BODY

KITTEN TAIL

leave open

leave open

KITTEN HEAD

Chenille Flag Pillow

Don't wait till the Fourth of July to show off your patriotic spirit! Our folk-style pillow features chenille stripes that you create by stitching and cutting layered fabric. Button "stars" help the scrappy pillow resemble Old Glory.

You will need paper-backed fusible web, $8^1/2$" x 12" rectangle of blue print fabric, $16^1/2$" x $24^1/2$" rectangles of cream fabric and blue fabric for pillow front and back, six 6" x 26" rectangles of red print fabrics, polyester fiberfill, hot glue gun, and assorted white buttons.

1. For pillow front, fuse smaller blue rectangle to top left corner of cream rectangle. Using a narrow zigzag stitch, sew along edges of blue rectangle.

2. For chenille "stripes," layer red print rectangles with right sides up; cut five stacks of 1" x 27" strips. Stitch lengthwise along center of each stack. Make cuts to stitching every $1/4$" along both sides of each stack. Wash and dry strips to fray. Cut two of the strips in half to make a total of four short strips and three long strips.

3. Beginning with a short strip even with bottom of blue rectangle and placing strips $2^1/2$" apart, stitch chenille strips to pillow front; trim ends if necessary.

4. Matching right sides and raw edges and leaving an opening for turning, sew pillow front and back together. Clip corners and turn pillow right side out; stuff with fiberfill. Sew opening closed.

5. For "stars," glue buttons to blue rectangle.

Table Coordinates

These table coordinates are perfect for a morning meal or an afternoon get-together! It's so easy to stitch strips of fabric together to make the colorful place mats, and you can cut motifs from your print fabric to fuse to muslin napkins.

You *will need* scraps of assorted fabrics (including one fabric with printed motifs), muslin, and paper-backed fusible web.

Use a ¼" seam allowance for all sewing.

1. For each place mat, cut seven 2½" x 21½" fabric strips and one 14½" x 21½" piece of muslin.

2. Matching right sides, sew long edges of fabric strips together; press. Matching right sides and leaving an opening for turning, sew pieced rectangle and muslin rectangle together. Clip corners, turn right side out, and press. Hand sew opening closed.

3. For each napkin, cut a 19" square of muslin. To hem, press raw edges ¼" to wrong side; press edges ¼" to wrong side again and stitch in place.

4. Fuse web to wrong side of print fabric; cut out desired motif. Remove paper backing and fuse motif to corner of napkin.

123

Rooster Table Topper

You can start every day with a cock-a-doodle-doo when these perky roosters are at your breakfast table! Fused appliqués, borders, and hems make the no-sew topper a cinch to finish.

For table topper to fit 30" diameter table, you will need $1^3/8$ yds 90"w muslin, $5/8$ yd 44/45"w fabric for borders, 7" x 6" piece of fabric for each rooster appliqué, 2" x 4" piece of fabric for each comb and wattle appliqué, 2" square of fabric for each beak appliqué, approx. 2 yds paper-backed fusible web, 11 yds 1"w paper-backed fusible web tape, fabric glue, black and white dimensional fabric paints in squeeze bottles, and waxed paper.

1. Cut a 48" square from muslin.
2. To hem, fuse web tape along one edge on wrong side of fabric (Fig. 1). Do not remove paper backing.

Fig. 1

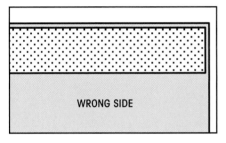

3. Press hem to wrong side along inner edge of tape. Unfold pressed edge and remove paper backing. Refold hem and fuse in place (Fig. 2). Repeat for remaining 3 sides.

Fig. 2

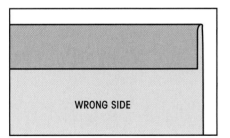

4. (Note: For instruction purposes, two opposite sides of topper will be referred to as side edges and the remaining sides will be referred to as top and bottom edges. Piece fabric strips for border, if necessary.) For side borders, cut two 3" x 47" strips from border fabric. For top and bottom borders, cut two 3" x $49^1/2$" strips from border fabric. Press one long raw edge of each strip $1^1/4$" to wrong side (Fig. 3a). This side will be the front of the border.

5. Press short ends of side borders $1/2$" to back. Press short ends of top and bottom borders $1/2$" to back; press $1/2$" to back again. Glue all pressed short edges to secure.
6. Fuse web tape along remaining long raw edge of each border strip (Fig. 3b). Remove paper backing.

Fig. 3a

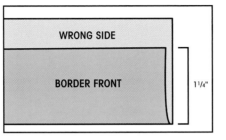

Fig. 3b

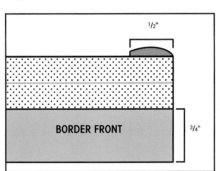

7. For side borders, align edge of topper with edge of fusible web so that $3/4$" of border fabric shows beyond topper; fuse in place. Repeat with remaining side border and opposite side of topper.
8. For top border, align edge of topper with edge of fusible web on border so that $3/4$" of border fabric shows beyond topper; fuse in place. Repeat with bottom border and bottom edge of topper.
9. Glue borders at each corner to secure.
10. For appliqués, place paper-backed fusible web (web side down) over each pattern. Trace patterns onto paper side of fusible web, spacing at least 1" apart; cut apart between drawn lines.
11. Follow manufacturer's instructions to fuse patterns traced on web to wrong side of appliqué fabrics; cut out along drawn lines. Remove paper backing.
12. Referring to photo, arrange appliqués approximately $4^1/2$" above hemline along each edge of topper, placing rooster appliqué slightly over edge of comb, wattle, and beak appliqués; fuse in place.
13. Place waxed paper under areas to be painted. Referring to photo, use fabric paints to paint legs and eye on each rooster; allow to dry.
14. Arrange topper on table skirt as desired.

WONDERFUL WATERMELONS

You will need paper-backed fusible web, green striped ticking, scraps of assorted fabrics, pinking shears, a hot glue gun, and buttons.

1. For each place mat, cut one 14^1/$_2$" x 19^1/$_2$" rectangle from web and two 14^1/$_2$" x 19^1/$_2$" rectangles from ticking. Fuse wrong sides of ticking rectangles together. Use pinking shears to trim place mat to 14"x19".

2. Using patterns, page 127, follow Making Appliqués, page 127, to make watermelon and rind appliqués and to make two 1^1/$_4$" x 12" and two 1^1/$_4$" x 17" border appliqués. Overlapping ends, fuse border appliqués to place mat. Arrange remaining appliqués on place mat and fuse in place. Glue one button to each corner of border.

3. For each napkin, cut an 18" square from ticking. Remove several threads from each edge to fringe.

4. Cut a 1" x 28" strip from fabric; notch ends. Tie strip into a bow around napkin.

What better symbolizes the laid-back days of summer than the watermelon? Now you can create place mats as delightful as the fruit itself! And there's no need for needle and thread to make these comely creations. All it takes is some cutting, fusing, and gluing.

MAKING APPLIQUÉS

To protect your ironing board, cover with muslin. Web material that sticks to iron may be removed with hot iron cleaner, available at fabric and craft stores.

To prevent darker fabrics from showing through, white or light-colored fabrics may need to be lined with fusible interfacing before being fused.

Trace appliqué pattern onto paper side of web. If pattern is a half-pattern or to make a reversed appliqué, make a tracing paper pattern (turn traced pattern over for reversed appliqué) and follow instructions using traced pattern. When making more than one appliqué, leave at least 1" between shapes. Cutting 1/2" outside drawn shape, cut out web shape. Fuse to wrong side of fabric. Cut out shape along drawn lines. Remove paper backing. Fuse appliqués in place.

CATNAP CUDDLE-UPS
(Continued from page 120)

For each project, you will need tracing paper; pencil; fabric marking pencil; medium weight cotton or cotton blend fabrics (two 18" squares for Cat Head and Body, two 6" x 8" pieces for Cat Tail, two 9" squares for each Kitten Head and Body, two 4" x 5" pieces for each Kitten Tail); thread to match fabrics; liquid fray preventative; polyester fiberfill; crochet hook; hand sewing needle; desired color embroidery floss; embroidery needle; craft glue; and one button (3/4" for Cat and 1/2" for Kitten).

1. For Body pattern, fold tracing paper in half and place fold on dashed line of pattern; trace. Cut out traced pattern; unfold. Trace Head and Tail patterns; cut out traced patterns.
2. Center and draw around each pattern on wrong side of one corresponding fabric piece with fabric marking pencil. Mark opening for turning and stuffing. Do not cut out.
3. Matching right sides and raw edges and leaving opening for turning and stuffing as indicated on pattern, use a short straight stitch and sew matching fabric pieces together directly on drawn line. Apply fray preventative to stitching at top of legs; allow to dry.

4. Leaving a 1/4" seam allowance, cut out each piece. Clip curves and into corners and turn right side out, carefully pushing curves outward with crochet hook. Stuff with fiberfill using crochet hook to stuff hard-to-reach areas. Blind stitch openings closed.
5. (Note: Satin Stitch and Straight Stitch should go through all layers to back of head and be pulled tightly to shape face.) Referring to grey lines on patterns, use 12 strands of floss for Cat and 6 strands for Kitten and embroidery needle to work Satin Stitch (page 29) for nose and Straight Stitch (page 201) for eyes, nose, and mouth.
6. For Cat whiskers, thread a 12" length of 12 strands of floss in embroidery needle. Knot one end approx. 4" from end. Referring to pattern for placement, insert needle at one dot and pull knot up to head. Bring needle from back of head to front at corresponding dot on other side of nose; knot floss as close as possible to head. Repeat to add remaining whiskers. To stiffen whiskers, rub craft glue into each whisker; shape and allow to dry. Trim whiskers as desired.
7. For Kitten whiskers, follow Step 6 using a 10" length of 6 strands of floss.
8. Referring to photo for placement, sew Head to Body. Sewing through all layers, attach Tail to Body through holes of button.

Designs by Susan Carson.

WATERMELON

RIND

EASY BALLOON SHADE

Bright, cheerful fabrics make charming window fashions. This colorful balloon shade is a breeze to create by using grosgrain ribbon sashes to gather the poufs.

You will need a $1/2$" spring-tension rod or conventional rod, fabric, 1"w paper-backed fusible web tape, 2"w grosgrain ribbon, liquid fray preventative, safety pins (if needed), and tissue paper (optional).

1. Allowing $2^1/2$" for header, mount rod in window. Use a pencil to lightly mark placement of rod in window.

2. To determine width of fabric piece, measure length of mounted rod; multiply by 3. To determine length of fabric piece, measure from top of rod to window sill; add 10". Cut a piece of fabric the determined measurements, piecing with web tape if necessary.

3. Press side edges 1" to wrong side. To make a double hem, fuse web tape along pressed edges; do not remove paper backing. Press pressed edges of fabric to wrong side 1" again. Unfold pressed edge and remove paper backing; refold edges and fuse in place. Repeat for bottom edge of panel. For a single hem on top edge of panel, fuse web tape along edge on wrong side of fabric; do not remove paper backing. Press edge to wrong side along inner edge of tape. Unfold edge and remove paper backing. Refold edge and fuse in place.

4. For header and casing, fuse web tape along top edge and 2" below top edge on wrong side of panel. Do not remove paper backing.

5. Press top edge of panel $4^1/2$" to wrong side. Unfold edge and remove paper backing. Refold edge and fuse in place.

6. Remove rod from window and insert into casing; replace rod in window.

7. For ribbon ties, measure length of shade; multiply by $1^1/2$ and add 1 yd for bow. Cut 2 lengths of ribbon the determined measurement.

8. With center of each ribbon length at bottom of shade, tie ends of each ribbon length into a bow at top of shade, gathering shade to desired length. Trim ribbon ends. Apply fray preventative to ribbon ends and allow to dry. If necessary, use safety pins to pin bows to shade to secure.

9. If desired, use safety pins to pin each bottom corner of shade to back of shade for added poufs. Arrange poufs in shade, stuffing lightly with tissue paper to maintain shape if desired.

Delightful Appliquéd Shade

Red and white — or any colors that suit your fancy — can be a delight when you combine them in a cozy corner. Just replace the vinyl shade on a roller window shade with a length of fabric and spruce up the bottom with fun appliqués, lacy linens, and a tassel pull.

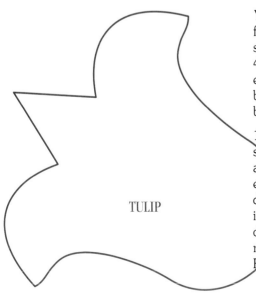

TULIP

You will need roller window shade, fabric for shade; fusible interfacing; scraps of assorted fabrics for appliqués; $4^{1}/_{2}$" long tassel; two 9" square, lace-edged handkerchiefs; rickrack; paper-backed fusible web; 1" dia. shank button; fabric glue; and a staple gun.

1. Remove slat from shade; remove shade from roller. Measure length and width of old shade and add 2" to each measurement. Cut fabric the determined measurement. Cut interfacing $1^{1}/_{2}$" narrower than determined measurement. Press long raw edges of fabric 1" to wrong side. Fuse interfacing to wrong side of fabric.

2. To make casing for slat, press bottom edge of shade $^{1}/_{2}$" to wrong side; press 1" to wrong side and stitch along first fold.

3. Cut handkerchiefs in half diagonally; arrange along bottom of shade. Glue cut edges to shade to secure. Glue a length of rickrack over cut edges of handkerchiefs.

4. Using pattern, left, follow Making Appliqués, page 127, to make desired number of tulip appliqués. Arrange appliqués on shade and fuse in place.

5. Stitch button to bottom center of shade; hang tassel from button.

6. Staple top edge of shade to roller and hang shade. Place slat in casing.

Halloween Wear

These black cats are prowling for a good time! Whether perched among the stars on a cardigan or sashaying across a sweatshirt, they'll definitely put you in the "spirit" of things.

130

For cardigan, you will need a sweatshirt with set-in sleeves, 3/4 yd 44/45"w black and white stripe fabric for binding, 15" x 8" piece of black and white stripe fabric and 11" x 5" piece of orange and yellow check fabric for square appliqués, 6" x 10" piece of black fabric for cat appliqués, eight 4" squares of assorted fabrics for star appliqués, six-strand white embroidery floss, ten 3/4" buttons for sleeves and appliqués, six assorted buttons, 2 yds paper-backed fusible web, tear-away fabric stabilizer, clear nylon sewing thread, pinking shears, tracing paper, and pencil.

For sweatshirt, you will need a sweatshirt with set-in sleeves, 44/45"w fabrics (1/4 yd orange and yellow check fabric and 1/8 yd black and white stripe fabric), 12" square of black fabric for cat appliqués, 1 yd paper-backed fusible web, four 1/2" star-shaped buttons, tear-away fabric stabilizer, clear nylon sewing thread, tracing paper, and pencil.

CARDIGAN

1. Wash, dry, and press sweatshirt and fabrics. Do not use fabric softener; fabric may not accept fusible web when fabric softener has been used.
2. Remove cuffs, neckband, and bottom band from sweatshirt. Cut off each sleeve at desired finished length. To find center front of sweatshirt, match shoulder and armhole seams and fold sweatshirt in half lengthwise; cut along fold on sweatshirt front.
3. Using a straight stitch and stitching approximately 1/4" from cut edge, stay stitch around raw edges of sweatshirt to stabilize edges.
4. Refer to Fig. 1 to fold fabric for binding. Cut along fold. Discard triangular piece of fabric.

Fig. 1

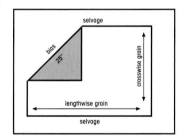

5. Cut a 10" x 25" piece of fusible web. Place web, paper side up, on wrong side of fabric with one long edge along bias edge of fabric. Follow manufacturer's instructions to fuse web in place.
6. For neckline binding, measure raw edge of neckline. Use pinking shears to cut a 1 1/4"w bias strip the determined measurement. Do not remove paper backing.
7. Matching wrong sides and raw edges, press binding in half lengthwise. Unfold binding and remove paper backing.

Refold binding.
8. Insert neckline edge in fold of binding; fuse in place.
9. Repeat Steps 6-8 to bind bottom edge and center front edges of sweatshirt, cutting as many strips as necessary.
10. For sleeve bindings, measure raw edge of one sleeve; add 1". Use pinking shears to cut two 1 1/4"w bias strips the determined measurement. Do not remove paper backing.
11. Matching wrong sides and raw edges, press each binding in half lengthwise. Unfold each binding and remove paper backing. Refold bindings.
12. Beginning at sleeve seam, insert one sleeve edge in fold of one binding; fuse in place, overlapping ends. Repeat to bind remaining sleeve.
13. Referring to Stitch Diagram, work Running Stitch around each bound edge of cardigan, using six strands of embroidery floss.
14. Use pencil to trace patterns onto tracing paper; cut out.
15. Cut a piece of fusible web slightly smaller than each fabric piece. Fuse web to wrong side of each fabric piece. Do not remove paper backing.
16. For square appliqués, cut two 5 1/4" squares from black and white fabric (we cut ours on the bias) and two 4 1/2" squares from orange and yellow check fabric. Remove paper backing.
17. For cat appliqués, position pattern, right side up, on paper-backed side of black fabric and draw around pattern. Reverse pattern and draw around again. Cut out along drawn lines. Remove paper backing.
18. For star appliqués, position patterns, right side up, and draw around patterns 4 times. Cut out along drawn lines. Remove paper backing.
19. Arranging two stars on bottom right of cardigan similarly to stars on upper left, refer to photo for placement and fuse appliqué pieces to cardigan.
20. Cut a piece of fabric stabilizer 1" larger on all sides than each appliqué. Pin stabilizer to wrong side of cardigan under each appliqué.
21. Using nylon thread and a narrow width zigzag stitch with a short stitch length, stitch over raw edges of each appliqué piece. Remove stabilizer.
22. Form a small pleat on lower edge of each sleeve. Secure by hand sewing a 3/4" button through all layers of pleat.
23. Hand sew a 3/4" button to each corner of square appliqués. Sew remaining buttons to cardigan.

SWEATSHIRT

1. Wash, dry, and press sweatshirt and fabrics. Do not use fabric softener; fabric may not accept fusible web when fabric softener has been used.
2. Measure front of sweatshirt from

armhole to armhole 2 1/2" below neckband; add 6". Cut one 5 1/4"w strip from orange and yellow check fabric and two 1"w strips from black and white stripe fabric the determined measurement.
3. Referring to photo and using a 1/4" seam allowance, machine stitch long edges of strips together to make a single strip. Press long raw edges of strip 1/4" to wrong side.
4. Cut a piece of fusible web 6" less than length of strip and 1/2" less than width of strip. Centering web on wrong side of strip and following manufacturer's instructions, fuse web to strip. Remove paper backing.
5. Center strip across front of sweatshirt with top long edge 2 1/2" below neckband. Use seam ripper to open armhole seams as far as necessary to insert ends of strip into shirt at seams. Fuse strip in place.
6. Topstitch along seams and pressed edges of strip on sweatshirt front. Trim short edges of strip even with raw edges of armholes.
7. Turn shirt wrong side out and stitch armhole seams closed along previous seamlines.
8. Use pencil to trace cat pattern onto tracing paper; cut out.
9. Cut a piece of fusible web slightly smaller than black fabric piece. Fuse web to wrong side of fabric piece. Do not remove paper backing.
10. Position pattern, right side up, on paper-backed side of fabric and draw around pattern two times. Reverse pattern and draw around pattern two times. Cut out along drawn lines. Remove paper backing.
11. Referring to photo for placement, fuse cat appliqués to strip on sweatshirt.
12. Cut a piece of fabric stabilizer 1" larger on all sides than each appliqué. Pin stabilizer to wrong side of cardigan under each appliqué.
13. Using nylon thread and a narrow width zigzag stitch with a short stitch length, stitch over raw edges of each appliqué piece. Remove stabilizer.
14. Hand sew a button to each appliqué.

STITCH DIAGRAM
RUNNING STITCH
These straight stitches form a broken line. Knot one end of floss. Bring needle up from wrong side of fabric at 1 and go down at 2; come up at 3 and go down at 4 (Fig. 2).

Fig. 2

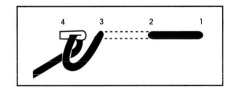

Winter Fun Jumper

It may not be snowing outside, but your favorite little girl can
still walk in a winter wonderland when she wears this fun outfit! Snowmen and
snowflakes made from buttons and appliquéd evergreens and snowdrifts add
a playful scene to a purchased jumper. We paired it with a white blouse
trimmed with blanket stitch for a special finishing touch.

You will need button-front jumper; button-front long sleeve white shirt; four $3^3/4$" x $4^1/2$" pieces of assorted green fabrics for trees; 8" x 12" piece of white fabric for snowmen and hills; covered button hardware for two $1^1/8$" buttons, one $1^7/8$" button, and one $3/4$" button; sewing thread to match fabrics; assorted white buttons for snowflakes; a $5/8$" x 5" torn fabric strip and a $3/8$" x 3" torn fabric strip for scarves; permanent pens (orange and black); six-strand embroidery floss; embroidery needle; $1/2$ yd paper-backed fusible web; tear-away stabilizer; tracing paper; and pencil.

1. For snowmen, follow manufacturer's instructions to cover buttons with white fabric.
2. Referring to pattern and photo, draw each face on indicated covered button using black pen. Color in noses using orange pen. Draw buttons on remaining covered buttons.
3. For each hill pattern, measure from side seam to center front along seam that joins skirt to bodice. On tracing paper, draw a horizontal line the determined measurement. At one end draw a 2" perpendicular line (this line will be placed on side seam). Referring to photo for shape, draw a curved line connecting top of perpendicular line to other end of horizontal line.
4. Trace tree patterns onto tracing paper. Cut out tree and hill patterns.
5. Follow manufacturer's instructions to fuse paper-backed fusible web to wrong side of tree and hill fabrics.
6. Draw around patterns on paper-backed side of fabric pieces. Cut out along drawn lines. Remove paper backing. Refer to photo to arrange appliqués; fuse in place.
7. Cut a piece of fabric stabilizer 1" larger on all sides than each appliqué. Pin stabilizer to wrong side of jumper under each appliqué.
8. (Note: For satin stitch, set sewing machine for a medium width zigzag stitch and a short stitch length. Test and adjust thread tension for even, balanced zigzag stitches. Small areas may require a more narrow zigzag stitch.) Use matching thread to satin stitch raw edges of each appliqué. Remove stabilizer.
9. For snowmen, refer to photo and hand sew covered buttons to jumper.
10. For scarves, tie 5" length around large snowman and 3" length around small snowman. Tack scarves to jumper to secure.
11. For snowflakes, hand sew remaining buttons to jumper.
12. Using six strands of floss, refer to photo and Stitch Diagram to work Blanket Stitch around cuffs and collar of shirt.

STITCH DIAGRAM

Blanket Stitch: Knot one end of floss. Bring needle up from wrong side of shirt at 1, even with edge of shirt. Go down into shirt at 2 and come up at 3, keeping floss below point of needle (Fig. 1). Continue to stitch in this manner, keeping stitches even (Fig. 2).

Fig. 1   Fig. 2

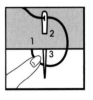

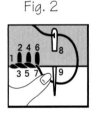

LARGE SNOWMAN FACE
(use $1^1/8$" button)

SMALL SNOWMAN FACE
(use $3/4$" button)

133

Easy Crewel Cardigan

Graceful flowers stitched with satin ribbon are the focus of our simple crewel embroidery design. Whether you purchase a new cardigan or select a favorite from your closet, feel free to choose the ribbon color to complement your sweater. You're going to love wearing this pretty wrap!

You will need a dry-cleanable wool cardigan jacket to accommodate a 5" x 5¾" design; 100% wool Persian yarn (We used DMC Floralia light green #7010, green #7009, and yellow #7027); 3 yds ³⁄₈"w blue satin ribbon; crewel embroidery needle; Sulky® Solvy Water Soluble Stabilizer; thread; and a permanent fine-point felt-tip pen.

1. Dry clean jacket, yarn, and ribbon (to prevent dyes from fading onto jacket).
2. Use pen to trace design (excluding numbers) twice onto stabilizer, spacing designs at least 1" apart; cut apart. Referring to photo for placement, baste one design, traced side up, to left jacket front. Baste remaining design, traced side down, to right jacket front.
3.(Note: For Steps 3-5, refer to Stitch Key and Stitch Diagrams and work stitches on jacket through stabilizer.) Use 1 strand of yarn to work leaves and stems.
4. Use ribbon to work flower petals.
5. Use one strand of yarn to work flower centers and buds.
6. Remove basting. Carefully tear away stabilizer. If necessary, spritz with water and remove excess.

STITCH DIAGRAMS

Satin Stitch: Come up at odd numbers and go down at even numbers with stitches touching but not overlapping (Fig. 1).

Fig. 1

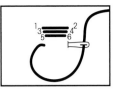

Stem Stitch: Come up at 1. Go down at 2 and come up at 3, keeping thread below point of needle. Go down at 4 and come up at 5 (Fig. 2).

Fig. 2

Japanese Ribbon Stitch: Come up at 1. Lay ribbon flat on fabric and go down at 2 (approx. ³⁄₄" from 1), piercing top of ribbon in the center and pulling ribbon gently through to wrong side of jacket (Fig. 3). Do not pull too tightly as this will change the effect of the stitch.

Fig. 3

French Knot: Bring needle up at 1. Wrap floss once around needle and insert needle at 2, holding end of floss with non-stitching fingers (Fig. 4). Tighten knot; then pull needle through jacket, holding floss until it must be released.

Fig. 4

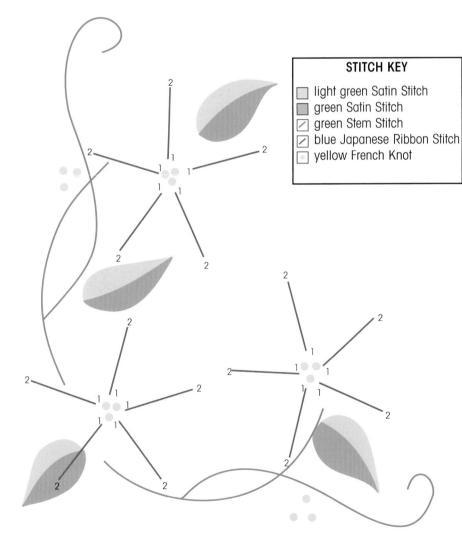

STITCH KEY
- light green Satin Stitch
- green Satin Stitch
- green Stem Stitch
- blue Japanese Ribbon Stitch
- yellow French Knot

135

Silk Ribbon Savvy

Y ou'll have a pocketful of fun with our silk ribbon sunflowers!
The cheery "flower garden" is created with easy embroidery
stitches, beads, and decorative buttons.

You will need a chambray shirt with pocket, yellow 4mm silk ribbon, green 7mm silk ribbon, six-strand embroidery floss (green, brown, and black), Mill Hill Buttons (we used Ladybug #86050, Bumblebee #86128, and Crow #86071), Mill Hill Seed Beads #02023, 7" x 6" piece of tissue paper, crewel embroidery needle, 9" embroidery hoop, thread for basting, and permanent pen.

1. Wash, dry, and press shirt.
2. Using permanent pen, trace design onto tissue paper.
3. Referring to photo, position traced design on shirt above pocket; pin in place. Baste tissue paper to shirt; remove pins.
4. Center design in embroidery hoop.
5. (Note: For Steps 5-7, refer to Stitch Diagrams and work stitches on shirt through tissue paper.) Use Stem Stitch and 3 strands of floss to work stems.
6. Use Japanese Ribbon Stitch and green ribbon to work leaves.
7. Bringing needle up at solid-line circle and going down at dotted-line circle, use Japanese Ribbon Stitch and yellow ribbon to fill in area between the two circles (Fig. 1).

Fig. 1

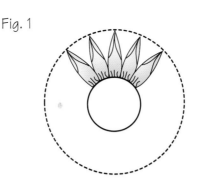

8. Remove basting. Carefully tear away tissue paper.
9. Use one strand of brown floss to attach beads to shirt, filling in center of each flower.
10. Using 3 strands of black floss, refer to photo to sew buttons to shirt. Remove hoop.

Design by Billie Click.

STITCH DIAGRAMS
Stem Stitch: Come up at 1. Go down at 2 and come up at 3, keeping thread below point of needle. Go down at 4 and come up at 5 (Fig. 2).

Fig. 2

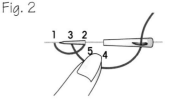

Japanese Ribbon Stitch: Come up at 1 (base of leaf or petal). Lay ribbon flat on fabric and go down at 2 (tip of leaf or petal), piercing ribbon (Fig. 3a). Gently pull needle through to back. Do not pull ribbon too tightly. Ribbon will curl at tip as shown in Fig. 3b.

Fig. 3a   Fig. 3b

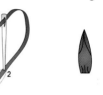

SILK RIBBON BASICS
Threading Needle with Ribbon: Cut a 12" length of ribbon; insert ribbon into the eye of needle. Bring the ribbon around to the point of the needle, piercing the ribbon approximately 1/4" from ribbon end (Fig. 4a). Grasp short end and pull back down over ribbon; gently tug long end, fastening ribbon to needle (Fig. 4b).

Fig. 4a   Fig. 4b

Beginning and Ending with Ribbon: To begin, form a soft knot in the ribbon by folding the ribbon end back approximately 1/4" and piercing needle through both layers (Fig. 5a). Gently pull the ribbon through to form a knot (Fig. 5b). To end, secure the end of the ribbon on the wrong side of the fabric by making a knot.

Fig. 5a   Fig. 5b

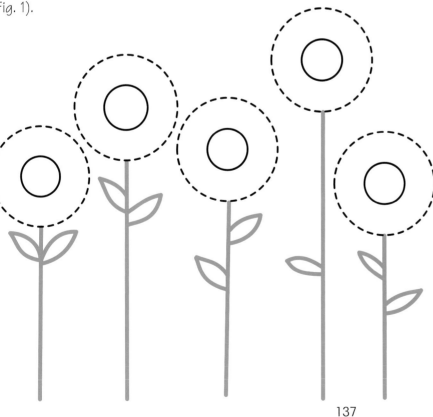

flirty jean jacket

Design by Patti Uhiren.

Unleash your creativity and turn a ho-hum jacket into an eye-catching fashion statement! Simply round up a flirty collection of beads and trims and attach them with glue or easy stitching.

3 DIFFERENT WAYS TO ATTACH TRIMS TO YOUR JACKET:

Heavy-Duty Paper-Backed Fusible Web

We used fusible web on all the fabric pieces on our jacket. Lay tracing paper on the jacket to trace a pattern; cut out. Cut a piece of fusible web a little bit larger than you will need for your pattern. Iron the web to the wrong side of your fabric, following the web instructions. On the right side of your fabric, trace around your pattern onto the fabric with a pencil or fabric pen. Cut out fabric along pattern lines, then peel off paper backing. Iron the fabric to your jacket. Let the fusible web cool completely before continuing.

Fabric Glue

We used fabric glue on the decorative trims for our jacket. Cut a piece of trim about 1/2" longer than you need. Squeeze fabric glue onto one end of wrong side of trim and attach it to the jacket. Hold the trim in place until the glue begins to adhere, then squeeze glue onto the rest of the trim, a small section at a time, and attach. When you get to the end of the decorated area, cut trim with scissors to fit. Let the fabric glue dry completely before continuing.

Sewing

You can sew trims and fabrics to your jacket. For better stability, we suggest first fusing fabric to your jacket with heavy-duty fusible web, then topstitching. Ribbon, trims, fringe, and beading can be stitched right onto the jacket.

BEFORE YOU START:

✳. Wash jacket to remove sizing.

✳. Use jacket measurements to purchase the correct amount of trims. Pin trims in place on your jacket to see how they will fit.

✳. Plan order of assembly. Fabric should be attached first, so that the raw edges will be covered with trims. Beads should be attached last since they are fragile.

1. Trace the flower pattern (page 138, bottom) onto tracing paper and cut out. Using pattern, cut flowers from felt. Read Felt Flowers, this page, to attach flowers on placket.

2. Trace jacket yoke shapes onto pink fabric. Cut out and attach to jacket. Add butterfly trim and bead trim along bottom edge of yoke.

3. Cover cuffs with strips of fabric and pink trim. Attach bead trim to edges where fabric and trim meet.

4. For waistband, attach pink trim and bead trim. Attach butterfly trim above the waistband.

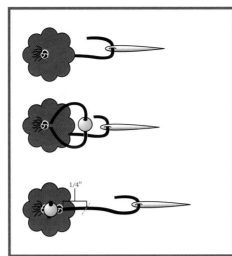

Felt Flowers

Thread your needle with six strands of embroidery floss and knot the thread about 1/4" from the end. Position your felt flower on the jacket and push your needle through the center of the flower from the right side of the jacket to the back. Bring needle back through the jacket to the front, thread a bead onto the needle, and push through to the back. Bring needle back through to the front, knot the thread close to the flower, and trim the floss 1/4" from knot. Repeat with each flower.

Beads

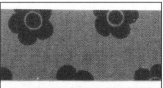

Pink Fabric

Butterfly Trim

Bead Trim

Pink Trim

You will also need:
Purple Felt

CRAFTY CLOTHES

collar

yoke

pocket flap

sleeve

pocket

cuff

pocket panel

placket

waistband

139

Measure These Jacket Lengths Before You Go Shopping:

Waistband: _____ inches
Cuff: _____ inches
Collar: _____ inches
Placket: _____ inches
Yoke: _____ inches
Pocket Panel: _____ inches
Pocket: _____ inches
Pocket Flap: _____ inches

Tie Dyed T-Shirts

These cool shirts are to "dye" for — and they're a cinch to make! By using the magic of the microwave or an iron to heat-set our coloring and scrunching techniques, you'll transform lifeless T-shirts into your own works of art in less than an hour. The possibilities are endless!

READY...SET...GO!

1. Wash and dry your shirt without using fabric softener. Clear your work area to keep dye from getting on something it shouldn't. Cover the work area with the garbage bags. Put paper towels and then the baking rack on top of the bags.

2. Put on the rubber gloves. Measure water into a glass jar, then add dye. (For **liquid dye**, stir 2 tablespoons dye into 1 cup warm water. For **powdered dye**, stir 1 package dye into 2 cups warm water.) Next, use the funnel to pour each dye color into a squeeze bottle.

3. Hold the rubber-banded shirt under running water, making sure that it's completely wet, even between the folds. Wring out the shirt, straighten the folds, and put it on your baking rack.

4. Squirt a little bit of your first dye color on both sides of the rubber bands — you can always go back over a color to make it darker. Keep squirting on different colors until you're happy with the look. Remember to dye the sides and the backs of pleated shirts! Next, squeeze the fabric in each dyed area to work the dye through all the layers.

5. Now your shirt needs to be heat-set for the dye to be permanent. There are two ways to do this:

Microwaving
Make sure the shirt is completely damp or wet. If there are any dry spots on the shirt, they could burn in the microwave.

Put your shirt in a gallon-size plastic storage bag making sure dyed areas don't overlap (you might need two bags if the shirt is very big). **Don't** seal the bag. Put the bag in the microwave and set it on medium power. Set the timer for 60 seconds at a time until the shirt is very hot and the inside of the bag is steamy. (It usually takes about 4 minutes for each shirt.) **Caution:** Steam can burn your hands.

Let the shirt cool in the microwave, then take it to the sink and remove the shirt from the plastic bag. Rinse the shirt under cold water until the water runs clear. Now, carefully cut the strings and rubber bands under running water and rinse the shirt completely. Wring water from the shirt. **Don't** put the shirt in the dryer because the dye might smear. Dry the shirt on a hanger.

Ironing
Rinse the shirt under cold water until the water runs clear. Carefully cut the strings and rubber bands under running water and rinse the shirt completely. Wring water from the shirt. **Don't** put the shirt in the dryer because the dye will smear. Completely dry the shirt on a hanger. Turn the shirt inside out and use a dry iron on the cotton setting to press the dyed areas for 20 seconds.

Designs by Patti Uhiren.

Hints

- The original shirt color will show through wherever you put a rubber band.
- The wetter the shirt is with water, the less intense the dye colors will become.
- After you mix up your dye colors, squirt the colors onto an old cotton shirt or a piece of cotton fabric. Heat-set the dye to see what the colors will look like on your shirt.
- You can get darker or lighter shades of the same color by adding more or less dye to the water in your jars.

Diagonal Pleat

Find the diagonal center of your shirt by slightly pulling on one shoulder seam and the opposite bottom side seam. Now, pleat the shirt diagonally.

Tie strings and then wrap rubber bands around the shirt the same way as in the Vertical Pleat instructions, page 142.

Tangerine Tingle
We made diagonal pleats on an orange shirt and used red fabric dye.

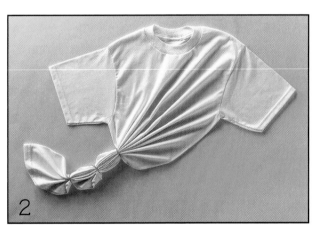

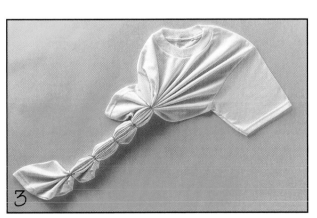

Scrunch

You can do several scrunches or just one big scrunch in the front center of your shirt. Use safety pins to mark where you want the scrunches.

Pinch the front of the shirt at one of the pins and pull up to create a tail. (If you're doing one big scrunch in the center of the shirt, pull up enough to get part of the sleeves in the tail.) Now, wrap a rubber band tightly around the base of the tail. Remove the pin and wrap more rubber bands between the base and the tip of the tail. Scrunch the rest of the shirt front and make horizontal pleats on the sleeves. The dye will drip through to the back of the shirt, creating a watercolor effect.

Vertical Pleat

Find the center of your shirt and make a pleat from the neck to the bottom. Pleat the shirt from the center to one side. Now, pleat the shirt going the other way.

Tie strings tightly around the shirt, working from the bottom to the middle of the shirt and then from the top to the middle (remember to pleat the sleeves!). Trim ends of string close to knots. Then, tightly wrap rubber bands over the strings.

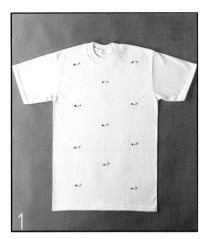

1

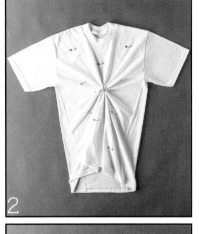

2

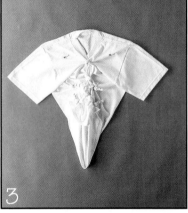

3

4

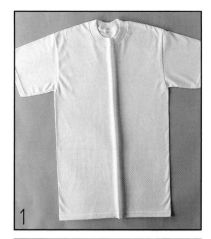

1

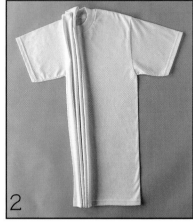

2

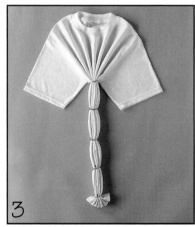

3

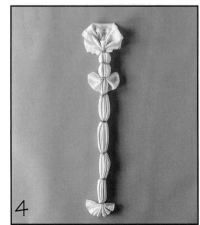

4

Horizontal Pleat

Start with the bottom hem and pleat one side of your shirt up to the shoulder (it will look like a fan). Tie a piece of string tightly around the shirt at the shoulder. Now, pleat the other side of the shirt and tie it at the shoulder.

Tie strings tightly around the shirt between the shoulders. Trim ends of string close to knots. Then, tightly wrap rubber bands over the strings and around sleeves.

Sunny Delight

We made one big scrunch from the neck to the shoulders, horizontal pleats on the sleeves, and vertical pleats on the lower half of a yellow shirt and used orange fabric dye.

Hints

- Every shirt will be different, so be creative and make your own one-of-a-kind masterpiece.
- Clean off the baking rack after dyeing each shirt so you don't get unwanted colors on your next project.
- Once you're comfortable dyeing T-shirts, try doing shorts, hats, socks, bed sheets. The sky's the limit!!
- Always use cool water and mild, non-bleaching detergent to wash your dyed shirts. Wash each shirt separately the first few times.
- Dye colors will be lighter on a shirt that's not 100% cotton.
- You can get fine lines of dye by using a squeeze bottle tip with a small opening. A larger opening will give you a broad line of dye. You can also drip dots and dashes over your shirt.

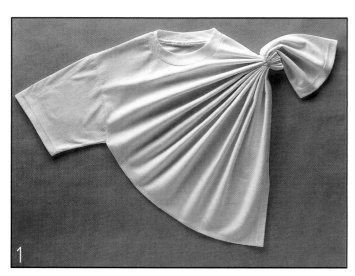

1

2

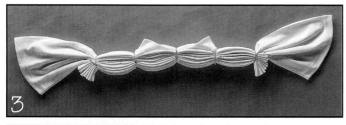

3

4

CRAFTY CLOTHES

143

FRIENDSHIP BRACELETS

*T*hese easy-to-make embroidery floss bracelets are so hot, they're cool! Wear them to make a fashion statement, show your team spirit, or share with best buds. Your choice of colors and beads will make each one unique.

READ THIS FIRST!
♥ Leave 3" to 4" of thread at both ends to tie around your wrist.
♥ Support threads are threads around which some knots are made. They must be taut as you work. Wrap the tail end around your shirt button or fasten with a pin.
♥ Tie knots with an upward motion.
♥ Tape start to something steady like a tabletop, a clipboard, or pin to your jeans.
♥ On Square Knots, Right Knots, & Left Knots remember to always tie twice.

Designs by Carolyn Yates.

144

2 Color Abstract Chevron Double
Colors: A-purple & B-green

1. You will need to cut six 36" lengths of each color.
2. Tie together & tape down in this order. In this design you use 2 threads together like a single thread.

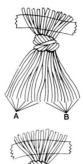

3. On the left side, make a left knot with 2 As onto 2 As (remember to tie twice). Repeat with 2 As onto the next 2 As.

4. On the right side, make a right knot with 2 Bs onto 2 Bs (remember to tie twice). Repeat with 2 Bs onto the next 2 Bs.
5. Knots will form a V when you now make a right knot in the center with 2 Bs onto 2 As.

6. Repeat knots - always working toward the center with your outside threads, until the length is right.
7. Tie a knot & trim.

3 Color Spaced Diagonal
Colors: A-purple, B-green, & C-yellow

1. You will need to cut two 36" lengths of each color.
2. Tie together & tape down in this order.
3. Start on the left side with A as your knotting thread. Make left knots with A across remaining 5 threads (remember to tie twice).

4. Start again on left side & make left knots across with the other A.
5. Repeat knots - always starting with the left thread. Work left to right. A diagonal pattern will form.
6. After 2 rows of each color, leave 1/2" unknotted space & start knotting again.
7. Repeat step 6 until the length is right. Tie a knot & trim.

Half Square Twist Foursome with Beads
Color: A & B- yellow

1. You will need to cut eight 36" lengths (A) & two 18" lengths (B). You will also need 6 beads.
2. Tie together & tape down in this order.
3. Put the beads onto your double support threads (B). Fasten the other end of the support threads to your shirt - put beads close to you. In this design you use 4 outside threads together as a single thread.

4. Make 1/2 of a square knot. Pull up tight - but not too tight or it will be stiff!
5. Make 4 of the 1/2 square knots & then slide down a bead.
6. Make next 1/2 square knot under the bead.
7. Repeat step 5 until the length is right. Tie a knot & trim.

KIDS' COOL STUFF

Square Knot Double With Beads
Color: A & B-blue

1. You will need to cut four 36" lengths (A) & two 18" lengths (B). You will also need 8 beads.
2. Tie together & tape down in this order. In this design you use 2 threads together like a single thread.
3. Put the beads onto your support threads (B). Put beads close to you. Fasten the other end of your support threads to your shirt.

A A B B A A

4. Make 4 square knots with double outside threads (remember to tie twice).
5. Slide down 1 bead & make 1 square knot under the bead.
6. Slide down 1 bead & make 4 or 5 square knots.
7. Repeat steps 5 & 6 until the length is right. Tie a knot & trim.

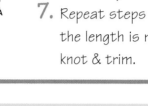

---

4 Color Zig-Zag Diagonal
Colors: A-purple, B-green, C-yellow, & D-blue

1. You will need to cut two 36" lengths of each color.
2. Tie together & tape down in this order.
3. Start on the left side with A as your knotting thread. Make left knots with A across remaining threads (remember to tie twice).

A A B B C C D D

4. Start again on left side & make left knots across with the other A.
5. Repeat knots - always starting with the left thread. Work left to right. A diagonal pattern will form.
6. Knot 8 rows - 2 rows of each color. Untape, turn over, & tape down again.
7. Knot another 8 rows in reverse color order - D, C, B, A.

8. Turn over & repeat steps 6 & 7.
9. Work until the length is right. Tie a knot & trim.

---

5 Color Abstract Chevron Single
Colors: A-red, B-light pink, C-dark pink, D-orange, & E-purple

1. You will need to cut two 36" lengths of each color.
2. Tie together & tape down in this order.
3. Make a left knot with A onto A (remember to tie twice), then onto B, B, & C. You have made 4 left knots.

A B C D E

4. On the right side, make a right knot with E onto E (remember to tie twice), then onto D, D, & C. You have made 4 right knots.
5. Knots will form a V when you now make a right knot with E onto A.
6. Repeat knots - always working toward the center with your outside threads - until the length is right. Tie a knot & trim.

CHARMING

*L*obster clasps make these beaded shoe charms quick to change.

idea!
Use leftover beads to create a choker slide for each day of the week!

Designs by Guniz Jernigan and Patti Uhiren.

CAT SHOE CHARM

We used: silver faceted (4mm), rondelle (6mm), opaque "E," & fluted (4mm) beads; silver charm

String one 5" long strand of bead wire through the ring on the lobster clasp. Fold the wire in half. String beads on the doubled wire using the Simple Chain pattern. String the wire through the charm ring. Twist to secure and trim.

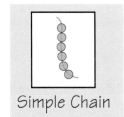

Simple Chain

HEART SHOE CHARM

We used: rondelle (6mm) & faceted (4mm) beads; silver charm

String one 5" long strand of bead wire through the ring on the lobster clasp. Fold the wire in half. String beads on the doubled wire using the Simple Chain and the Mini Flower patterns. String the wire through the charm ring. Twist to secure and trim.

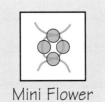

Mini Flower

BEAD HEART SHOE CHARM

We used: faceted (4mm), miracle (6mm), & silver heart (10mm) beads

String one 5" long strand of bead wire through the ring on the lobster clasp. Fold the wire in half. String beads on the doubled wire using the Simple Chain pattern. Twist the wire around the last bead and trim.

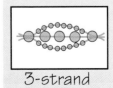

3-strand Bubble

BUBBLE SHOE CHARM

We used: silver faceted (6mm), faceted (4mm), & silver-lined rochaille beads

String two 5" long strands of bead wire through the ring on the lobster clasp. Fold the wires in half. String beads on the doubled wires using the 3-strand Bubble pattern. (Treat the 2 middle wires as 1 wire.) Twist the wire around the last bead and trim.

Clay Magnets

You won't believe how easy it is to make cool clay figures! Using polymer clay and a few simple supplies you probably have on hand, you can sculpt and then bake these fun shapes in a snap.

Don't be afraid of making a mistake — if you do, just roll the clay into a ball and start again!

Designs by Becky Meverden.

148

Working with
Polymer Clay

Make sure your work area and hands are clean. Use pre-moistened towelettes to clean your hands and your work area when you are switching colors.

Polymer clay needs to be conditioned before you begin the project. Cut it into small pieces and roll into a rope, again and again, until pliable. Any tool or surface that is used for clay should not be used for food.

Clay is measured in balls. Use the Circle Templates, below, for sizing all balls.

Other pattern pieces needed to complete each magnet are included with project instructions.

To use the Circle Templates and pattern shapes, we recommend that you make a copy of the templates and patterns and either laminate the copies or place them in sheet protectors so that you can use them again and again.

Place project on a piece of parchment paper or an index card on a baking dish or heavy-duty cookie sheet to bake. The paper is necessary to protect your cookie sheet and prevent shiny spots on your project.

A coffee cup or a crumpled piece of parchment paper are great props for your project. They will keep it from falling over during the baking process. Place parchment paper between project and coffee cup during baking.

Bake project in a preheated 265° oven for 30 minutes. Turn oven off and remove project when cool.

Use an oven thermometer to check the actual temperature of your oven. Undercooking can leave your project weak and overcooking can burn it.

Place unused clay into sealable plastic bags to store.

Circle Templates

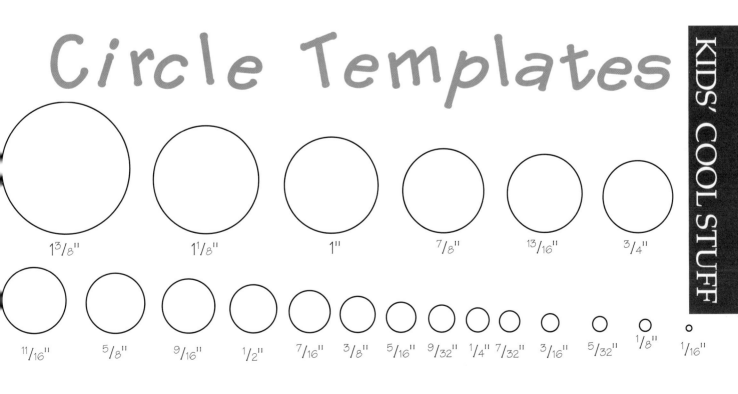

1³/₈"   1¹/₈"   1"   ⁷/₈"   1³/₁₆"   ³/₄"

¹¹/₁₆"   ⁵/₈"   ⁹/₁₆"   ¹/₂"   ⁷/₁₆"   ³/₈"   ⁵/₁₆"   ⁹/₃₂"   ¹/₄"   ⁷/₃₂"   ³/₁₆"   ⁵/₃₂"   ¹/₈"   ¹/₁₆"

Ladybug Magnet

Materials
Premo! Sculpey™: Cadmium Red, Black
Parchment paper or index card
Baking dish or cookie sheet
Oven thermometer
Household cement
$1/2$" magnet

Instructions

Read Working with Polymer Clay, pg. 149.

1. Body – Roll a 1" ball of cadmium red into an oval. Using body pattern as a guide, flatten into body.

2. Head – Roll a $5/8$" ball of black. Using head pattern as a guide, shape into head. Press onto end of body. **Stripe** – Roll a $1/16$" wide black log. Press onto center of body and flatten slightly. **Spots** – Roll $1/8$" balls of black. Flatten slightly and press onto body.

3. After baking, cement magnet to back of body.

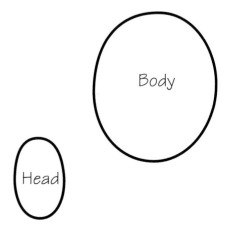

Body

Head

Bee Magnet

Materials

Premo! Sculpey™: Cadmium Yellow,
   Black, White
Round toothpick
24 gauge black Fun Wire™
Parchment paper or index card
Baking dish or cookie sheet
Oven thermometer
Household cement
1/2" magnet

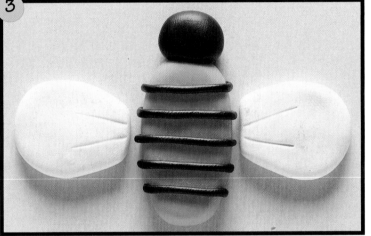

Instructions

Read Working with Polymer Clay, pg. 149.

1. **Body** – Roll a 7/8" ball of cadmium yellow. Using body pattern as a guide, roll into an oval and flatten into body.
Stripes – Roll five 1/16" wide logs of black. Lay stripes across the body, about 1/4" from each other, and press down slightly.

2. **Head** – Roll a 1/2" ball of black. Using head pattern as a guide, shape into head. Press head onto body.

3. **Wings** – Roll two 5/8" balls of white. Using wing pattern as a guide, flatten into wings. Use toothpick to make two score lines in each wing. Press wings onto sides of body. For antennas, cut two 1" long pieces of wire. Curl one end of each wire and press other end into top of head. **Stinger** – Roll a 3/16" ball of black. Using stinger pattern as a guide, shape into stinger. Press onto body.

4. After baking, cement magnet to back of body.

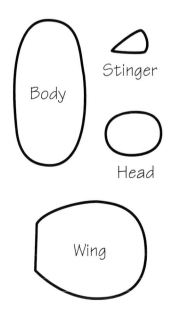

Body

Stinger

Head

Wing

KIDS' COOL STUFF

Santa Magnet

Materials

Premo! Sculpey™: White, Cadmium Red, Beige
2 black E beads
Round toothpick
Parchment paper or index card
Baking dish or cookie sheet
Oven thermometer
Household cement
1/2" magnet

Instructions

Read Working with Polymer Clay, pg. 149.

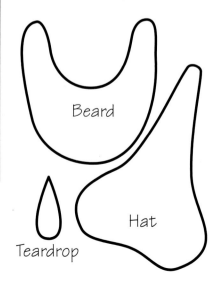

Beard

Teardrop

Hat

1. **Head** – Roll a 3/4" ball of beige and flatten to 1 1/8" round. For eyes, press two beads into head. Use toothpick to make two squint lines from each eye.

2. **Beard** – Roll a 3/4" ball of white. Using beard pattern as a guide, flatten into beard. Press onto head.

3. **Mustache** – Roll two 5/16" balls of white into teardrops. Using teardrop pattern as a guide, flatten slightly and curl ends. Press both pieces of the mustache together. Press mustache onto head. **Nose** – Roll a 1/16" ball of beige and press onto the center of the mustache. For mouth, use a toothpick to make a hole under the mustache.

4. **Hat** – Roll a 7/8" ball of cadmium red. Using hat pattern as a guide, shape into hat. Press onto head. **Brim** – Roll a 7/32" wide log of white. Flatten to 1/4" wide and press onto hat. **Pom-pom** – Roll a 3/8" ball of white and press onto end of hat.

5. After baking, cement magnet to back of head.

Reindeer Magnet

Materials
Premo! Sculpey™: Raw Sienna, Ecru, Cadmium Red
Paring knife
2 black E beads
Round toothpick
Parchment paper or index card
Baking dish or cookie sheet
Oven thermometer
Household cement
1/2" magnet

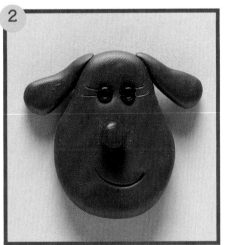

Instructions

Read Working with Polymer Clay, pg. 149.

1. Head – Roll a ⁷/₈" ball of raw sienna. Using head pattern as a guide, flatten into head. For eyes, press two beads into head. Use toothpick to make two squint lines from each eye.

2. Nose – Roll a ³/₁₆" ball of cadmium red and press onto center of head. Use toothpick to draw mouth. **Ears** – Roll two ³/₈" balls of raw sienna into teardrops. Using teardrop pattern as a guide, flatten into shape of ears. Press ears onto sides of head.

3. Antlers – Roll a ⁵/₃₂" wide log of ecru. Cut the following lengths: two – 1" pieces, four – ³/₈" pieces. Press two of the ³/₈" pieces onto each of the 1" pieces. Press antlers onto back of head.

4. After baking, cement magnet to back of head.

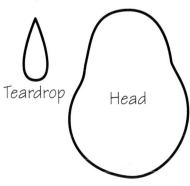

Teardrop   Head

153

Mini-Momento

ACCORDION BOOKLET

two 2-1/2" x 2" cardboard pieces
two 3-1/2" x 3" decorative paper pieces
20" x 30" piece of white art paper
gold elastic beading cord
4 decorative beads
craft scissors
Tacky Glue
scissors, ruler, pencil

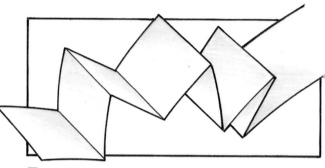

3. Cut a 2-1/2" x 30" strip of white art paper. Carefully accordion-fold the strip into "pages" 1-3/4" wide.

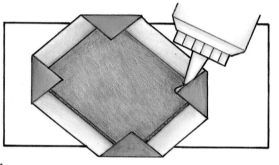

1. Cover the cardboard pieces with decorative paper. Begin by gluing a cardboard piece in the center of each paper. Fold down each corner of the paper and glue in place, as shown.

GREAT GIFT IDEAS

♥ Secret Pals
♥ Party favors
♥ Buddy journals
♥ Anyone who loves to write

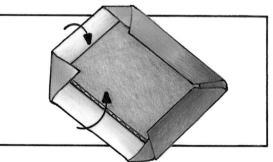

2. Fold the edges of the paper around the cardboard as tightly as possible. Glue in place.

KIDS' COOL STUFF

154

4. Trim each end of the strip with craft scissors.

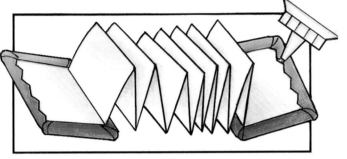

5. Glue the first and last pages to the front and back cardboard covers, as shown.

6. Tie a piece of elastic cord around the booklet tight enough so that the booklet stays closed. Knot the cord, leaving two 1" ends. Thread two beads through each end, and knot the cord to secure beads in place.

7. Use the booklet to keep special sayings, poems, autographs, small photos, and other memorabilia.

Design by Pamela Thomson

Autograph Pillowcase

Hold on to those exciting slumber party memories! For an inexpensive keepsake, draw a face and other designs onto a pillowcase using fabric crayons. Then autograph each other's cases and add ribbon bows for a cute final touch.

WHAT TO BUY
White pillowcase, fabric crayons, and 1/2 yd. of 3/8"w ribbon

THINGS YOU HAVE AT HOME
Safety pin

WHAT TO DO
1. Following crayon manufacturer's instructions, draw face and desired designs on pillowcase. (**Note:** Some crayons must be drawn on paper, then transferred to fabric.)

2. Brush excess color flecks from pillowcase.

3. Tie ribbon into a bow; pin to pillowcase.

156

BUTTON BULLETIN BOARD

An assortment of colorful buttons makes this eye-catching project so much fun! An ordinary cork bulletin board is bordered with buttons of all shapes and sizes for a kid-friendly look.

WHAT TO BUY
11" x 17" wood-framed bulletin board, large craft buttons (¼-lb. bag), and assorted buttons (200-piece bag)

THINGS YOU HAVE AT HOME
Scrap of ribbon and a hot glue gun

WHAT TO DO

1. Glue buttons onto frame of bulletin board as desired.

2. Tie ribbon into a bow; glue to center top of bulletin board.

Wild About

Thinking of rescuing that shabby chest of drawers from the jungle of furnishings at the resale shop? Don't let its poor condition tame your creativity. Give it an exotic flair by dressing up the drawers with wallpaper in animal prints. Your family will be wild for it!

WALLPAPERED CHEST

You will need a wooden chest of drawers, painter's masking tape, primer, paintbrush, pre-pasted wallpaper in assorted animal prints, and decorative drawer pulls (optional).

1. Remove drawer pulls. Use tape to mask outer $1/4"$ of each drawer front.

2. Apply primer to front of each drawer; allow to dry. Remove tape.

3. Using a different print for each drawer, cut a piece of wallpaper to fit each primed area. Follow manufacturer's instructions to apply wallpaper to drawer fronts.

4. Replace drawer pulls with original or decorative pulls.

JUST GLUE IT!

Animal Prints

A special present deserves a gr-r-reat presentation! Decorate a papier-mâché gift bag with tissue paper and ribbon printed in big cat or other wild animal designs.

GR-R-EAT! GIFT BAG

You will need a papier-mâché gift bag, $7^1/2$"h; animal-print tissue paper; spray adhesive; craft glue; $^3/_4$ yd animal-print ribbon, $1^1/2$"w; $^3/_4$ yd beaded trim; $1^3/_8$ yd narrow gimp; and $^3/_4$ yd wired open-weave ribbon, $^1/_2$"w.

Remove handles from gift bag. Add 5" to height of bag; cut tissue paper to determined measurement. Crumple paper then smooth slightly. Spray bag with spray adhesive. Apply tissue paper, overlapping slightly in back. Fold top of tissue paper to inside of bag and fold bottom as if wrapping a gift box. Glue to secure; allow to dry. Glue animal-print ribbon around bag below the holes for the handles; allow to dry. Glue beaded trim along bottom edge of ribbon; allow to dry. Turning ends under to hide raw edges, glue gimp on top of beaded trim and along top edge of ribbon; allow to dry. Cut two lengths of open-weave ribbon for handles. Insert ribbon through handle holes; knot on inside of bag to secure.

With layers of exotic trims added to its corners, this purchased zebra-print photo album captures the eye.

FREE-SPIRITED PHOTO ALBUM

You will need a zebra-print photo album, $9^1/2$" x 9"; craft glue; $^1/2$ yd beaded trim; $^1/2$ yd animal-print trim; and 1 yd narrow gimp.

Glue beaded trim diagonally across opposite corners of photo album wrapping ends to inside; allow to dry. Glue animal-print trim just above beaded trim; allow to dry. Glue gimp along both edges of animal-print trim; allow to dry.

Bead-Dazzling

COVERED BOX

You don't have to be an artist to recreate this exquisite box! Just prime and paint a round papier mâché box. Then, using decoupage glue, attach torn pieces of crumpled tissue paper to the box. Sponge paint with desired colors. After the box has dried, punch a hole in the lid and attach a decorative drawer knob. Finish by hot gluing a gemstone on top of the knob and beaded trim, then gimp, around the rim of the box. Magnificent!

FEATHERED & BEADED LAMPSHADE

Pluck a garland of feathers from the fabric store and you're almost finished with this appealing lampshade. Just glue it on and top with beaded trim and gimp.

Home Accents

STACKED GLASS PLATES

Skirted with dangling crystal trim, pretty glass pedestal plates serve up lots of style. Stack them in graduated sizes for a glitzy way to showcase jewelry.

WROUGHT-IRON CANDLE SET

Adding "the Midas touch" to this wrought-iron candle set saved it from simply blending into the background. A fascination with world cultures was the muse that led us to skirt the underside of each pedestal with ethnic-inspired beading. Just glue the trim in place and you're done! Then sit back and admire the glowing results.

161

Tasseled Baubles

Ideal for dressing up the knobs of a china cabinet or armoire, these romantic tasseled adornments are made from common glass drawer pulls, beads, and an assortment of fringe, gimp, and other trims. You'll be amazed at how quickly these decorative baubles open the door to a new look for the entire room!

DRAWER PULL TASSELS

Bullion Fringe Tassel

You will need 1 yd. of gold 20-gauge craft wire, wire cutters, $3^3/4$" long straight wooden clothespin, pliers, hot glue gun, $5^1/2$" long bullion fringe, $1^1/2$" long brush fringe, $1/2$"w decorative gimp trim, glass drawer pull with hole through center, and one each 18mm and 16mm faceted glass beads.

1. For hanger, cut two 18" lengths of wire; twist wires together. Place slit in clothespin over center of twisted wires; bring ends of wires to top of clothespin and twist once to secure.

2. Wrap and glue a length of bullion fringe around bottom of clothespin. Wrap and glue two layers of fringe just above first layer; repeat to add a third layer above second layer.

3. Wrap and glue a length of brush fringe over top of last layer of bullion fringe. Glue gimp trim around head of clothespin. Cut one strand from bullion fringe; beginning with cut end, glue strand around tassel on top of brush fringe.

4. Thread hanger wires through drawer pull, 18mm bead, then 16mm bead. Form wire into a loop; wrap wire ends around loop close to bead; trim ends.

Brush Fringe Tassel

You will need two skeins #5 pearl cotton, one skein embroidery floss, 5" square of cardboard, hot glue gun, $5^1/2$" long brush fringe, $1/2$"w gimp trim, glass drawer pull with hole through center, 18mm faceted glass bead, and an 8mm glass bead.

1. For hanger, cut four 12" lengths of pearl cotton; place lengths together and set aside. For tassel tie, cut a 6" length of pearl cotton; set aside.

2. For tassel, wrap embroidery floss and remaining pearl cotton together around cardboard. Thread hanger to center under threads at one end of cardboard (Fig. 1); knot hanger tightly around threads. Cut threads at bottom of cardboard. Knot tassel tie around tassel $3/4$" from hanger.

3. Beginning at tassel tie and working toward hanger, glue brush fringe around tassel. Wrap and glue gimp trim around top of fringe.

4. Thread hanger ends through drawer pull, 18mm bead, then 8mm bead. Split hanger threads in half; wrap around, then back up though 8mm bead (Fig. 2). Knot ends of hanger together.

Fig. 2

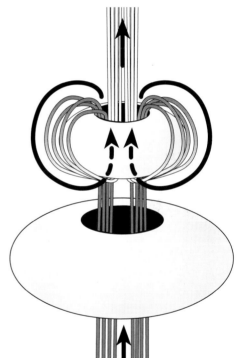

Fig. 1

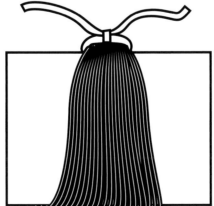

JUST GLUE IT!

Skeleton leaves are used to embellish this picture frame and hurricane globe. The leafy frame exhibits a colorful botanical print mounted on handmade paper. Our leaf-graced globe is easily adorned and placed on a lacy paper doily.

BOTANICAL PRINT IN FRAME

You will need a 4" x 6" botanical print, 8" x 10" piece of handmade paper, spray adhesive, 8" x 10" acrylic picture frame, preserved skeleton leaves, waxed paper, $^{7}/_{8}$"w wired ribbon, and a hot glue gun.

1. Use spray adhesive to mount print in center of handmade paper. Place mounted print in frame.

2. Spray wrong sides of leaves with spray adhesive. Use waxed paper to press leaves in place along outer edge of frame; allow to dry.

3. Tie ribbon into a bow; trim and notch streamer ends. Use hot glue to attach bow to frame.

HURRICANE GLOBE

You will need lavender acrylic paint, paintbrush, 8" dia. wooden plate, preserved skeleton leaves, spray adhesive, waxed paper, 7" dia. paper doily, and a 12"h hurricane globe.

1. Paint plate; allow to dry.

2. Spray wrong sides of leaves with spray adhesive. Use waxed paper to press leaves in place on globe; allow to dry.

3. Place doily, then globe on plate.

Sassy Style

Notice this! Important messages will get more attention on a beaded bulletin board. We tell you how to make a "note-able" board of your own below. For razzle-dazzle style, add gleaming beaded trim and rickrack to your favorite scented gel candles.

Sassy Bulletin Board

Bulletin board, 11" x 17"
Hot glue gun
1⅝ yd beaded trim
1⅝ yd grosgrain ribbon, ¼"w
1⅝ yd tri-color rickrack

Glue beaded trim around side edges of bulletin board. Glue grosgrain ribbon on top of beaded trim. Glue rickrack around front edges of bulletin board.

Razzle-Dazzle Candles

Three gel candles, 2"dia.
Hot glue gun
24" beaded trim
24" tricolor rickrack

Glue beaded trim to each gel candle approximately ¼" from top edge. Glue rickrack on top of beaded trim.

The glass in an old picture frame provides an ideal surface for writing notes with a dry-erase marker. Simply decorate the back of the glass as you please and spray it with white paint; then dress up the frame with whimsical stripes and swirls. The result is a fanciful memo board guaranteed to catch the eye of all passersby!

You will need spray primer, picture frame, assorted colors of acrylic paint, paintbrushes, matte clear acrylic spray sealer, glass to fit in frame, paint pens, and matte-finish white spray paint.

Refer to Painting Techniques, page 204, before beginning project. Allow primer, paint, and sealer to dry after each application. Use only a grease pencil or dry-erase pen on glass.

1. Apply primer to frame. Paint frame as desired (we painted striped borders, dots, and swirls over our basecoat colors). Apply sealer to frame.

2. Paint design on glass as desired (we used a paint pen to draw swirled lines and the end of a paintbrush handle to paint the dots). Spray paint same side of glass white.

3. With unpainted side of glass facing front, mount glass in frame.

FUN & EASY

Garden Luminaries

Filled with votive candles, prettily painted tin-can luminaries dangle from the tines of a garden rake to welcome guests to the garden. The decorative vine takes shape from medium-gauge wire and leaves cut from aluminum beverage cans.

FUN & EASY

You will need three tin vegetable cans; garden rake without handle; drill and bit; utility scissors; five 12-oz. aluminum beverage cans; tracing paper; medium-gauge wire for vines; wire cutters; welding compound; hammer; awl; yellow, peach, blue, green, and dark green spray paint; yellow, peach, blue, and green acrylic paint; paintbrushes; and three votive candles.

Allow primer, paint, and sealer to dry after each application.

1. Fill vegetable cans with water; freeze.

2. Drill a hole through metal ferrule of rake.

3. Use utility scissors to cut through opening and down side of beverage cans; cut away and discard tops and bottoms of cans. Flatten remaining pieces.

4. Trace leaf pattern, this page, onto tracing paper; cut out. Use pattern to cut desired number of leaves from can pieces. Fold each leaf in half lengthwise to form crease.

5. Cut two 36" lengths of wire for vines and three 18" lengths for can hangers.

6. Wrap one end of each leaf around vine; following manufacturer's instructions, use welding compound to secure in place. Repeat to attach remaining leaves to vines.

7. For each luminary, remove can from freezer and use hammer and awl to punch holes in can; punch a hole in opposite sides of can 1/2" below rim for hanger. Let ice melt from can; wipe dry.

8. Spray paint ferrule of rake, wire hangers, and vines and leaves dark green, then spray lightly with green paint. Spray paint remainder of rake yellow. Spray paint one can yellow, one peach, and one blue. Use acrylic paint to paint desired designs on each can.

9. Thread 6" of one end of one vine through hole in ferrule; form a loop for hanging and twist wire around itself to secure. Curl, twist, and wrap remainder of vine and second vine around upper portion of rake. From outside, thread handle ends into side holes in cans; curl wire ends to secure.

10. Place a candle in each can; hang cans from rake tines.

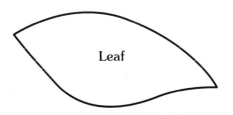

Leaf

Patio Set Pizzazz

That drab table and chair that went unnoticed before are sure to get a second glance after being revived with paint and decoupaged gift-wrap posies. Hand-painted stripes give both pieces pizzazz, so they won't be wallflowers anymore!

You will need spray primer, two colors of acrylic paint to coordinate with wrapping paper, paintbrushes, wooden folding chair with slatted back and bottom, small round wooden table, natural sponge pieces, wrapping paper, decoupage glue, foam brushes, and clear acrylic spray sealer.

Allow primer, paint, glue, and sealer to dry after each application.

CHAIR
1. Apply primer, then two coats of paint to chair. Paint stripes on chair back as desired.
2. Cut a strip from paper to cover each chair slat. Follow Decoupage, page 205, to apply strips to slats.
3. Apply two coats of sealer to chair.

TABLE
1. Apply primer to table. Paint table desired color. Sponge Paint, page 204, outer 2$^1/_2$" of tabletop with coordinating color of paint; paint stripes along edge of tabletop.
2. Draw around tabletop on wrong side of paper; cut out 2" inside drawn line. Follow Decoupage, page 205, to apply paper piece to tabletop. Decoupage a piece of paper around spindle.
3. Apply two coats of sealer to table.

TRICK OR TREAT!

Make a festive container to hold Halloween treats! Just paint a grinning pumpkin face on a simple glass fish bowl, add craft-foam leaves, and fill it with goodies. The trick-or-treaters will be standing in line!

PUMPKIN LEAF

WHAT TO BUY
6"w hexagonal fish bowl; white, orange, and black enamel glass paint; two green chenille stems; and one sheet of green craft foam

THINGS YOU HAVE AT HOME
Tracing paper, tape, paintbrushes, pencil, craft knife, and craft glue

JACK-O'-LANTERN BOWL
1. Trace pumpkin leaf pattern, this page, and face pattern, page 171, onto tracing paper. Cut out leaf pattern. Tape face pattern to inside of bowl.

2. Painting on outside of bowl, paint face orange and eyes and mouth white; allow to dry.

3. Use black paint to outline eyes and mouth, add pupils to eyes, and detail lines to teeth and pumpkin sections; allow to dry.

4. Leaving ends free, twist chenille stems together 3" from one end. Wrap stems around rim of bowl; twist remaining ends together to secure. Wrap each end around pencil to curl.

5. Draw around leaf pattern twice on craft foam. Using craft knife, cut out leaves. Glue leaves to stems.

Stepping Stones

These keepsake stepping stones will be enchanting in your flower garden! Brick mortar is decorated with impressions, handwriting, inlaid pebbles, or mosaic designs and then allowed to harden in sturdy containers. We used broken pieces of china to make our bright sunflower. You can also use seashells, marbles, bits of colorful polished glass, or other items for your mosaics, or finish your stone with just a hand print and signature. Let your imagination be your guide!

For each project, you will need brick mortar mix (available at home centers), 1-gallon heavy-duty plastic bags with reclosable zipper seal, and coarse sandpaper.

For square stone, you will also need a 13" square take-out pizza box, 4 wire coat hangers, a large heavy-duty garbage bag, various small stones, a sharpened pencil with lead tip broken off, utility knife, and 2"w packing tape.

For small round stone, you will also need two $8^1/_2$" dia. foil cake pans, 2 wire pant hangers, and yellow and green ceramic dishes.

For large round stone, you will need a plastic utility bucket with $10^1/_2$" dia. bottom (available at home centers), 2 wire pant hangers, 1 tablespoon vegetable oil, paper towel, small fresh pinecones, 8 magnolia leaves, craft stick, and tracing paper.

MORTAR RECIPE
Place one 1-gallon plastic bag inside another. Fill inner bag with $5^1/_2$ cups brick mortar mix and $1^1/_4$ cups water. Close inner bag, squeezing as much air out as possible. Mix mortar and water by squeezing bags, releasing air frequently from inner bag to prevent bag from bursting. Mixture will be thick.

SQUARE STONE
1. Use utility knife to cut lid from box.
2. To strengthen sides of box, apply several layers of tape to top edges and sides of box.
3. Cut a square from garbage bag about 3" larger on all sides than box. Line box with plastic square.
4. To reinforce mortar, refer to Fig. 1 to place hangers in bottom of box.

Fig. 1

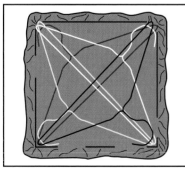

5. Make Mortar Recipe 5 times to fill box.
6. Tap box on hard surface to remove air bubbles and smooth surface.
7. Referring to photo and using pencil with lead broken off:
    a. Write "tip toe through …".
    b. Draw flowers, leaves, and stems.
8. Push stones into mortar, smoothing mortar around stones.
9. Let set for 4 hours. Mortar may fill in designs while settling; retrace with pencil as needed.
10. Allow mortar to harden completely (approximately 48 hours).
11. Using edges of plastic to lift stone, remove stone from box. Remove plastic from bottom of stone. Use sandpaper to smooth edges of stone.

SMALL ROUND STONE
1. Place one foil pan inside the other.
2. To reinforce mortar, remove cardboard from wire pant hangers; discard. Place hangers in bottom of pan, bending to fit circular shape.
3. Make Mortar Recipe once to fill pan.
4. Tap pans on hard surface to remove air bubbles and smooth surface.
5. Break dishes into various shapes and sizes.
6. Referring to photo, press pieces into mortar to form design.
7. Allow mortar to harden completely (approximately 48 hours).
8. Remove pans from stone, peeling foil edges back if necessary. Use sandpaper to smooth edges of stone.

LARGE ROUND STONE
1. Pour oil in bottom of bucket. Use paper towel to spread oil over bottom and approximately 3" up sides of bucket.
2. To reinforce mortar, remove cardboard from wire pant hangers; discard. Place hangers in bottom of bucket, bending to fit circular shape.
3. Make Mortar Recipe twice to fill bucket 2" from bottom.
4. Tap bucket on hard surface to remove air bubbles and smooth surface.
5. For flower center pattern, draw a 4" circle on paper; cut out. For placement guide for leaves, draw around bottom of bucket on paper.
6. Arrange leaves on guide circle as desired, forming flower shape. Place flower center pattern over center of leaves. Draw around pattern on leaves. Cut on drawn line. Discard bottom portion of leaves.
7. Pick leaves up from placement guide and place, right side up, on mortar. Gently press leaves into mortar, using stones to hold in place.
8. To texture center, press pinecones into mortar in center of leaves. Let set for 4 hours.
9. Remove pinecones. If necessary, finish texturing center, using craft stick to lift areas of mortar.
10. Remove leaves. If necessary, smooth edge of center.
11. Allow mortar to harden completely (approximately 48 hours).
12. Remove stone from bucket. Use sandpaper to smooth edges of stone.

PUMPKIN FACE

JACK-O'-LANTERN BOWL (Continued from page169)

FUN & EASY

Beaded Stars

Here's an elegant twist on beaded ornaments: just thread those beautiful jewels onto gold tinsel chenille stems. Dazzling! Use them on the Christmas tree, on packages, tied with ribbon around your party napkins, or in other creative ways.

A. Red Star

1. For star, leave a 1" tail and thread one spaghetti bead and one dark red bead onto chenille stem. Use needle nose pliers to bend stem to form inner corner of star. Thread one spaghetti bead and one dark red bead. Bend outer corner.

2. Repeat pattern four more times.

3. For hanger, twist ends together to form a small loop.

Materials

❖ spaghetti beads (10)

❖ dark red transparent silver-lined glass beads (10)

❖ 3mm x 12" gold tinsel chenille stem

B. Metallic Star

1. For star, attach 10mm rings to split ring. Leaving a 1" tail, thread one gold bead, five red beads, and one 10mm ring onto chenille stem. Use needle nose pliers to bend stem to form inner corner of star. Thread five red beads. Bend outer corner.

2. Repeat pattern four more times. Thread stem through first gold bead.

3. For hanger, twist ends together to form a small loop.

C. Simple Star

1. For star, leave a 1" tail and thread beads approximately $^3/_8$" apart onto chenille stem. Use needle nose pliers to bend stem at 1" intervals to form inner and outer corners of star.

2. For hanger, twist ends together to form a small loop.

Materials

❖ dark red transparent silver-lined glass beads (25)

❖ 3mm x 12" gold tinsel chenille stem

Materials

❖ 8mm gold beads (5)

❖ dark red transparent silver-lined glass beads (50)

❖ 10mm gold washed rings (5)

❖ 16mm gold split ring (1)

❖ 3mm x 12" gold tinsel chenille stem

Clay Pot Santa

This snazzy Santa snack keeper had its humble beginnings as a couple of terra-cotta flower pots. Isn't it amazing what you can do with a little paint, pom-poms, and other trims!

SUPPLIES

- 6¹/₂" dia. clay pot
- 3¹/₂" dia. clay pot
- 6¹/₂" dia. clay saucer
- Acrylic paints — red, white, black, pink, yellow, and flesh
- Paintbrushes
- Small sponge piece
- 1¹/₄" dia. wooden ball
- 1¹/₄"w red pom-pom for nose
- Two ¹/₂"w black buttons for eyes
- White felt scrap
- Tracing paper
- Transfer paper
- Dull pencil
- Cement glue
- Black fine-point permanent pen
- Sealer

INSTRUCTIONS

For further information, please read Clay Pot Techniques, page 100.

1. Paint large pot white. Paint small pot and saucer red.
2. For hat, transfer star pattern to small pot. Paint transferred design. When dry, draw "stitches" and "X" in star using pen. Paint wooden ball white. Paint white dots on small pot and saucer.
3. For face, transfer face pattern to large pot. Paint transferred design. Lightly sponge paint over cheeks using white paint.
4. Paint black ⁷/₈" long dashes on rim.
5. Seal pots and saucer.
6. For mustache, use mustache pattern to make cutouts from felt.
7. To complete face, glue buttons, felt pieces, and pom-pom to large pot.
8. Glue small pot to bottom of saucer. Glue wooden ball to bottom of small pot.
9. Place saucer on top of large pot.

Design by Holly Witt.

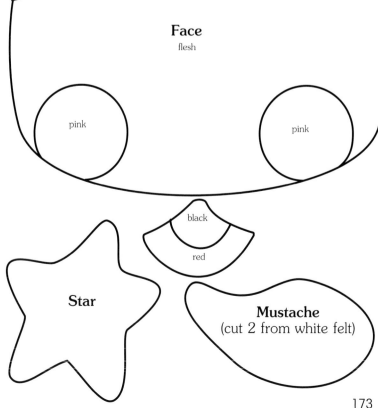

Face
flesh

pink   pink

black

red

Star

Mustache
(cut 2 from white felt)

SNAZZY BEADED PINS

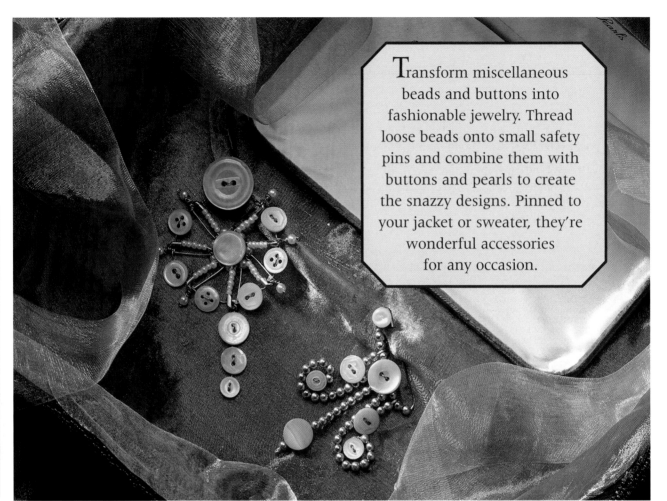

Transform miscellaneous beads and buttons into fashionable jewelry. Thread loose beads onto small safety pins and combine them with buttons and pearls to create the snazzy designs. Pinned to your jacket or sweater, they're wonderful accessories for any occasion.

SAFETY PIN JEWELRY

BROOCH WITH CURLS

Recycled items: two jumbo paper clips; 1¹/₂"-long safety pin; 4mm gold beads; one large, two medium, and two small two-hole buttons; and one large and one small shank button.

You will also need 24-gauge gold jewelry wire, wire cutters, two pairs of needle-nose pliers, and clear silicone adhesive.

Using two pairs of pliers makes it easier to work with small paper clip and wire pieces. Use silicone for all gluing; allow to dry after each application.

1. Use pliers to straighten paper clips; cut two 1" lengths for short dangles, two 3¹/₂" lengths for curled dangles, and one 2¹/₂" length for straight dangle. Form a small loop, large enough to thread onto safety pin, at one end of each dangle piece.

2. For each short dangle, thread two gold beads onto 1" paper clip length. Use gold wire to attach medium button to dangle. Bend end of dangle to back to secure.

3. For each curled dangle, thread seventeen gold beads onto 3¹/₂" paper clip length. Use wire to attach small two-hole button to end of dangle. Bend end of dangle to back to secure. Curl button end of dangle.

174

4. For long dangle, thread eleven gold beads, shank button, then two gold beads onto 2¹/₂" paper clip length. Bend end of dangle to secure.

5. Straighten safety pin. Refer to Brooch with Curls Diagram, below, to thread beads and dangles onto safety pin close to clasp. Rebend pin to latch.

6. Use gold wire to attach large two-hole button to top of long dangle. Use gold wire to attach small shank button to clasp. Cover ends of wires on back of brooch with silicone.

STARBURST BUTTONS BROOCH

Recycled items: seven gold ³/₄"-long safety pins; one extra-large, one large, seven medium, and one small pearl button; and one large white shank button.

You will also need pearl seed beads, thirteen 4mm round pearl beads, 24-gauge jewelry wire, wire cutters, needle-nose pliers, small pin back, and clear silicone adhesive.

1. Thread five seed beads onto each safety pin and latch closed.

2. Referring to Fig. 1, below, and alternating beads and pins, tightly thread 4mm beads and safety pins onto wire to form inner ring. Twist wire ends together to secure; trim ends.

3. Placing extra-large button at top, and referring to Fig. 2, below, to attach a 4mm bead to end of each safety pin except pin opposite top button, thread wire through holes in medium buttons and top of safety pins to form outer ring. Twist wire ends together to secure; trim ends.

4. For dangle, twist one end of wire through safety pin at bottom of brooch. Thread wire through large, medium, and small buttons; twist end of wire into a curl at back of small button to secure.

5. Use wire to attach shank button to inner ring; trim wire ends.

6. Glue clasp to back of extra-large button at top of brooch. Cover ends of wires on back of brooch with silicone.

STARBURST BUTTONS BROOCH

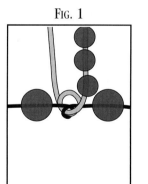

FIG. 1   FIG. 2

BROOCH WITH CURLS
ASSEMBLY DIAGRAM

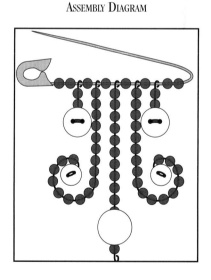

175

A Touch of Class

Sprayed with color stain, a plain apothecary jar becomes a conversation piece with its necklace of beaded silver wire.

A pillar candle rises to the occasion when you coil it with threaded beads and scatter on a few more using beading pins.

JAR NECKLACE
Apothecary jar
Spray color stain
24 gauge wire, silver
Assorted beads
Wire cutters

Using light coats, spray jar with stain until desired coverage is achieved. Wrap a 14" piece of wire around neck of jar; twist ends together. Add beads to each end of wire, coiling wire at ends to secure. Repeat two times. Cut four 5" pieces of wire. Loop onto wire around neck of jar. Add beads to each end of wire, coiling wire at ends to secure.

BEAD-EMBELLISHED CANDLE
Candle
Beads
Beading needle
Thread
Beading pins

Attach thread to a beading pin and insert into candle. Thread beading needle and string beads onto thread. Wrap around candle as desired. To end, tie end of thread onto another pin and insert pin into candle. Push pins through beads and insert pins into candle as desired.

CRITTER KEEPER

This appliquéd wall hanging is just the thing to keep a youngster's room clutter-free! We found a ready-made canvas organizer, then dressed it up with colorful fabrics, trims, and buttons. The pockets are great for holding stuffed animals or other toys.

You will need paper-backed fusible web; scraps of assorted fabrics, rickrack, and ribbon; canvas organizer with pockets; hot glue gun; and assorted buttons.

1. Using patterns, below, follow Making Appliqués, page 127, to make flower and leaf appliqués. Arrange appliqués on organizer and fuse in place.

2. Glue rickrack and buttons to organizer.

3. Tie three 10" lengths of ribbon into bows; glue to top of organizer.

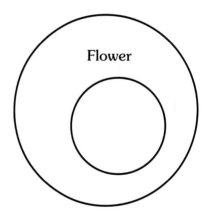

Flower

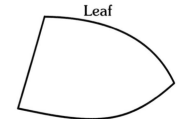

Leaf

MIRRORING NATURE

Mirrors and candles add life to any room, especially when they're garden-inspired. Create these ornate accents by cutting leaf shapes from flattened aluminum cans. Apply a painted faux-patina finish, then attach the leaves around a framed mirror and onto candlesticks to complete this alfresco project.

SOMETHING FOR NOTHING

Leaf-Edged Mirror

Recycled items: aluminum beverage cans, newspaper, and mirror with a wooden frame

You will also need: utility scissors; tracing paper; decorative-edge craft scissors (we used pinking shears); craft foam; stylus; $1/8$" dia. and $1/4$" dia. hole punches; rust-colored spray primer; copper, bronze, green, and pearl mint green acrylic paint; paintbrushes; natural sponge pieces; painter's masking tape; clear acrylic spray sealer; small brass nails; small $3/8$" dia. brass washers; and a hammer.

Refer to Painting Techniques, page 204, before beginning project. Allow glue, primer, paint, and sealer to dry after each application.

1. Cut through openings in beverage cans and down to bottom rims; cut away and discard tops and bottoms of cans. Flatten can pieces.

2. Trace leaf pattern, page 181, onto tracing paper; cut out. Using pattern and craft scissors, cut leaves from can pieces to fit around frame.

3. To emboss each leaf, place leaf on craft foam. Place pattern on leaf, then, pressing firmly to make indentions, use stylus to draw over embossing lines on pattern and to make mark for hole in leaf. Punch a $1/8$" hole in each leaf where indicated. Apply primer to front and back of leaf.

4. Paint leaf copper, then *Sponge Paint* with bronze paint. For faux-patina, mix unequal parts of green and mint green paint; lightly *Sponge Paint* mixture onto leaves.

5. Use tape and newspaper to mask mirror for painting; repeat Step 4 to paint frame.

6. Apply two coats of sealer to leaves and frame; remove paper and tape.

7. For spacers, use $1/4$" dia. hole punch to cut one circle from craft foam for each leaf.

8. Arrange leaves, embossed sides up, along edges of frame. To attach each leaf, insert nail through center of one spacer, through one washer, then into hole in leaf; hammer nail into frame.

Stacked Spools Candlesticks

Recycled items: heavy cardboard (such as the back of a writing tablet) and aluminum beverage cans

For each candlestick, you will also need: utility scissors; pinking shears; craft glue; large wooden spools (ours measure $1 1/2$" dia. x 2"h); two $3/4$"-long pieces of $3/8$" dia. dowel; drill and $1/32$" bit; 2" dia. wooden candle cup; 1"-long thin brass screws; tracing paper; decorative-edge craft scissors (we used pinking shears); craft foam; stylus; $1/8$" dia. and $1/4$" dia. hole punches; rust-colored spray primer; copper, bronze, green, and pearl mint green acrylic paint; paintbrushes; natural sponge pieces; $3/8$" dia. brass washers; and clear acrylic spray sealer.

Refer to Candlestick Assembly Diagram, page 181, to assemble candlesticks. Allow glue, primer, paint, and sealer to dry after each application.

1. For base, use utility scissors to cut two $3 1/2$" dia., one $3 1/4$" dia., and one 3" dia. circle from cardboard; use pinking shears to cut one $2 1/2$" dia. circle. Glue $3 1/2$" dia. circles together, then center and glue $3 1/4$" dia., 3" dia., then $2 1/2$" dia. circles on top.

2. Glue spools together for spindle. Glue dowel pieces into holes at top and bottom of spindle. Drill a hole through center of dowel pieces, base, and candle cup. Insert one screw through bottom of base and into hole in dowel at bottom end of spindle.

3. Follow Steps 1 – 3 of Leaf-Edged Mirror to make five leaves.

4. Apply primer to front and back of leaves, candlestick, and candle cup. Follow Step 4 of Leaf-Edged Mirror to paint leaves, candlestick, and candle cup.

5. For spacer, use $1/4$" dia. hole punch to cut a circle from craft foam.

6. Insert screw through candle cup, center of spacer, holes in leaves (embossed sides up), and washer, then into hole in dowel at top of candlestick; arrange leaves, then tighten screw. Apply two coats of sealer to candlestick.

Lend Mother Nature a hand while you perk up your patio or garden with this earthy collection of yard ornaments. Utilize those tossed aluminum cans to make the various insect shapes, then cut lengths of metal hangers to create the stakes. Our simple rusting technique gives each bug its charming timeworn appearance.

RUSTED METAL YARD BUGS

Recycled items: 12-oz. aluminum beverage cans and heavy-duty metal coat hangers

You will also need utility scissors, tracing paper, stylus, hammer and awl, craft wire, wire cutters, pliers, and household cement.

1. For each bug, start at opening in can and cut down one can to bottom rim; cut away and discard top and bottom of can. Flatten remaining piece. Trace desired pattern, page 181, onto tracing paper; cut out. Use pattern to cut bug from can piece.

2. Use stylus to emboss details on bug. Use hammer and awl to punch two small holes in bug head. For antennae, cut a 5" length of craft wire. From bottom, thread ends of wire through holes; use pliers to curl wire ends. Apply a small amount of cement to underside of head to secure antennae and allow to dry.

3. For stake, cut an 18" length of wire from hanger. Form a small, flat curl at one end of wire; cement bug to curl and allow to dry.

4. Follow *Rusting* to rust bug.

RUSTING

This technique creates a faux-rusted finish on project's surface.

1. Spray surface of project with a rusty-red color primer.
2. For paints, unevenly mix one part water to one part orange acrylic paint; unevenly mix one part water to one part dark orange acrylic paint.
3. (*Note:* To create a more natural rusted look, use a paper towel or a clean damp sponge piece to dab off paint in some areas after applying paint. Also, drip a few drops of water onto painted surface while paint is still wet, let them run, and then allow to dry.) Dip a dampened sponge into paint; blot on paper towel to remove excess paint. Allowing to dry after each coat, use a light stamping motion to paint project with orange, then dark orange paint mixtures. Apply sealer to project and allow to dry.

RUSTED METAL YARD BUGS

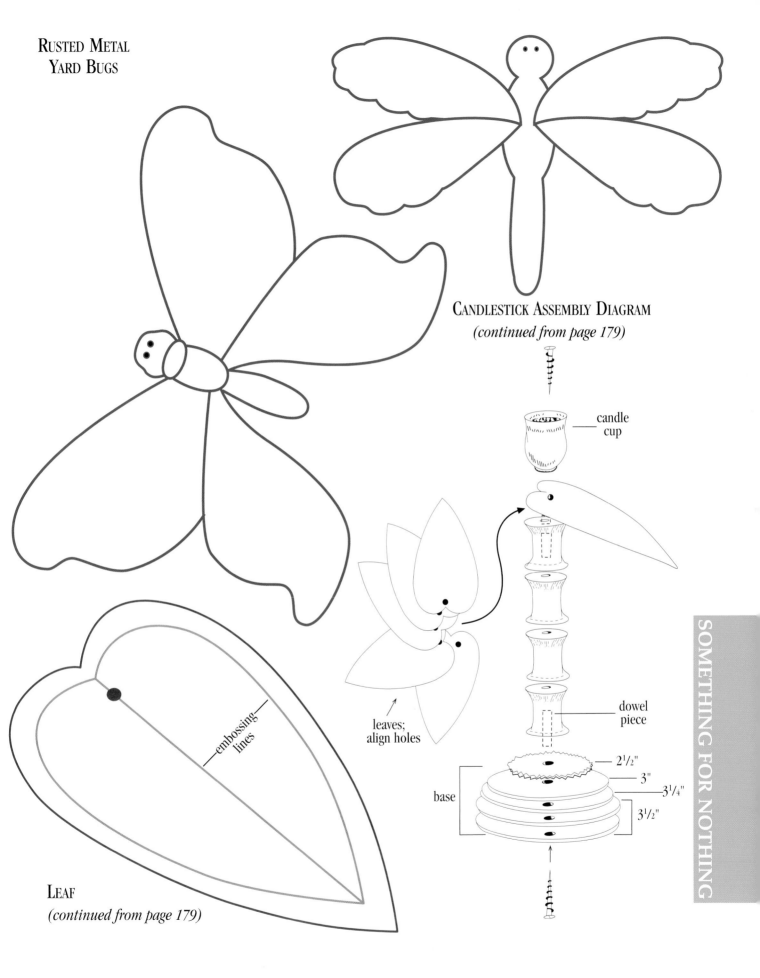

CANDLESTICK ASSEMBLY DIAGRAM
(continued from page 179)

candle cup

leaves; align holes

dowel piece

base

$2^{1}/_{2}$"

3"

$3^{1}/_{4}$"

$3^{1}/_{2}$"

embossing lines

LEAF
(continued from page 179)

SOMETHING FOR NOTHING

Faux-Simple Stained Glass

Searching for the perfect stained glass piece can be time-consuming — and costly. Especially when you can use a castaway window frame to create your own designer accent — inexpensively. Simply outline your pattern on the window with silver liquid leading and fill in the areas with colorful glass paint!

FAUX STAINED GLASS WINDOW FRAME

You will need a washable felt-tip marker, ruler, window, silver liquid leading, and desired colors of glass paint.

1. Use marker and ruler to draw desired design on back of glass.
2. Follow manufacturer's instructions to apply leading over lines on front of glass.
3. Follow manufacturer's instructions to paint window with glass paint.
4. Remove marker lines from back of glass.

*O*rdinary brown paper bags are transformed into glimmering gift totes when you découpage them with torn pieces of crumpled tissue paper and dry brush with metallic paint. Luminescent wired ribbon creates gorgeous bows, and shiny twisted wire trim provides both functional and decorative handles.

DÉCOUPAGED GIFT BAGS

Recycled items: white tissue paper and paper bags (we used a lunch-size bag and a small grocery bag)

You will also need découpage glue, foam brush, gold and silver acrylic paint, paintbrushes, wired ribbon, hot glue gun, wire cutters, and wired trim.

Allow paint to dry after each application. Use découpage glue for all gluing unless otherwise indicated.

1. For each bag, tear tissue paper into small pieces. Working in small sections and overlapping pieces, apply glue to bag, then press and scrunch pieces of tissue paper into glue, covering outside of bag completely and overlapping slightly to inside; allow to dry. Apply a layer of glue over covered part of bag to seal and allow to dry.

GLIMMERY GIFT TOTES

2. Dry Brush, page 204, bag with paint. (We used gold paint on our large bag, and silver and gold for the stripes on our smaller bag.)

3. Overlapping at front of bag, glue a length of ribbon along top edge of bag. Tie another length of ribbon into a bow; hot glue knot to ribbon on front of bag.

4. For handles, hot glue lengths of trim at inside top of bag.

183

Set the tone for holiday fun right at your doorstep with our one-man welcoming committee. Wrapped in a "recycled" muffler and mittens (just like a traditional snowman), this snow buddy is crafted using scraps of vinyl flooring. He's embellished with tree limb arms, bottle cap eyes, and a smile made with stones.

VINYL FLOORING SNOWMAN

Recycled items: vinyl flooring scraps, two wide-mouth jar lid inserts, two metal bottle caps for eyes, rocks for mouth, 2¹/₂' x 5' piece of cardboard (pieced as necessary), mittens, plastic bags, small tree limbs, and scarf

You will also need string; pencil; thumbtack; utility knife; tracing paper; white, orange, and black acrylic paint; natural sponge; black spray paint; paintbrushes; clear acrylic spray sealer; hot glue gun; nail; and jute twine.

Allow paint and sealer to dry after each application. Use utility knife to cut all vinyl pieces.

1. For head, tie one end of an 18" length of string to pencil. Insert thumbtack through string 6" from pencil, then into wrong side of vinyl. Draw circle on vinyl (Fig. 1); cut out. Repeat inserting thumbtack through string 9" and 12" from pencil to make two additional circles.

Fig. 1

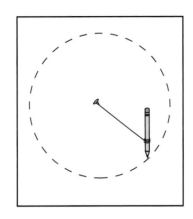

2. For hat, cut one 7¹/₂" x 8" and one 2¹/₂" x 12" piece from vinyl. Trace nose pattern, below, onto tracing paper; cut out. Draw around pattern on wrong side of vinyl; cut out.

3. Follow *Sponge Painting,* page 204, to paint wrong side of circles white. Spray paint wrong side of hat pieces, jar lid inserts, and eyes black. For buttons, use white paint to paint "buttonholes" and "stitches" on jar lid inserts. Paint nose orange. Use black paint to add details to nose. Apply sealer to all pieces.

4. Glue circles together to make snowman. Glue hat to top of head. Draw around snowman on cardboard; cut out ¹/₂" inside drawn line.

5. For hanger assembly, use nail to punch ten holes in hat of cardboard snowman (Fig. 2). Lace a 1 yd. length of twine through holes. Tie ends of twine together. Glue cardboard snowman to back of vinyl snowman.

Fig. 2

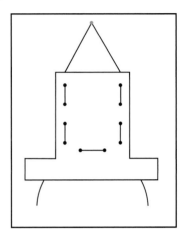

6. Glue eyes, nose, and mouth to head for face. Glue buttons to body.

7. Stuff mittens with plastic bags. Insert one limb into each mitten. Tie a length of twine around wrist of mitten to secure. For arms, glue limbs to back of body. Cut two 3" x 5" pieces from vinyl; glue one piece across each limb on back of body to secure.

8. Tie scarf around neck.

Nose Pattern

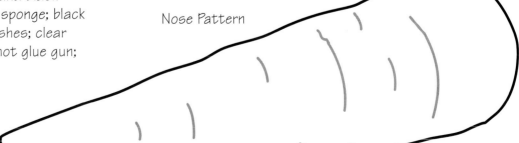

185

Impressive Wall Art

Get your creative juices flowing with our beautiful wall ornament! A wonderful way to enjoy the art of paper making, this fun project is crafted using paper egg carton pulp that's pressed into a metal trash can lid "mold." Use the lid's contours to inspire your creation — we fashioned a sun face because of the "ray" impressions on our lid. Terra-cotta paint and wood-tone spray give the decorative medallion its aged clay appearance.

Egg Carton Sun

Recycled items: metal trash can lid, twelve paper egg cartons, and 10" of jute twine

You will also need craft glue; spray primer; terra-cotta, raw sienna, and brown acrylic paint; paintbrushes; natural sponge pieces; wood-tone spray; clear acrylic spray sealer; and a hot glue gun.

Allow craft glue, primer, paint, wood-tone spray, and sealer to dry after each application.

1. Place lid upside down on level surface.

2. (Note: Reserve one carton cup for nose.) Use egg cartons and follow *Paper Making* to make paper pulp. Set aside two cups of pulp for facial features.

3. Press pulp firmly into and up sides of lid to a thickness of $1/2$", covering inside of lid completely. Gently press pulp with a towel to remove as much moisture as possible; allow to dry. Remove dried pulp shape from lid.

4. Use remaining pulp to form crescents for eyes and mouth, and flattened circles for cheeks. For nose, cut a section from reserved egg carton cup and cover with pulp. Place eyes, mouth, cheeks, and nose on curved surface on outside of lid and allow to dry.

5. Use craft glue to adhere shapes to face.

6. Apply primer, then two coats of terra-cotta paint to both sides of sun. Follow *Sponge Painting* to paint sun raw sienna, then brown. Apply wood-tone spray and two coats of sealer to sun.

7. For hanger, knot ends of jute; hot glue knot to back of sun.

Sponge Painting

This technique creates a soft, mottled look on project's surface.

1. Dampen sponge with water.

2. Dip dampened sponge into paint; blot on paper towel to remove excess paint.

3. Use a light stamping motion to paint project. Allow to dry.

4. If using more than one color of paint, repeat Steps 1 – 3, using a fresh sponge piece for each color.

5. If desired, repeat technique using one color again over areas of other colors, to soften edges or to lighten up a heavy application of one color.

Paper Making

1. Tear paper to be recycled into pieces about $1/2$" square; place in bucket. Fill bucket with hot water and soak for at least one hour.

2. Wearing rubber gloves, squeeze excess water from a small handful of pre-soaked paper pieces and place in blender; cover with water until blender is half full. Blend at low speed for fifteen seconds, increasing speed to medium, then high, at fifteen second intervals; decrease speed in the same manner. When pulp is no longer lumpy, pour it into a second bucket.

3. With one handful of soaked paper pieces at a time, repeat the blending process until all pieces have been processed.

4. Lay a towel on a flat surface and cover with a piece of screen wire. Scoop pulp from bucket and press onto screen; place another piece of screen, then another towel on pulp and press to let towels absorb excess water. Use prepared pulp to complete project.

Blooming Luminaries

*I*lluminate your patio party in style with this "blooming" garland of pretty lights. Simply cut aluminum cans to cover selected sockets on a string of miniature lights and curl narrow strips into "petals."

CAN FLOWER LIGHT COVERS

Recycled items: two 12-oz. aluminum beverage cans for each light cover and a string of miniature lights

You will also need utility scissors, awl, white spray primer, desired colors of spray paint, and silicone adhesive.

Allow primer, paint, and adhesive to dry after each application.

1. For each light cover, draw a line around one can $3^{1}/2$" from can bottom; cut top from can along line. Use awl to make a hole at center bottom of can large enough to fit over lightbulb socket.

2. Cutting through opening in can, cut down second can to bottom rim; cut away and discard top and bottom of can. Cut a $2^{3}/4$" x $3^{1}/2$" rectangle from remaining piece.

3. For petals, make cuts $1/4$" apart to within $1/2$" from bottom of can and from one long edge of rectangle.

4. Apply primer, then two coats of paint to can pieces.

5. Wrap each petal around a pencil to curl.

6. For inner petals, overlap ends of rectangle piece $1/2$" and glue to secure, using a paper clip to hold in place until dry. Center and glue inner petals to can bottom.

*B*righten the day of a secret pal with our cute memo chalkboard. Hand-painted flowers decorate the border, and a ribbon-tied stick of chalk makes it easy to leave an uplifting message.

What To Buy

6⅝" x 8⅝" wood-framed chalkboard; white, yellow, light blue, and green acrylic paint; 1 yd. of ⅝"w blue grosgrain ribbon; ⅔ yd. of ¼"w blue grosgrain ribbon; and one box of chalk

Things you have at home

Paintbrushes, household sponge, pencil with a new eraser, black fine-point felt-tip pen, masking tape, and a hot glue gun

Secret Pal Chalkboard

1. Paint wood frame of chalkboard white; allow to dry.

2. Cut a ¾" square from sponge. Referring to Painting Techniques (pg. 204), use sponge square and blue paint to stamp checkerboard design on frame; allow to dry.

3. For each flower, dip eraser in yellow paint and stamp three dots close together; allow to dry. Use green paint to paint stems and leaves between flowers. Use pen to outline flowers and draw detail on stems.

4. Place masking tape ¼" from inside edge of chalkboard frame. Use yellow paint to paint border on chalkboard; allow to dry.

5. For streamer, cut a 20" length of ⅝"w ribbon; fold in half. Leaving a 1½" loop at top, glue streamer to center back of chalkboard. Cut a 12" length of ⅝"w ribbon; tie into a bow and glue over loop of streamer.

6. For chalk holder, glue one end of ¼"w ribbon to back of chalkboard. Tie remaining end around one piece of chalk.

7. Write message on chalkboard.

Great Gifts

miles of smiles

Every girl is unique, and one-of-a-kind jewelry is just what she needs to help make her personal statement. She'll charm everyone she meets when wearing one of these easy necklaces!

DRAGONFLY NECKLACE

We used: small twist, rainbow seed, free-form, & plated round pearl (4mm) beads; pewter charm; round jump ring (4mm)
String beads on 1 strand of nylon bead thread using the **Simple Chain** pattern. Attach the jump ring to the charm. Use jewelry pliers to clamp the jump ring to the center of the necklace. Attach the thread ends to mini clasps and a barrel clasp.

FLOWER NECKLACE

We used: rainbow seed & pastel seed beads; pewter charm; round jump ring (4mm)
String beads on 1 strand of nylon bead thread using the **Picot** pattern. Attach the jump ring to the charm. Use jewelry pliers to clamp the jump ring to the center picot. Attach the thread ends to mini clasps and a barrel clasp.

SMILEY NECKLACE

We used: round (3mm) & 2/cut rochaille beads; pewter charm; 2 round jump rings (4mm)
String beads on 1 strand of nylon bead thread using the **Simple Chain** pattern. Attach 2 jump rings to the charm. Thread the top jump ring through the center bead of the necklace. Use jewelry pliers to clamp the ends of the jump ring together. Attach the thread ends to mini clasps and a barrel clasp.

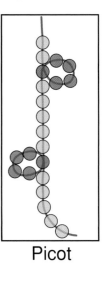

Picot

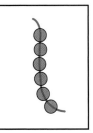

Simple Chain

BEST FRIENDS

A gift between friends should be special — that's why an easy-to-make bracelet is the perfect idea for young folks! Inexpensive waxed thread is laced with alphabet beads to spell "best friends," along with colorful accents to add flair.

WHAT TO BUY

Black waxed-linen thread, alphabet beads, solid and striped opaque beads, and a hook and eye clasp

FRIENDSHIP BRACELET

*Finished project yields a 7¹/₂"
bracelet.*

1. Cut a 4¹/₂ ft. length of linen thread. Thread eye clasp onto thread 12" from one end; fold down. Tie an Overhand Knot (Fig. 1) below eye.

Fig. 1

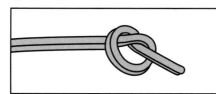

2. Thread a bead onto short end of thread. Work a Buttonhole Knot (Fig. 2) around bead with longer thread length; repeat with four more beads. Knotting between beads, thread alternating alphabet beads and opaque beads until "BEST FRIENDS" has been spelled out, threading a heart bead and two opaque beads between the words.

Add five more beads to end of bracelet.

Fig. 2

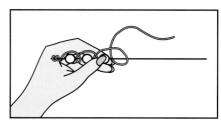

3. Tie hook onto bracelet with remaining 12" length using Overhand Knot.

4. Working toward eye clasp, use remaining longer end of thread to work Buttonhole Knot on opposite sides of beads; tie off to finish.

191

Romantic Monograms

Pretty little accessories for your boudoir become treasured heirlooms when monogrammed with our hearts and flowers alphabet. The tiny keepsakes make beautiful gifts for loved ones, too.

Heart-Shaped Sachet

The letter "M" was stitched on a 6" x 5" piece of linen. For sachet, cut backing fabric same size as stitched piece. Trace heart pattern onto tracing paper; cut out pattern.

With right sides facing and matching raw edges, place stitched piece and backing fabric together. Center pattern on wrong side of stitched piece. Use fabric marking pencil to draw around pattern. Cut out fabric pieces.

For lace ruffle, cut one 11" length of 1/2"w pregathered lace. Matching edges and beginning at top of stitched piece, use a 1/4" seam allowance to sew lace to right side of stitched piece. With right sides facing and matching raw edges, pin stitched piece and backing fabric together. Using a 1/4" seam allowance and leaving an opening for turning, sew pieces together. Clip seam allowance at curves and corners, and turn heart right side out. Stuff heart with polyester fiberfill. Place a few

drops of scented oil on a small amount of polyester fiberfill and insert in middle of sachet. Sew final closure by hand.

Jar Lid

The letter "P" was stitched on a 4" square of linen. It was inserted in the lid of a 2 3/4" dia. porcelain jar.

Sachet Bag

The letter "R" was stitched on a 5" x 7 1/2" piece of linen. For bag, center and stitch letter with the bottom 1 1/2" from one short edge of the fabric. For backing, cut a second 5" x 7 1/2" piece of same fabric as stitched piece. Fold a 24" length of 1/8" w ribbon in half. On right side of stitched piece 2" from top, pin folded edge of ribbon even with left raw edge. With right sides facing and leaving top edge open, sew stitched piece and backing fabric together along sides and bottom using 1/2" seam allowance. Trim corner seam allowances diagonally. Fold top edge of bag 1/4" to wrong side; press.

Fold 1/4" again; hem. Sew desired pregathered lace trim to top edge and turn right side out. Stuff with polyester fiberfill. Place a few drops of scented oil on a small amount of polyester fiberfill and insert in middle of sachet. Tie ribbon in bow.

Square Sachet

The letter "A" was stitched on a 5" square of linen. For sachet, cut backing fabric same size as stitched piece. With finished edge toward center of sachet and gathered edge 3/4" from design on all sides, baste desired pregathered lace trim to right side of stitched piece. With right sides facing and leaving an opening for turning, sew stitched piece and backing fabric together on basting line. Trim seam allowance to 1/4" and turn right side out. Stuff with polyester fiberfill. Place a few drops of scented oil on a small amount of polyester fiberfill and insert in middle of sachet. Sew final closure by hand.

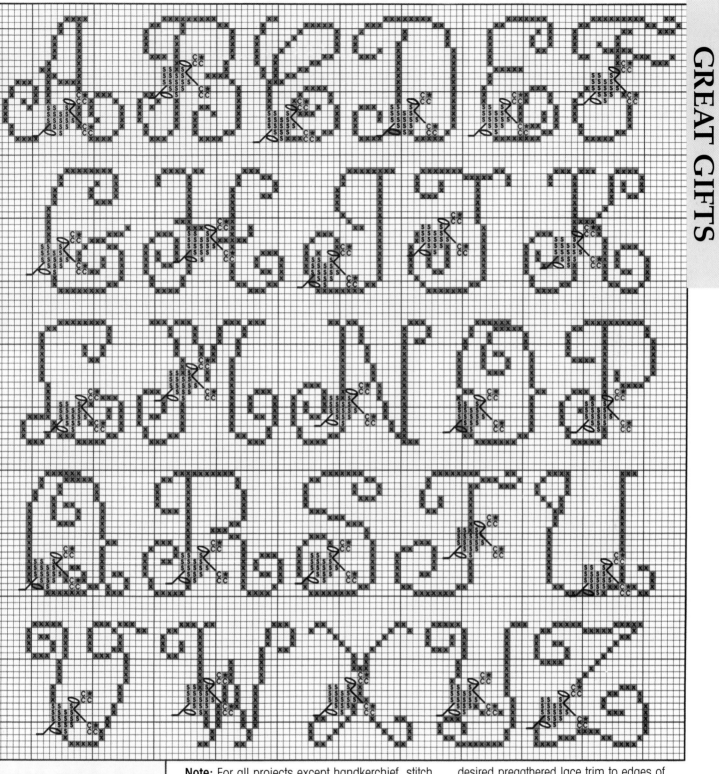

X	DMC	B'ST	JPC	COLOR
S	223		3241	pink
	501	✓	6878	green
✕	640		5393	brown
★	930		7052	blue
C	931		7051	lt blue
∅	501			green Lazy Daisy Stitch

Note: For all projects except handkerchief, stitch over 2 fabric threads on Cream Belfast Linen (32 ct). For all projects, use strands of floss for Cross Stitch and 1 for all other stitches.

Handkerchief: The letter "H" was stitched over a 2¹/₂" x 2¹/₂" piece of waste canvas (18 ct) in the corner of an 11" square of cotton fabric (see Working on Waste Canvas, page 201). For handkerchief, refer to photo for placement and stitch letter. Fold each edge of fabric ¹/₄" to wrong side; press. Fold ¹/₄" again; hem. Sew

desired pregathered lace trim to edges of handkerchief.

Towel: The letters "D", and "K", and "B" were stitched on a 12" x 20" piece of linen. For towel, center and stitch letters 2 squares apart with the bottom of letters 2¹/₂" from one short edge. Fold each edge ¹/₄" to wrong side; press. Fold each edge ¹/₄" to wrong side; press. Fold ¹/₄" again; hem. Sew desired pregathered lace trim to bottom edge of towel.

Tea-Towel Tote

Yo-yo flowers and buttons adorn this charming tote, which is created from an ordinary tea towel. The old-fashioned basket shape is cut from a lace-trimmed napkin. Whether presented alone or filled with goodies, this useful gift will please a sentimental friend.

WHAT TO BUY

18½" x 27" tea towel; 12" square white cloth napkin with crocheted edge; and ⅛ yd. each of pink, yellow, green, and blue fabric

THINGS YOU HAVE AT HOME

Paper-backed fusible web, thread, tracing paper, drawing compass, and three assorted white buttons

TEA-TOWEL TOTE

1. For bag handles, cut a 2½"w strip from each long edge of towel. Remove stitching from hemmed long edge of each strip. Folding handles in half lengthwise, insert raw edge into hem; re-stitch hem and press.

2. Cut an 8" square from one corner of napkin. Matching wrong sides, fold crocheted corner down 3¼"; press.

3. Referring to Making Appliqués, page 127, use basket pattern, this page, to make appliqué, aligning top of basket pattern with folded edge of 8" square. Use basket handle pattern, this page, to make appliqué from remaining piece of napkin. Center appliqués on one end of towel; fuse in place. Using a narrow zigzag stitch, sew around edges of appliqués.

4. Matching right sides and short edges, fold towel in half. Using a ¼" seam allowance, sew sides of bag together.

5. Referring to Fig. 1, match each side seam to fold line at bottom of bag; sew across each corner 1" from point.

Fig. 1

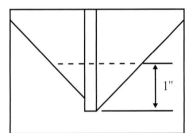

6. Turn bag right side out. Press top edge of bag ¼" to wrong side; stitch in place.

7. Use tracing paper and compass to draw a 4½" dia. circle pattern. For each flower, use pattern to cut a circle from fabric. Turn raw edge of each fabric circle ¼" to wrong side. Using a double strand of thread, hand baste along turned edge. Pull ends of thread to tightly gather circle; knot thread and trim ends. Flatten circle. Sew a button over center of flower.

8. For each leaf, cut a 2½" square of green fabric; fold square in half. Bring corners of folded edge to center of straight edge; press. Baste along straight edge of leaf; gather and knot threads.

9. Arrange leaves and flowers on front of tote; stitch in place.

10. Spacing ends of tote handles 6" apart, sew ends of handles to inside top of bag.

BASKET HANDLE

BASKET

Letter-Perfect Gift

Wonderfully easy and inexpensive, this feature-packed stationery set will delight anyone who enjoys corresponding with friends. The handy ensemble includes note cards edged using a gold paint pen and coordinating envelopes lined with wrapping paper. For the look of an expensive writing tablet, a cover of rag paper and fabric is glued onto a purchased notepad. A little spray adhesive and gift wrap turn an accordion file folder into a decorative organizer for the entire set. By choosing a wrapping paper that reflects your friend's personality, you'll deliver a gift that's letter-perfect!

STATIONERY GIFT SET

For stationery file folder, you will need an accordion-style file folder, wrapping paper, lightweight cardboard, $1^1/2$"w wired ribbon, spray adhesive, hot glue gun, glue sticks, and paint pen with fine point (optional). *For notepad,* you will need a plain notepad (ours measures 5" x 8"), heavy handmade paper, fabric piece for front of notepad, paper-backed fusible web, paint pen with fine point, $3/8$"w ribbon, hot glue gun, and glue sticks. *For note cards,* you will need plain note cards with matching envelopes, paint pen with fine point, wrapping paper, and paper-backed fusible web.

STATIONERY FILE FOLDER

1. Remove elastic strap from file folder.
2. To cover back and flap of folder, position open folder on wrapping paper. Cut a piece of wrapping paper approx. 1" larger on all sides than open folder. Apply spray adhesive to back and flap of folder. Center open folder adhesive side down on wrong side of paper piece; press firmly to secure. Trim paper even with edges of folder.
3. To cover front of folder, cut a piece of cardboard same size as front of folder. Cut a piece of wrapping paper approx. 1" larger on all sides than cardboard. Apply spray adhesive to wrong side of paper piece. Center cardboard on paper piece; press in place. Fold edges of paper to back over edges of cardboard and press in place. Hot glue covered cardboard to front of folder.
4. If desired, use paint pen to write headings on tabs inside folder.
5. Tie ribbon into a bow around folder; trim ends.

NOTEPAD

1. To determine width of paper to cover notepad, measure width of notepad. To determine length of paper to cover notepad, measure length of notepad and thickness of gummed edge. Cut a piece of handmade paper the determined measurements.
2. Matching 1 short edge of paper to bottom edge of notepad, place handmade paper on notepad. Fold top edge of paper over gummed edge of notepad; crease. Glue folded portion of paper to gummed edge of notepad.
3. Follow manufacturer's instructions to fuse web to wrong side of fabric piece. Cut fabric piece $1/2$" smaller on all sides than top of covered notepad. Remove paper backing. Center and fuse fabric to covered notepad.
4. For label, cut a small rectangle from handmade paper. Use paint pen to write "Notes" on paper piece. Glue paper piece to center of fabric on notepad.
5. Tie ribbon into a bow around notepad; trim ends.

NOTE CARDS

1. (*Note:* Follow Steps 1 - 3 to line each envelope.) Follow manufacturer's instructions to fuse web to wrong side of wrapping paper. Do not remove paper backing.
2. Use a pencil to draw around open envelope on paper backing side of wrapping paper. Cutting just inside drawn lines, cut shape from wrapping paper. Remove paper backing.
3. Place wrapping paper piece in envelope, trimming side edges to fit if necessary; trim paper to expose gummed edge of envelope. Fuse paper to inside of envelope.
4. For each note card, use paint pen to draw a border on card to coordinate with wrapping paper.

Spiced-Up Candles

Just by adding a few kitchen ingredients to store-bought candles, you can easily craft creative candles with an expensive gift-shop look. These are textured with whipped wax or rolled in warm wax and ground spices or other naturals.

CAKE CANDLES

INSTRUCTIONS

1. For 3" dia. x 3"h candle, place bottle cap over candle wick.
2. Cover work area with newspaper.
3. Heat 1" of water to boiling in an electric skillet or bottom of double boiler.
4. Break wax into chunks. Place wax in coffee can or top of double boiler. If using coffee can, place in boiling water. Reduce heat to simmer. If applicable, melt candle dye pieces in wax. Use craft stick to stir.
5. Pour wax into coffee can. Add spices, if applicable, to wax. Allow wax to harden slightly.
6. Using whisk, whip wax until fluffy. Working in small sections, use plastic fork to apply whipped wax to pillar candle. Whip wax periodically so wax remains fluffy. For candle #3, work in small sections and dab on dry cake mix while applying whipped wax.
7. Remove bottle cap.

SUPPLIES

*(**Note:** Supplies given are for crafting one candle.)*

Project	Purchased Pillar Candles	Candle Wax or Paraffin	Yaley Concentrated Candle Dye	Spices	Food Items	General Supplies
#1	3" dia. x 3"h ivory pillar	1 lb.	—	1 tsp. each of ground cinnamon, nutmeg, and allspice	—	electric skillet and coffee can **or** double boiler plastic fork bottle cap from 20 oz. soft drink craft stick coffee can wire whisk newspaper
#2	3" dia. x 3"h cranberry pillar	1 lb.	5 bars cranberry	4 tsp. ground cinnamon	—	
#3	3" dia. x 3"h ivory pillar	1 lb.	½ bar gold	—	spice cake mix	

Caution: Wax is flammable; continue to add water to skillet or double boiler as necessary to avoid overheating. Do not melt wax in a pan placed directly on burner.

ROLLED CANDLES

INSTRUCTIONS

1. Follow Steps 2-4 of **Cake Candles.**
2. Line jelly roll pans with aluminum foil.
3. While wax is melting, grind naturals if necessary. Pour naturals in a thin layer on bottom of one jelly roll pan.
4. Pour just enough wax to cover bottom of remaining jelly roll pan.
5. Covering candle evenly, roll candle in wax. Roll candle in naturals while wax is still warm. Repeat as desired, ending with a coat of wax. Allow to harden.
6. To cover top of candle, use craft stick to dab wax on top of candle. Sprinkle with naturals.

SUPPLIES

*(**Note:** Supplies given are for crafting one candle.)*

Project	Purchased Candle	Wax	Naturals	General Supplies
#4	2" dia. x 9"h white pillar	1 lb. candle wax or paraffin	coarsely ground cloves coarsely ground dried orange peel	electric skillet and coffee can **or** double boiler 2 old jelly roll pans aluminum foil craft stick newspaper coffee/spice grinder (optional)
#5	3" dia. x 6"h green pillar	1 lb. candle wax or paraffin	ground cinnamon, cloves, and allspice	
#6	3" dia. x 6"h blue pillar	1 lb. candle wax or paraffin	oatmeal	
#7	2½" dia. x 6"h white pillar	1 lb. candle wax or paraffin	ground cinnamon, cloves, and allspice	
#8	2½" dia. x 3"h red pillar	12 oz. Berry Red Candle Magic® Wax Crystals™	ground cinnamon, cloves, and allspice	

BABY-SOFT BLANKETS

Beautiful crocheted edgings give these blankets a loving touch. Made from snuggly flannel, they're as baby-soft as the skin they were created to cover — and almost as sweet.

Finished Size: 37" square
Please read General Instructions, pages 202-203, before starting project.

MATERIALS
Bedspread Weight Cotton Thread (size 10):
Edging #1 - Yellow, 2 balls (150 yards per ball)
Edging #2 - Pink, 2 balls (150 yards per ball)
Edging #3 - White, 1 ball (225 yards per ball)
Steel crochet hook, size 4 (2.00 mm) or size needed for gauge
1 1/8 yards cotton flannel for each blanket
Scissors
6" diameter cardboard circle
Fabric marking pen
Sewing needle and thread
GAUGE: 25 sc = 4"

PREPARATION
Wash, dry, and press flannel. Trim flannel to a 36" square. To round corners, place cardboard circle on one corner of flannel with edge of circle even with edges of flannel. Use fabric marking pen to draw along edge of circle in corner; cut away excess flannel along drawn line. Repeat for remaining corners. Press all edges of blanket 1/4" to wrong side and hand baste in place.
Note: Remove basting stitches after first round of Edging has been added. When working stitches on first round of each Edging, insert hook through blanket 1/4" from pressed edge.

EDGING #1
Rnd 1 (Right side): With right side of blanket facing, join thread with slip st at center of one rounded corner; ch 1, ★ work 216 sc evenly spaced across to center of next rounded corner; repeat from ★ 3 times **more**; join with slip st to first sc: 864 sc.
Rnd 2: Ch 5, dc in same st, skip next 2 sc, ★ (dc, ch 2, dc) in next sc, skip next 2 sc; repeat from ★ around; join with slip st to third ch of beginning ch-5: 288 ch-2 sps.
Rnd 3: Slip st in first ch-2 sp, ch 3, (dc, ch 3, 2 dc) in same sp, (2 dc, ch 3, 2 dc) in next ch-2 sp and in each ch-2 sp around; join with slip st to top of beginning ch-3, finish off.

EDGING #2
Rnd 1 (Right side): With right side of blanket facing, join thread with slip st at center of one rounded corner; ch 1, ★ work 216 sc evenly spaced across to center of next rounded corner; repeat from ★ 3 times **more**; join with slip st to first sc: 864 sc.
Rnd 2: Ch 3, dc in next sc and in each sc around; join with slip st to top of beginning ch-3.
Rnd 3: Ch 3, (2 dc, ch 2, 3 dc) in same st, skip next dc, sc in next dc, skip next dc, ★ (3 dc, ch 2, 3 dc) in next dc, skip next dc, sc in next dc, skip next dc; repeat from ★ around; join with slip st to top of beginning ch-3, finish off.

EDGING #3
Rnd 1 (Right side): With right side of blanket facing, join thread with slip st at center of one rounded corner; ch 1, ★ work 216 sc evenly spaced across to center of next rounded corner; repeat from ★ 3 times **more**; join with slip st to first sc: 864 sc.
Rnd 2: Ch 6, sc in same st, dc in next 2 sc, ★ (dc, ch 3, sc) in next sc, dc in next 2 sc; repeat from ★ around; join with slip st to third ch of beginning ch-6: 288 ch-3 sps.
Rnd 3: Slip st in first ch-3 sp, (sc, ch 3, 3 dc) in same sp and in each ch-3 sp around; join with slip st to first sc, finish off.
Designs by Lorraine White.

GENERAL INSTRUCTIONS

CROSS STITCH

Preparing floss: If your project will be laundered, soak floss in a mixture of one cup water and one tablespoon vinegar for a few minutes and allow to dry before using to prevent colors from bleeding or fading.

Counted Cross Stitch (X): Work one Cross Stitch to correspond to each colored square on the chart. For horizontal rows, work stitches in two journeys.

Fig. 1

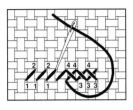

For vertical rows, complete each stitch as shown.

Fig. 2

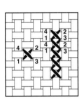

When working over 2 fabric threads, work Cross Stitch as shown.

Fig. 3

Quarter Stitches (¹/₄X and ³/₄X): Quarter Stitches are denoted by triangular shapes of color on the chart and on the color key. Come up at 1 **(Fig. 4)**; then split fabric thread to go down at 2. When stitches 1-4 are worked in the same color, the resulting stitch is called a Three-Quarter Stitch (³/₄X).

Fig. 4

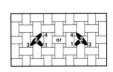

Backstitch (B'ST): For outline detail, Backstitch (shown in chart and color key by black or colored straight lines) should be worked after all Cross Stitch has been completed.

Fig. 5

French Knot: Bring needle up at 1. Wrap floss once around needle and insert needle at 2, holding floss with non-stitching fingers **(Fig. 6)**. Tighten knot; then pull needle through fabric, holding floss until it must be released. For larger knot, use more strands; wrap only once.

Fig. 6

Working on Waste Canvas: Cut pieces of waste canvas and lightweight interfacing about 1" larger on all sides than finished design size. Center and pin interfacing to inside front of garment. Cover edges of canvas with masking tape. Find center of stitching area on **canvas** and mark with a pin. Find center of stitching area on **garment** and mark with a pin. Matching center of canvas to pin on garment, pin canvas in place. Stitching through all layers, baste along edges of canvas, from corner to corner, and from side to side. Mark center of canvas by using pink thread to baste down center. Beginning 1" from top of canvas, use a sharp needle to stitch design. Remove basting threads and trim canvas to about ¹/₂" from design. Use tweezers to pull out canvas threads one at a time. If necessary, slightly dampen canvas until it becomes soft enough to make removing threads easier.

EMBROIDERY

Preparing floss: If using embroidery floss for a project that will be laundered, soak floss in a mixture of one cup water and one tablespoon vinegar for a few minutes and allow to dry before using to prevent colors from bleeding or fading.

Fig. 7

Straight Stitch: Referring to **Fig. 7**, come up at 1 and go down at 2.

Running Stitch: Referring to **Fig. 8**, make a series of straight stitches with stitch length equal to the space between stitches.

Fig. 8

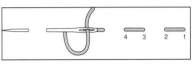

Blanket Stitch: Referring to **Fig. 9**, bring needle up at 1. Keeping thread below point of needle, go down at 2 and come up at 3. Continue working as shown **(Fig. 10)**.

Fig. 9   **Fig. 10**

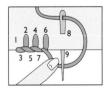

(**Note:** For more embroidery stitches, see page 29.)

PLASTIC CANVAS

Unless otherwise indicated, bring threaded needle up at 1 and all odd numbers and down at 2 and all even numbers.

Backstitch: This stitch is worked over completed stitches to outline or define (**Fig. 11, page 202**). It is sometimes worked over more than one thread. Backstitch may also be used to cover canvas as shown in **Fig. 12 (page 202)**.

201

GENERAL INSTRUCTIONS (continued)

Fig. 11

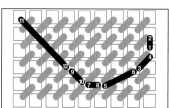

Fig. 12

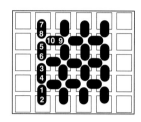

Cross Stitch: This stitch is composed of two stitches **(Fig. 13)**. The top stitch of each cross must always be made in the same direction. The number of intersections may vary according to the chart.

Fig. 13

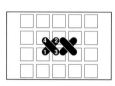

French Knot: Bring needle up through hole. Wrap yarn around needle once and insert needle in same hole **(Fig. 14)**. Tighten knot as close to the canvas as possible as you pull the needle and yarn back through canvas.

Fig. 14

Fringe Stitch: Fold a length of yarn in half. Thread needle with loose ends of yarn. Bring needle up at 1, leaving a 1" loop on the back of the canvas. Bring needle around the edge of canvas and through loop **(Fig. 15)**. Pull to tighten loop **(Fig. 16)**. Trim fringe to desired length. A dot of glue on back of fringe will help keep stitch in place.

Fig. 15

Fig. 16

Gobelin Stitch: This basic straight stitch is worked over two or more threads or intersections. The number of threads or intersections may vary according to the chart **(Fig. 17)**.

Fig. 17

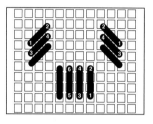

Lazy Daisy Stitch: Bring needle up at 1. Insert needle in the same hole, leaving a loop on top of the canvas. Bring needle up at 2 and through the loop **(Fig. 18)**. To secure loop, insert needle at 2 and gently pull yarn back through canvas until loop lies flat on the canvas.

Fig.18

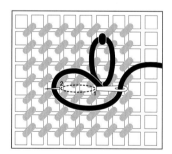

Mosaic Stitch: This three-stitch pattern forms small squares **(Fig. 19)**.

Fig. 19

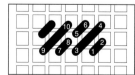

Overcast Stitch: This stitch covers the edge of the canvas and joins pieces of canvas **(Fig. 20)**. It may be necessary to go through the same hole more than once to get even coverage on the edge, especially at the corners.

Fig. 20

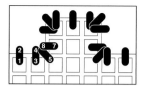

Scotch Stitch: This stitch may be worked over three or more threads and forms a square. **Fig. 21** shows the Scotch stitch worked over three threads.

Fig. 21

Tent Stitch: This stitch is worked in horizontal or vertical rows over one intersection as shown in **Fig. 22**.

Fig. 22

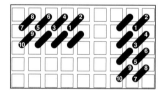

CROCHET
Abbreviations

BLO	Back Loop(s) Only
BPdc	Back Post double crochet(s)
BPtr	Back Post treble crochet(s)
ch	chain(s)
dc	double crochet(s)
FLO	Front Loop(s) Only
FPdc	Front Post double crochet(s)
FPdtr	Front Post double treble crochet(s)
FPtr	Front Post treble crochet(s)
hdc	half double crochet(s)
Rnd(s)	Round(s)
sc	single crochet(s)
sp(s)	space(s)
st(s)	stitch(es)
tr	treble crochet(s)
YO	yarn over

★ — work instructions following ★ as many **more** times as indicated in addition to the first time.

( ) — work enclosed instructions **as many** times as specified by the number immediately following **or** work all enclosed instructions in the stitch indicated **or** contains explanatory remarks.

Gauge: Gauge is the number of stitches and rows or rounds per inch to make sure your project will be the right size. The hook size given in the instructions is only a guide. The project should never be made without first making a sample swatch about 4" square using the thread or yarn, hook, and stitch specified. Measure the swatch, counting stitches and rows carefully. If your swatch is smaller than what is specified in the instructions, try again with a larger hook; if it's larger, try again with a smaller one. Keep trying until you find the size hook that will give you the specified gauge.

Slip stitch (slip st): Insert hook in st or sp indicated, YO and draw through st and through loop on hook.

Fig. 23

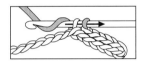

Single crochet (sc): Insert hook in st or sp indicated, YO and pull up a loop, YO and draw through both loops on hook.

Fig. 24

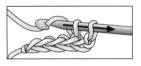

Half double crochet (hdc): YO, insert hook in st or sp indicated, YO and pull up a loop, YO and draw through all 3 loops on hook.

Fig. 25

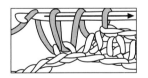

Double crochet (dc): YO, insert hook in st or sp indicated, YO and pull up a loop, YO and draw through two loops on hook (**Fig. 26a**), YO and draw through remaining two loops on hook (**Fig. 26b**).

Fig. 26a   **Fig. 26b**

Treble crochet (tr): YO twice, insert hook in st or sp indicated, YO and pull up a loop (four loops on a hook, **Fig. 27a**), (YO and draw through two loops on hook) three times (**Fig. 27b**).

Fig. 27a   **Fig. 27b**

Post stitch: Work around post of stitch indicated, inserting hook in direction of arrow (**Fig. 28**).

Fig. 28

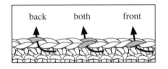

Back or Front Loop Only (BLO, FLO): Work only in loop(s) indicated.

Fig. 29

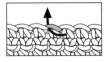

Free loops of a chain: When instructed to work in free loops of a chain, work in loop indicated by arrow.

Fig. 30

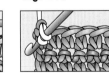

Reverse sc: Working from left to right, insert hook in st or sp to right of hook (**Fig. 31a**), YO and draw through, under and to left of loop on hook (two loops on hook, **Fig. 31b**), YO and draw through both loops on hook (**Fig. 31c**) (reverse sc made, **Fig. 31d**).

Fig. 31a   **Fig. 31b**

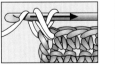
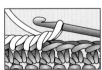

Fig. 31c   **Fig. 31d**

Fringe: Cut a piece of cardboard 5" wide and 9" long. Wind yarn **loosely** and **evenly** around the cardboard lengthwise until the card is filled, then cut across one end; repeat as needed.

Hold together as many strands of yarn as specified in individual instructions; fold in half.

With **wrong** side facing and using a crochet hook, draw the folded end up through a row or stitch and pull the loose ends through the folded end (**Fig. 32a** or **32c**); draw the knot up **tightly** (**Fig. 32b** or **32d**). Repeat, spacing as desired. Lay flat on a hard surface and trim the ends.

Fig. 32a   **Fig. 32b**

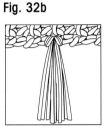

Fig. 32c   **Fig. 32d**

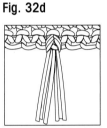

KNIT

(**Note:** For general knitting instructions and more stitches, see pages 64-75.)

Abbreviations

K	knit
LT	Left Twist
M1	make one
mm	millimeters
P	purl
PSSO	pass slipped stitch over
P2SSO	pass 2 slipped stitches over
RT	Right Twist
SSK	slip 2 sts as if to knit, knit together
st(s)	stitch(es)
tog	together
YO	yarn over

★ — work instructions following ★ as many **more** times as indicated in addition to the first time.

† to † — work all instructions from first † to second † **as many** times as specified.

( ) or [ ] — work enclosed instructions **as many** times as specified by the number immediately following **or** work all enclosed instructions in the stitch indicated **or** contains explanatory remarks.

colon (:) — the number(s) given after a colon at the end of a row or round denote(s) the number of stitches you should have on that row or round.

Gauge: Correct gauge is essential for proper size. Needle size given in instructions is merely a guide and should never be used without first making a sample swatch approximately 4" square in the stitch, yarn, and needles specified. Then measure it, counting your stitches and rows carefully. If you have more stitches per inch than specified, try again with larger size needles; if fewer, try again with a smaller size. Keep trying until you find the size that will give you the specified gauge. DO NOT HESITATE TO CHANGE NEEDLE SIZE TO OBTAIN CORRECT GAUGE.

Slip, Slip, Knit (SSK): Separately slip two stitches as if to **knit (Fig. 33a)**. Insert the **left** needle into the **front** of both slipped stitches **(Fig. 33b)** and knit them together **(Fig. 33c)**.

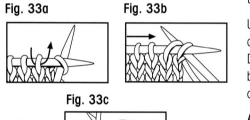

Fig. 33a   Fig. 33b

Fig. 33c

PAINTING TECHNIQUES

A disposable foam plate makes a good palette for holding and mixing paint colors. It can easily be placed in a large resealable plastic bag to keep remaining paint wet while waiting for an area of applied paint to dry.

As well, when waiting for large areas to dry, before applying a second coat, wrap your paintbrush in plastic wrap and place in the refrigerator to keep paint from drying on your brush. Always clean brushes thoroughly after use to keep them in good condition.

Transferring a Pattern

Trace pattern onto tracing paper. Place transfer paper, coated side down, between project and traced pattern. Use removable tape to secure pattern to project. Use a pencil to transfer outlines of design to project (press lightly to avoid smudges and heavy lines that are difficult to cover). If necessary, use a soft eraser to remove any smudges.

Transferring Details

To transfer detail lines to design, position pattern and transfer paper over painted basecoat and use a pencil to lightly transfer detail lines onto project.

Adding Details

Use a permanent marker or paint pen (usually with a fine-tip) to draw over transferred detail lines or to create freehanded details on project.

Painting Basecoats

A basecoat is a solid color of paint that covers the project's entire surface.

Use a medium round brush for large areas and a small round brush for small areas. Do not overload brush. Allowing to dry between coats, apply several thin coats of paint to project.

Aged Finishes

This technique creates a faux-aged finish.

Allowing to dry between applications, paint project the desired basecoat color. Randomly apply a thin layer of floor paste wax with a soft cloth, or rub a candle over areas on project to be aged (such as the edges). Paint project the desired top coat color and allow to dry. Lightly sand project to remove some of the paint for a gently-aged look. Wipe project with a tack cloth to remove dust, then seal with clear acrylic sealer.

"C" Stroke

Dip an angle or flat paintbrush in paint. Touch tip to surface, pulling brush to the left. Pull brush toward you while applying pressure. When stroke is desired length, lift brush gradually while pulling to the right to form the tail of the stroke.

Color Wash

A color wash is a light coloration of a project surface. It is similar to Dry Brush, yet creates a softer look that penetrates the project's surface.

To create a color wash, mix one part acrylic paint with two to three parts water. Dip paintbrush in color wash and brush across the area to receive color. Decrease pressure on the brush as you move outward. Repeat to create desired effect.

Dots

Dip handle end of paintbrush for larger dots or the end of a toothpick for smaller dots, into paint; touch to painting surface and lift straight up. Dip tip into paint frequently to maintain uniform dots.

Dry Brush

Do not dip brush in water. Dip a stipple brush or old paintbrush in paint; wipe most of the paint off onto a dry paper towel. Lightly rub the brush across the area to receive color. Decrease pressure on the brush as you move outward. Repeat as needed to create the desired coverage of color.

Spatter Painting

Dip the bristle tips of a dry toothbrush into paint, blot on a paper towel to remove excess, then pull thumb across bristles to spatter paint on project.

Sponge Painting

This technique creates a soft, mottled look on project's surface.

1. Dampen sponge with water.

2. Dip dampened sponge into paint; blot on paper towel to remove excess paint.

3. Use a light stamping motion to paint project. Allow to dry.

4. If using more than one color of paint, repeat Steps 1 – 3, using a fresh sponge piece for each color.

5. If desired, repeat technique using one color again over areas of other colors, to soften edges or to lighten up a heavy application of one color.

Stenciling

1. Cut a piece from stencil plastic 1" larger than entire pattern. Center plastic over pattern and use a permanent pen to trace outlines.

2. Place plastic piece on cutting mat and use a craft knife to cut out stencil along solid lines, making sure edges are smooth.

3. Hold or tape stencil in place. Using a clean, dry stencil brush or sponge piece, dip brush or sponge in paint. Remove excess paint on a paper towel. Brush or sponge should be almost dry to produce best results. Beginning at edge of cutout area, apply paint in a stamping motion over stencil. If desired, highlight or shade design by stamping a lighter or darker shade of paint in cutout area. Repeat until all areas of first stencil have been painted. Carefully remove stencil and allow paint to dry.

Dimensional Paint

Turn bottle upside down to fill tip before each use. While painting, clean tip often with a paper towel. If tip becomes clogged, insert a straight pin into opening to unclog.

To paint, touch tip to project. Squeezing and moving bottle steadily, apply paint to project, being careful not to flatten paint line. If painting over trasferred line on project or freehand details as desired.

To correct a mistake, use a paring knife to gently scrape excess paint from project before it dries. Carefully remove stain with non-acetone nail polish remover on a cotton swab. A mistake may also be camouflaged by incorporating it into the design.

DÉCOUPAGE

1. Cut desired motifs from fabric or paper.

2. Apply découpage glue to wrong sides of motifs.

3. Arrange motifs on project as desired, overlapping as necessary. Smooth in place and allow to dry.

4. Allowing to dry after each application, apply two to three coats of sealer to project.

MAKING PATTERNS

Blue line on pattern indicates where traced pattern is to be placed on fold of fabric.

When patterns are stacked or overlapped, place tracing paper over pattern and follow a single colored line to trace pattern. Repeat to trace each pattern separately onto tracing paper.

For a more durable pattern, use translucent vinyl template material instead of tracing paper.

Transferring a pattern: Make a tracing paper pattern. Position pattern on project. Place transfer paper coated side down between pattern and project. Use a stylus or ballpoint pen to trace over lines of pattern.

SEWING SHAPES

1. Center pattern on wrong side of one fabric piece and use fabric marking pen to draw around pattern. Do not cut out shape.
2. Place fabric pieces right sides together. Leaving an opening for turning, carefully sew pieces together directly on drawn line.
3. Leaving a $^1/_4$" seam allowance, cut out shape. Clip seam allowance at curves and corners. Turn shape right side out and press.

(**Note:** For Making Appliqués, see page 127).

STITCHING APPLIQUÉS

Place paper or stabilizer on wrong side of background fabric under fused appliqué. Set machine for a narrow zigzag stitch. Beginning on a straight edge of appliqué if possible, position project under presser foot so that most of stitching will be on appliqué. Take a stitch in fabric and bring bobbin thread to top. Hold both threads toward you and sew over them for several stitches to secure; clip threads. Stitch over all exposed raw edges of appliqué(s) and along detail lines as indicated in instructions.

When stitching is complete, remove stabilizer. Clip threads close to stitching.

MAKING A FABRIC YO-YO

1. Use a compass to draw a circle on tracing paper the diameter indicated in project instructions. Use pattern to cut out fabric circle.

2. Turn raw edge of circle $^1/_4$" to wrong side.

3. Using a double strand of thread, work a Running Stitch, page 201, along turned edge.

4. Pull ends of thread to tightly gather circle; knot thread.

5. Flatten circle with gathers at center.

QUILTING

PIECING AND PRESSING
Precise cutting, followed by accurate piecing and careful pressing, will ensure that all the pieces of your quilt top fit together well.

Piecing

Set sewing machine stitch length for approximately 11 stitches per inch. Use a new, sharp needle suited for medium-weight woven fabric.

Use a neutral-colored general-purpose sewing thread (not quilting thread) in the needle and in the bobbin. Stitch first on a scrap fabric to check upper and bobbin thread tension; make any adjustments necessary.

For good results, it is **essential** that you stitch with an **accurate** $^1/_4$" **seam allowance**. When piecing, **always** place pieces **right sides together** and **match raw edges**; pin if necessary. (If using straight pins, remove the pins just before they reach the sewing machine needle.)

Sewing Strip Sets

When there are several strips to assemble into a strip set, first sew the strips together into pairs, then sew the pairs together to form the strip set. To help avoid distortion, sew 1 seam in 1 direction and then sew the next seam in the opposite direction **(Fig. 34)**.

Fig. 34

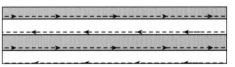

Sewing Across Seam Intersections
When sewing across the intersection of 2 seams, place pieces right sides together and match seams exactly, making sure seam allowances are pressed in opposite directions **(Fig. 35)**. To prevent fabric from shifting, you may wish to pin in place.

Fig. 35

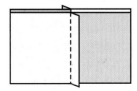

GENERAL INSTRUCTIONS (continued)

Sewing Sharp Points

To ensure sharp points when joining triangular or diagonal pieces, stitch across the center of the "X" (shown in pink) formed on the wrong side by previous seams **(Fig. 36)**.

Fig. 36

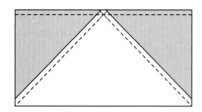

Pressing

Use a steam iron set on "Cotton" for all pressing. Press as you sew, taking care to prevent small folds along seamlines. Seam allowances are almost always pressed to one side, usually toward the darker fabric. However, to reduce bulk it may occasionally be necessary to press seam allowances toward the lighter fabric or even to press them open. In order to prevent a dark fabric seam allowance from showing through a light fabric, trim the darker seam allowance slightly narrower than the lighter seam allowance. To press long seams, such as those in long strip sets, without curving or other distortion, lay strips across the width of the ironing board.

INVISIBLE APPLIQUÉ

This method of appliqué is an adaptation of satin stitch appliqué that uses clear nylon thread to secure the appliqué pieces. Transparent monofilament (clear nylon) thread is available in 2 colors: clear and smoke. Use clear on white or very light fabrics and smoke on darker colors.

1. Referring to diagram and/or photo, arrange appliqués on the background fabric and follow manufacturer's instructions to fuse in place.
2. Pin a stabilizer, such as paper or any of the commercially available products, on wrong side of background fabric before stitching appliqués in place.
3. Thread sewing machine with transparent monofilament thread; use general-purpose thread that matches background fabric in bobbin.

4. Set sewing machine for a very narrow (approximately $^1/_{16}$") zigzag stitch and a short stitch length. You may find that loosening the top tension slightly will yield a smoother stitch.
5. Begin by stitching 2 or 3 stitches in place (drop feed dogs or set stitch length at 0) to anchor thread. Most of the zigzag stitch should be done on the appliqué with the right edges of the stitch falling at the very outside edge of the appliqué. Stitch over all exposed raw edges of appliqué pieces.

BORDERS

Adding Squared Borders

1. Mark the center of each edge of quilt top.

2. Squared borders are usually added to top and bottom, then side edges of the center section of a quilt top. To add top and bottom borders, measure across center of quilt top to determine length of borders **(Fig. 37)**. Trim top and bottom borders to the determined length.

Fig. 37

3. Mark center of 1 long edge of top border. Matching center marks and raw edges, pin border to quilt top, easing in any fullness; stitch. Repeat for bottom border.

4. Measure center of quilt top, including attached borders, to determine length of side borders. Trim side borders to the determined length. Repeat Step 3 to add borders to quilt top **(Fig. 38)**.

Fig. 38

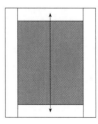

ASSEMBLING THE QUILT

1. Examine wrong side of quilt top closely; trim any seam allowances and clip any threads that may show through the front of the quilt. Press quilt top.
2. If quilt top is to be marked before layering, mark quilting lines.
3. Place backing **wrong** side up on a flat surface. Use masking tape to tape edges of backing to surface. Place batting on top of backing fabric. Smooth batting gently, being careful not to stretch or tear. Center quilt top **right** side up on batting.
4. If hand quilting, begin in the center and work toward the outer edges to hand baste all layers together. Use long stitches and place basting lines approximately 4" apart. Smooth fullness or wrinkles toward outer edges.

HAND QUILTING

The quilting stitch is a basic running stitch that forms a broken line on the quilt top and backing. Stitches on the quilt top and backing should be straight and equal length.

1. Secure center of quilt in hoop or frame. Check quilt top and backing to make sure they are smooth. To help prevent puckers, always begin quilting in the center of the quilt and work toward the outside edges.
2. Thread needle with an 18" - 20" length of quilting thread; knot 1 end. Using a thimble, insert needle into quilt top and batting approximately $^1/_2$" from where you wish to begin quilting. Bring needle up at the point where you wish to begin **(Fig. 39)**; when knot catches on quilt top, give thread a quick, short pull to "pop" knot through fabric into batting.

Fig. 39

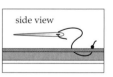

side view

3. Holding the needle with your sewing hand and placing your other hand underneath the quilt, use thimble to push the tip of the needle down through all layers. As soon as needle touches your finger underneath, use that finger to push the tip of the needle only back up through the layers to top of quilt. (The amount of the needle showing above the fabric

determines the length of the quilting stitch.) Referring to **Fig 40,** rock the needle up and down, taking 3-6 stitches before bringing the needle and thread completely through the layers. Check the back of the quilt to make sure stitches are going through all layers. When quilting through a seam allowance or quilting a curve or corner, you may need to make 1 stitch at a time.

Fig. 40

4. When you reach the end of your thread, knot thread close to the fabric and "pop" knot into batting; clip thread close to fabric.

5. Stop and move your hoop as often as necessary. You do not have to tie a knot every time you move your hoop; you may leave the thread dangling and pick it up again when you return to that part of the quilt.

BINDING

(**Note:** To make continuous bias strip binding, see page 78.)

Attaching French-Fold Binding with Mitered Corners

1. Matching wrong sides and raw edges, press strip in half lengthwise. Press 1 end of binding diagonally (**Fig. 41**).

Fig. 41

2. Beginning with pressed end several inches from a corner, lay binding around quilt to make sure that seams in binding will not end up at a corner. Adjust placement if necessary. Matching raw edges of binding to raw edge of quilt top, pin binding to right side of quilt along 1 edge.

3. When you reach the first corner, mark ¹/₄" from corner of quilt top (**Fig. 42**).

Fig. 42

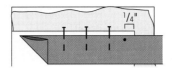

4. Using a ¹/₄" seam allowance, sew binding to quilt, backstitching at beginning of stitching and when you reach the mark (**Fig. 43**). Lift needle out of fabric and clip thread.

Fig. 43

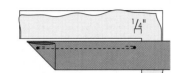

5. Fold binding as shown in **Figs. 44** and **45** and pin binding to adjacent side, matching raw edges. When you reach the next corner, mark ¹/₄" from edge of quilt top.

Fig. 44   **Fig. 45**

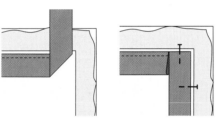

6. Backstitching at edge of quilt top, sew pinned binding to quilt (**Fig. 46**); backstitch when you reach the next mark. Lift needle out of fabric and clip thread.

Fig. 46

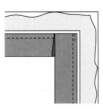

7. Repeat Steps 5 and 6 to continue sewing binding to quilt until binding overlaps beginning end by approximately 2". Trim excess binding.

8. If using 2¹/₂"w binding (finished size ¹/₂"), trim backing and batting a scant ¹/₄" larger than quilt top so that batting and backing will fill the binding when it is folded over to the quilt backing. If using narrower binding, trim backing and batting even with edges of quilt top.

9. On 1 edge of quilt, fold binding over to quilt backing and pin pressed edge in place, covering stitching line (**Fig. 47**). On adjacent side, fold binding over, forming a mitered corner (**Fig. 48**). Repeat to pin remainder of binding in place.

Fig. 47   **Fig. 48**

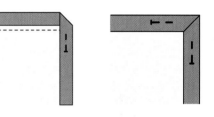

10. Blindstitch (**Fig. 49**) binding to backing, taking care not to stitch through to front of quilt.

Fig. 49

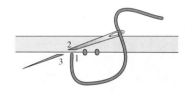

Come up at 1. Go down at 2 and come up at 3. Length of stitches may be varied as desired.